William Joseph Amherst

The History of Catholic Emancipation

Vol. I

William Joseph Amherst

The History of Catholic Emancipation
Vol. I

ISBN/EAN: 9783744664622

Printed in Europe, USA, Canada, Australia, Japan

Cover: Foto ©Lupo / pixelio.de

More available books at **www.hansebooks.com**

THE HISTORY OF
CATHOLIC EMANCIPATION

THE HISTORY

OF

CATHOLIC EMANCIPATION

AND

*THE PROGRESS OF THE CATHOLIC CHURCH
IN THE BRITISH ISLES (CHIEFLY IN ENGLAND)*

FROM 1771 TO 1820

BY

W. J. AMHERST, S.J.

"The ways of Providence are incomprehensible, and we know not in what times, or by what methods, God will restore His Church in England, or what farther tryalls and afflictions we are yet to undergo. Onely this we know, that if a Religion be of God, it can never fail, but the acceptable time we must patiently expect, and endeavour by our lives not to undeserve."—*From* DRYDEN'S *Dedication of the Life of St. Francis Xavier to the Queen.*

IN TWO VOLUMES
VOL. I.

LONDON
KEGAN PAUL, TRENCH & CO., 1, PATERNOSTER SQUARE
1886

(The rights of translation and of reproduction are reserved.)

TO

THE CATHOLIC YOUNG MEN OF ENGLAND

I DEDICATE THIS WORK,

IN THE HOPE,

THAT FROM ITS PERUSAL THEY MAY

THANK GOD FOR THE BLESSINGS HE HAS SHOWERED UPON US,

AND MAY LEARN WHAT TO AVOID AND WHAT TO DO,

AS FAITHFUL MEMBERS OF THE CHURCH,

AS LOYAL SUBJECTS OF THE QUEEN,

AND AS TRUE MEN,

RESOLVED TO USE THEIR LIBERTIES AS ENGLISHMEN

IN DEFENCE OF THEIR RELIGION AS CATHOLICS.

PREFACE.

ELEVEN years ago I accidentally discovered that the year 1874 was the centenary of the first Act of Parliament which relaxed the penal code against Catholics. It was an Act of the Irish Parliament, and therefore did not affect the English. But it was the beginning of a better order of things. It was the prelude to the Act of 1778, which passed unanimously at Westminster, and was the first Relief Act in favour of English Catholics. The circumstance of this Act of 1774 having been brought to my notice, suggested to me the idea of collecting, as far as my limited opportunities would permit, all the facts which should come under my notice connected with the progress of Emancipation and of the Catholic Church in England during the last hundred years. I had then no intention of publishing the result of my note-taking. I thought that I might perhaps collect matter which would be useful to some future historian. But I was strongly advised by a friend to take notes only with the view of working them into a history myself, as no one else, he said, would be likely to do so. I took the advice; and when, five years afterwards, the year 1879 brought us to the fiftieth year since the passing of the great act of 1829, a good opportunity was afforded of beginning the history.

It was accordingly commenced as a serial in *Catholic Progress*, and the greater part of this first volume has already appeared in that magazine; many of the first chapters being written under the heading of "The Jubilee of Emancipation."

I am quite sensible that this history is very imperfect and very incomplete. No history of Catholic Emancipation has as yet been written. The only full and connected account of any portion of the great contest which has been published is Mr. Wyse's most valuable and interesting "History of the Catholic Association."[1] If my attempt should have no other value, I hope that at least it may induce some one of more ability, and of greater powers and opportunities of research, to enter more fully into the details of one of the most remarkable events of modern times. For if Lord Beaconsfield could speak of the "Clare Election" alone as "not the least memorable of historical events," the whole agitation and the victory which followed must, taken together, occupy a high place amongst those great things which God has brought about through the instrumentality of willing men.

This history will, I fear, be found to be most incomplete precisely where a history of Emancipation ought to be least defective. I mean in the details of the agitation in Ireland. The introduction of Ireland into this history was, of course, absolutely necessary in more respects than one. It is true that an account of the proceedings for redress in England, from the year 1791 to the year 1826,

---

[1] A great deal of some of the most interesting portions of the history is related in the various lives of Bishop Milner and O'Connell, and in Sir Robert Peel's "Memoirs," in Mr. Butler's "Historical Memoirs," and Dr. Milner's "Supplementary Memoirs;" but no continued history has yet appeared of the whole period which I propose to embrace.

might have been written with Bishop Milner as the principal figure; but a history of Emancipation without O'Connell would give a much more absurd result than the representation of *Hamlet* with the omission of the character of the Prince of Denmark.

The object of an historian should be to state the facts correctly, and to draw his conclusions with as impartial a judgment as possible. I have endeavoured to write with as much accuracy as can be obtained, when not unfrequently conflicting accounts make the task somewhat difficult. For instance, it is not always easy to decide between Charles Butler and Bishop Milner. And with regard to the reflections which are frequently introduced to point the moral of the history, many of them have required a good deal of consideration. But I may say with the orator Cicero, "Dicam tamen quod sentio, et dicam brevius, quam res tanta dici possit:"[1] and with the Psalmist King David, "Credidi, propter quod locutus sum."[2]

W. J. AMHERST, S.J.

St. Mary's Hall, Stonyhurst,
Michaelmas Day, 1885.

[1] *Paradoxa*, sc. 2.   [2] Ps. cxv.

CONTENTS.

PAGE

INTRODUCTION   1

CHAPTER I.

THE ACTS OF 1771 AND 1774.

The Act of 1771—The unsuccessful bills of 1774—The Act of 1774 introduced—Prejudice against Catholics—Preamble of Act of 1774—Address of the Irish Catholics to the King—Relief granted by the Act of 1774—Tom Moore, Mr. Fagan, Charles Butler, and George Canning on the Act of 1774—Suggestions of disloyalty in the Act of 1774—The power and influence of Ireland—Fear the great motive of relief—Combination amongst Catholics   50

CHAPTER II.

STATE OF CATHOLICS PREVIOUS TO ACT OF 1778.

State of Catholics previous to the Act of 1778—and Lord Mansfield's charge to the jury at the trial of Mr. Webb   76

CHAPTER III.

THE ACT OF 1778.

Edmund Burke on the Act of William III.—Address of English Catholics to George III.—Remarks on the address—Debates on the bill of 1778—Sir George Savile, Mr. Dunning, Attorney-General Thurlow, Lord Beauchamp, and Henry Dundas on the bill—Second reading of the bill—A specimen of bigotry—A liberal speaker—The bill passes the Commons—Second reading of the bill in the Lords—Speech of a bishop—and of two future prime ministers—Lord Shelburne on the trial of Mr. Malony—The bill of 1778 passes the Lords—Relief given by the Act 91

CHAPTER IV.

REMARKS SUGGESTED BY THE ACT OF 1778 ... 111

CHAPTER V.

THE IRISH RELIEF ACT AND THE GORDON RIOTS.

The Irish Act—The riots in Scotland—Scotch and English bigotry—Compensation to the Scotch Catholics—Petition for compensation—Debate on the petition—Lord George Gordon—The Gordon riots—Services of Catholic priests not appreciated—Human respect and bad manners—Inconsistency of statesmen—Conduct of Dissenters—The Wesleyan Methodists 122

CHAPTER VI.

THE ACT OF 1791.

The Committee of Five—Letters of the Committee to the Catholics of England and to the Vicars Apostolic—The Committee and Milner—The Committee of Ten—The Protestation—The oath proposed by the Committee—The bishops condemn the oath—The schismatical protest—Milner attacks the Committee—Milner defeats the Committee—The passing of the bill of 1791—Relief given by the bill of 1791—Religious Orders under the Act of 1791—Further relief given by the Act 149

CHAPTER VII.

THE ACT OF 1791, AND SUBSEQUENT EVENTS.

Why the committee failed—Meeting at the Crown and Anchor—The Cisalpine Club—The Mediation—The "Buff-book"—Father Charles Plowden—The "Roman Catholic Meeting" 187

CHAPTER VIII.

THE RECEPTION OF THE FRENCH CLERGY AND OF THE ENGLISH COMMUNITIES IN ENGLAND.

The French clergy—Letter of the Bishop of St. Pol de Léon—English Communities abroad—Douay and St. Omer's—The Benedictine dames of Brussels—The providence of God over the Church in England—Mean action of some Cisalpines—Kindness of the Royal Family to the religious—George III. and the Taunton nuns—The Prince Regent and the Princethorpe nuns 207

CHAPTER IX.

REV. MR. WILKS AND THE "STAFFORDSHIRE CLERGY" ... 238

CHAPTER X.

PROGRESS OF EMANCIPATION IN IRELAND.

PAGE

The influence of Ireland—Duty of English Catholics towards Ireland—Catholic associations in Ireland—John Keogh—Keogh and O'Connell—O'Connell—Union is strength 245

CHAPTER XI.

FIRST SCOTCH RELIEF ACT.

English and Scotch bigotry—The Church in Scotland—The Act of 1793 274

CHAPTER XII.

THE RESIGNATION OF PITT IN 1801—THE VETO.

The resignation of Pitt—Lord Stanhope on Pitt's resignation—The Veto—Gregory XVI. and Lord Melbourne 286

CHAPTER XIII.

THE VETO QUESTION.

Origin of the veto question in the United Kingdom—Burke on the veto—Resolutions of the Irish bishops in 1799—First public mention of the veto—Milner's interview with Ponsonby—Debate in the Commons—Milner and Ponsonby—Indignation in Ireland—Milner's "Letter to a Parish Priest" 306

THE HISTORY OF CATHOLIC EMANCIPATION.

INTRODUCTION.

BOSSUET begins his treatise on universal history by observing, that if the time should ever come when the study of history would be useless to other people, it would still be necessary that princes should read it. It may be said with as much truth that if no others should take an interest in the progress of the Church in England during the last hundred years, Catholics at least should be well acquainted with the course of events. From a want of knowledge, there follows as a matter of course an absence of reflection. A Catholic who does not think of the past is uninfluenced by those strong motives which exist for gratitude to God, and for a desire to do his duty as a loyal member of the Church.

Some five and forty years ago, as two young Catholics were talking together on the duties of English Catholic laymen, the elder of the two observed to the younger, that he could not conceive a grander position for a young man than that in which the Catholic youth of England then stood. The fact is that the young men of that time were the firstfruits of the season of emancipation. They had gone to school about the time when the great Act was passing through Parliament; they had no personal experience of the times when their elders were living deprived of the liberties of British subjects. They had of course heard a great deal about the penal laws, and the dark days, and the hard times through which their forefathers had passed. Their grandfathers had lived in the deep gloom of the night, but had been spared to see at least the advancing dawn; their fathers had witnessed the aurora breaking into daylight, but the young men themselves had lived only under the risen sun. It was, no doubt, an interesting time when the generation which had never felt the pressure of the penal laws first stepped upon the stage of life. But it was not merely their freedom that gave them cause for joy and an eager desire for action. Their minds and hearts had been prepared by Kenelm Digby's famous works, the "Broad-stone of Honour," and the "Mores Catholici." Some narrow-minded unenthusiastic people, and, it may be added, some envious and jealous people, discouraged the reading of those most Christian books. But they did their good work, and infused into hundreds of young Catholics a spirit which, at the time those books were first published, breathed nowhere else but in them. When the Catholic young men of those days had been thus prepared and were ready to act, they found older men ready to receive them and to welcome them to manly life. There was the loyal, the vigilant and practical Langdale, to show in its greatest perfection how clergy and laity could work together; there was the large-hearted Wiseman, whose abiding thought was not, "How can I alone, discharging every one else, conduct English-Catholic affairs?" but, on the contrary, "Whose services can be engaged to-day in the grand work, to forward which the services of all who can give help are needed?" there was the enthusiastic and energetic Pugin, who was enlisting all whom he could in a crusade to revive Christian taste, and banish the spirit of paganism which was threatening to destroy the beauty of God's house; there was Father Ignatius Spencer, rallying all together in a holy league to pray for the conversion of our countrymen; there was Frederick Lucas, arguing, beseeching, and upbraiding in the pages of his Journal, and gradually forming a school of spirited action which evil counsels broke up, and whose place is known no more; there was increasing emigration from Ireland to great Britain, adding to the number of Catholics in England, and adding stone upon stone to the newly rising Church; there was the movement at Oxford, to which the eyes of all were directed, of which every one was speaking, and which filled the Catholics of England with joy and hope. The movement at Oxford, and other things which grew out of it, like the "Cambridge Camden Society," besides the substantial good which they contained within themselves, made the study of everything relating to the Catholic Church fashionable for the time, and the general aspect of things was very bright and very cheering. On the Continent, too, there were many signs of a Christian revival; and Donoso Cortes in Spain and Montalembert in France were speaking orations fit to rouse whatever remains of Catholic chivalry might be slumbering in the world.

If God in His mercy should prosper His English Church, those days, now nearly half a century gone by, will be looked upon as the early spring of the new life. And certainly the effect which the events of those days produced upon thousands of Catholics in England, was like the effect of the first fine days of spring after a long and dreary winter. There were hundreds of young laymen whose first thought was, "How can I best do my duty to the Church?" Besides enthusiasm, there was a persevering determination which certainly promised well for the future. This state of mind was produced not merely by the almost sudden change for the better which undoubtedly began to show itself about the year 1840, but by the recollection of what young Catholics had heard of the days which had passed away. The patience and fidelity of their forefathers under suffering, the long struggle which their grandfathers and fathers had maintained to regain their rights, were such glorious memories that those who lived in the times I am speaking of looked upon their peaceful and happy days as the fruit of victory. Though the number is fast diminishing, there are, I hope, still many amongst us who will bear me out in saying that there was a large number of young Catholic men then in England who would not have been content to incur the reproach that they did not know how to use the victory which their parents had gained. If the memory of the contest for emancipation added vigour to youthful minds and hearts forty-five years ago, it ought to produce some effect even now. The fruit of victory may be lost by the men who gained it, or it may be lost by their sons and their grandsons. The fresh enthusiasm of the conquerors may wear away; but, at least, duty should prevent the descendants of the conquerors from throwing away the advantages gained.

I am well aware that there is a tendency in human nature to depreciate the present as compared with the past in which a man has lived; and this tendency is more in the direction of unfavourably criticizing the actions of men than in that of complaining of material changes. But times do change, and the changes are either for a state of things as good, under the circumstances, as the former things, or they are changes for the better, or changes for the worse. But notwithstanding the tendency I have just now alluded to, it is not generally supposed that those who have lived in the past are the worst judges of the present. Experience teaches wisdom and prudence; and it is only those who have lived long who can be personally acquainted with the contrasts which the lapse of time produces. With every desire to make that allowance for the prejudice which naturally exists in the mind of one who has laboured in a cause to think lightly of the labours of his successors, I must deliberately say that the action of the young Catholic men of England in Catholic affairs at the present day, is mere idleness and sloth as compared with the energetic action of their fathers: it is as the indolent working of the men who used to be employed in excavating amongst the ruins of the Roman Forum, compared with the stout and vigorous labour of an English, or Irish navvy earning his bread on a railway embankment. And I say this advisedly. A layman in every way eminently qualified to judge has made the remark, that "it is not now the law or Acts of Parliament that prevent us taking our proper position, but our own apathy;" that, as far as he can judge, "the Catholic youth of this day is as worldly as his Protestant neighbour," as shown particularly in his disinclination "to giving up any of his time beyond his own personal enjoyment." If such be the case, perhaps the perusal of what has been done in the past may help to fan into a flame the spark that no doubt still remains in some who love their religion and have the hearts of Englishmen.

In the dedication of this volume, it has been noticed that history teaches us what to avoid as well as what to do. Many of the things done, as related in the first part of the history of emancipation, are more to be regretted than imitated. By far the greater number of Catholics in these days would no doubt condemn the actions of the English-Catholic committees, boards, and clubs, in the question of the Veto, and would at the same time loudly extol the stern orthodoxy and the manly spirit of the doughty champion Milner, who, almost single-handed, kept the lists against all comers. But the most enthusiastic admirer of the great bishop may be well advised to be cautious, and to restrain a little his thoughts and measure his words, lest he should find himself including bishops and priests in the terms of condemnation. The reader will also have to remember that the very exceptional circumstances under which the opponents of Milner acted, give them a title to be at least heard in mitigation of punishment. And there is one thing which we must always bear in mind, namely, that the sons and grandsons of those men who formed the early English-Catholic associations were, and some who remain still are, amongst the most faithful and devoted lovers and supporters of the Holy See. This seems to show that the Cisalpine spirit was only a temporary aberration caused by passing events.

If we count from the beginning of the struggle for emancipation, the two great heroes on the Catholic side were undoubtedly Milner and O'Connell. In Milner we see all that a loyal priest could do, and in O'Connell all that a loyal layman could do, to place their Catholic fellow-countrymen in the position which was their right, both as members of the Church and as British subjects. We see these two men, by the grace and favour of Almighty God, both victorious. We see them in the fight, opposed not only by Protestants, but in many battles by sections and sometimes by large divisions of their own people. They both of them had to be on the watch against open attacks and sneaking underhand advances. They were both roundly abused, not only by those from whom abuse might be expected, but by those who ought to have been ashamed of their words. Milner was spoken of sometimes as a blockhead and sometimes as a blackguard, and no foul and insulting word was spared when the actions of O'Connell were criticized.* When Milner was fighting for the rights of the Holy See, he was covertly reported to Rome as a mere turbulent priest; when O'Connell was agitating, well within the lines of the constitution, he was fiercely denounced as a rebel. And yet the actions for which these two men were so foully traduced are the very actions the memory of which surrounds their names with a halo of glory. But their conduct was not merely glorious; it was exemplary. They are models for all Catholics who have rights to obtain from State authorities. They teach us that when God designs to make man the instrument for attaining an end, an unflinching determination to give to God what belongs to God will often make Cæsar retire within his proper domain. They teach us also that detraction and calumny and unfair opposition are but the penalties which we must pay for doing our duty. All that they had to endure from the tongues of their enemies were mere sufferings which ended with time. We may notice in the lives of great men, men who have conferred some signal benefits on their fellow-men, what is always observed in the history of the Church. Almighty God seems sometimes to say to the evil spirits, " Now is your hour, and power of darkness." These evil spirits may inflict great and intense suffering, but they cannot prevent a glorious resurrection. It is, in fact, rather a good sign when a Catholic is abused for his political acts. The abuse is pretty sure to be occasioned by something very Christian and very Catholic in what he does. The political position

* O'Connell used often to say that he was "the best abused man in the world."

of an English Catholic is such that to some extent he must always be in opposition. In many, and perhaps in all, questions of mere civil policy, he may take his side in party warfare. But so long as Catholics are not in every respect on a perfect equality with Protestants, there must be questions on which we are at variance with one party or the other, and sometimes with both. In political action in the United Kingdom everything depends on the power of fighting. In our constitutional system, the redress of a grievance is obtained in a manner completely different from that in which it is obtained under an absolute monarchy. In a monarchy, and even in a limited monarchy, but one in which the sovereign has much more power than is possessed by the sovereign in England, the object of a class of persons suffering under a grievance is to conciliate the head of the State, or the minister to whom the direction of affairs is left. Hence it is the best policy of the aggrieved to consult the feelings and wishes of the authorities as much as possible, and to abstain from everything which might annoy, embarrass, and irritate them. For the redress of a wrong where there is absolute authority is not a party, but a personal affair; if they who are asking for justice can secure the favour of one man, they will soon get what they want. But in our parliamentary government it is a totally different thing. A wrong is not remedied by a person, but by a party. Whenever there is a refusal or a reluctance to do right, or an unreasonable delay in doing right, it is not by conciliating an individual that justice is obtained, but by making justice the interest of a party. A good example of what is here meant was the conduct of Lord John Russell in 1847, when he refused to include Catholics in the grant for education. Lord John cared nothing for the past services and the present conciliatory letters and speeches of all the Catholic Whigs in both Lords and Commons. The threat of the Wesleyan Methodists to oppose the grant if Catholics were included made, in the mind of a Russell, all the conciliatory conduct of the Catholics kick the beam. But no sooner did Sir William Molesworth get up in the House, and threaten the party leader with a serious defection from his ranks if Catholics were not included, than the minister immediately promised that Catholics should share in the grant. Political life and political action under the English constitution are certainly a warfare; and a wrong which affects religion must be remedied by the same means as are employed to put an Englishman into a better position as to his franchise, or his house, or his food, or anything else.[1] Those who never look threatening, who never organize, who are always saying, "We don't want to fight," are looked on by Englishmen as soldiers are looked upon who shun the combat. All the world knows what great things may be done by a small but well-disciplined force. And yet we Catholics of England but too often neglect to learn wisdom by experience. The consequence is, that our position is something like that of the Chinese people when they have a quarrel with a European state and a disciplined army. When men stand up boldly for some demand in which the bulk of the people do not sympathize, or which has a large party of opponents, they are sure to meet with abuse. In the heat of the contest nothing may be heard but hooting and yells; but "when the battle's lost and won," the hooting and the yells cease, and we hear nothing but praise of the bravery and, as we say, "thorough English conduct" of those who have been most hooted and yelled at. It is true that in the case of O'Connell the English people never completely forgave him. He had done what

[1] By "political action" is here meant the use of any civil right to promote an object, whether civil or religious.

no other man ever did do: he, an Irishman and a Catholic, had fought and beaten the British nation. But still, the vexation caused by that one great crime did not destroy admiration for his boldness and persevering determination to use every liberty he possessed, to obtain other liberties of which he was unjustly deprived. Who does not now admire in Milner and O'Connell all that which is summed up in the expressive word *pluck?* They *must* be admired, because, having to fight the English on English ground, they fought not as Chinese would fight, but as Englishmen are accustomed to fight and to conquer. The abuse they got was only the harmless cries of an exasperated and retiring enemy. But irritating as those discordant cries may have been, they were sweet and harmonious compared with the groans of contempt which would have followed them if they had chosen un-English weapons and un-English tactics in a fight with Britons to obtain British rights; if, in a word, they had foolishly relied on personal influence with the minister, or on secret underhand diplomacy, instead of on the only kind of political warfare which finds favour with the English people. Milner has taught us what one man alone can do by open and plain speech and a determined will; O'Connell gives us the brightest example in Christian times of what one leader can accomplish without breaking a tittle of the law, but with a united people at his back to support his public but peaceful demand.

It will be necessary to introduce a good deal of what has been done in Ireland. The Irish portion of the Church and the English portion of the Church stand in two very different positions. In both countries, it is true, Catholics were persecuted and kept down: but in England they were well-nigh exterminated; whereas in Ireland, while the political influence of Catholics was destroyed, the faith increased as the English tried to stamp it out, and the green blade sprang up in luxuriance beneath the feet of the oppressors. A hundred years ago, in England, Catholics had everything to gain; in Ireland they had religion to preserve, and political influence to acquire. It was a consequence of this state of things that, as soon as the legislature began to relax the penal laws, and the Irish Catholics could act with greater freedom, their numbers, their larger middle class, their more numerous gentry, began to exercise their legitimate influence in public affairs. This influence increased, and became at last an overwhelming power, when, under the command of the great O'Connell, it forced the power of England to yield, and to grant the emancipation of 1829. This power of the Irish Catholics had its effect in Great Britain. Here we had no force, physical or moral, to use; but what had been granted to the Irish could hardly have been refused to the English Catholics. It may be said that the Irish were relieved because they became too strong to be any longer ill-treated; we English were relieved because we were too weak to be feared. As the great Catholic power in the United Kingdom during the last hundred years had been, and still is, in Ireland, that power has, under good Providence, been exerted in many ways to improve the position of Catholics in England. It is impossible, therefore, to tell the history of British Catholics, and to recount the progress we have made, without frequently alluding to this great motive-power which our good God has made use of to bring about the happy result.

There are one or two matters which are always thrown upon the carpet whenever there is a difference between Catholics and Protestants in this country, and which it will be well to notice before beginning the history of the contest for emancipation. One of these matters is the expression,

"Catholic before everything." This phrase is quoted against us sometimes by well-intentioned persons who do not understand its meaning, and at other times by men who know its meaning well, who know that there is no harm in it, but who want to exasperate their Protestant fellow-subjects against us by charging us with being disloyal and un-English.

The origin of the expression, "*Catholique avant tout*," or "Catholic before everything," is its use by the great Christian orator of our time, Montalembert. He found himself almost alone in the House of Peers, and afterwards in the National Assembly, opposed to the liberal spirit of the time, in its constant attacks upon the Church. If in the House of Peers, and in the Assembly, Montalembert was supported by others, it was chiefly by men whom his eloquence roused to exertion. The liberty of the Church was attacked on all sides. Those who are old enough to remember it, will recall to mind that manly energy and those glorious bursts of eloquence with which the great champion defended the liberty of parents to bring up their children Catholics, the liberty of Religious Orders, and the liberty of the Holy Father.

Montalembert was the spokesman of Catholics in a Catholic country. But France had in his time, and has now, many wayward children. The infidel principles which burst forth at the commencement of the great Revolution have, in greater or less degree, dominated in the government of the country down to our own time. In spite of so much that is greatest and best in France, she was gradually becoming an un-Christian country. In this state of things, the Christian champion rushed to the front, and loudly proclaimed, "Remember, we are Catholic before everything." What did he mean? He meant that nothing that was un-Christian could be for the good of

France.¹ He meant that un-Christian principles disgraced his country, and that Christian principles honoured her; and it was necessary in France then, and over the whole of Europe it is now necessary, to raise the cry of "Catholic before everything," if they who wish to give to God what belongs to God are to be rallied to stand the shock of the enemy, who would give everything to Cæsar. We might, indeed, express the meaning of Montalembert, in the words used by Mr. Gladstone. When speaking of the words, "A Catholic first, an Englishman afterwards," he says, they "properly convey no more than a truism; for every Christian must seek to place his religion even before his country in his inner heart." Yes, the thought of Montalembert's inner heart was that, being a Christian, he must seek to place his religion even before his country. But he was not the man to be content to preserve Christian thoughts in his inner heart, and by word and by deed to flatter and help on the un-Christian principles of those around him. He was no gigantic hypocrite, pandering to tastes which in his heart he detested; he was no coward, "letting *I dare not* wait upon *I would.*" He was a man whose mouth spoke out of the abundance of his inner heart. He was a man who could and did raise his voice when necessary, to proclaim what his heart believed. And herein was his great offence in the opinion of such men as Mr. Gladstone. Let a Catholic keep his Christian principles in his inner heart, while with voice or with pen he denies them, and he is well pleasing in the eyes of the Liberal party. But let a Catholic give utterance to his principles; let him, as becomes a man, act upon them, and the chief men of the Liberal party will denounce him

¹ Those who are not Catholics should know that the words "Christian" and "Catholic" are practically, and in a Catholic country are understood to be, synonymous.

as incapable of being loyal, and of discharging his civil duty. It is no sin in England to be a Christian; but to act, under all circumstances, as a Christian should act, is treason.

Having said thus much about the words "Catholic before everything," I wish now to draw the reader's attention to the free translation of those words which Mr. Gladstone gave in one of his Vatican pamphlets. This is Mr. Gladstone's version: "A Catholic first, an Englishman afterwards." Mr. Gladstone puts these words into inverted commas, and says they "have become notorious." Being in inverted commas, Mr. Gladstone meant them for a quotation. Where did he take them from? Who has ever written them? Who ever spoke them? He has taken them from newspapers. Many Protestants have written, and many Protestants have said, that these words were said and written by Catholics. What Catholic ever said them? What Catholic ever wrote them? The impression intended to be conveyed by Mr. Gladstone is the same as the impression intended to be conveyed by the newspapers, which published the words as if spoken by a Catholic. The fact is that the words, "A Catholic first, an Englishman afterwards," have not a Catholic origin: they have been invented by Protestants to fix odium upon Catholics. Being invented, they have been quoted over and over again, and even by Mr. Gladstone, as having been uttered by a Catholic, and all England believes it, and, in believing it, believes what is false. But why should we be so anxious to deny the Catholic origin of the words, seeing that Mr. Gladstone himself thinks them capable of a very good interpretation? And we ourselves must admit that they contain an excellent meaning. We object to the phrase for this reason. It has been invented and put into our mouths in order to create a wrong impression. Two impressions may be created by the words, " A Catholic first, an Englishman afterwards." One, the impression which, as Mr. Gladstone says, they " properly convey," and the other, the impression which persons ill-disposed to the Catholic religion take from them ; as when Mr. Gladstone says, "We take them to mean that the 'convert' intends, in case of any conflict between the Queen and the Pope, to follow the Pope, and let the Queen shift for herself." Of the first and the true impression I have spoken above, in what has been said of the words " Catholic before everything." Of the false impression it will be necessary to say a few words, in order to explain what I have called the free translation into English of Montalembert's motto, "Catholique avant tout." When Mr. Gladstone spoke of a conflict between the Queen and the Pope, he did not, of course, speak of a conflict in spiritual matters. If a Catholic in spiritual matters speaks and acts as "a Catholic first," he is simply faithful in his conduct to what Mr. Gladstone calls a truism : that "every Christian must seek to place his religion even before his country in his inner heart." By a conflict between the Queen and the Pope, Mr. Gladstone meant, therefore, a conflict in civil matters ; and the wrong impression he meant to convey is that, in a conflict between the Queen and the Pope in civil matters, Catholics who adopt the expression, "Catholic before everything"—for we won't accept his distinction of "converts "— would "follow the Pope, and let the Queen shift for herself." Now, if the words "Catholic before everything" are changed into " A Catholic first, an Englishman afterwards," an antithesis is created which fixes the attention on the words "an Englishman afterwards," and so seems to place the interests of our country in a lower and secondary place. Our fellow-countrymen have been, and still are, so persistent in charging us, against all historical facts, with not being loyal, that they will not stop to make a distinction between spiritual matters and civil matters. When, therefore, they are told that we are Catholic first and English afterwards, they immediately take the words to mean that in civil matters we give our country the second place; which we do not. Those amongst our countrymen who know better, know also how easy it is to pervert the judgment of Englishmen in any Catholic question, by exciting their prejudices against us. A word can do it; a word has often done it.

The history of the expression, "A Catholic first, an Englishman afterwards," is therefore this. The great and noble utterance of Montalembert had its echo in England. It was calculated to rouse the spirit of Catholics, who had just shaken off the chains of persecution, and were thinking how they could, by all legal means, use their liberties as Englishmen in defence of their religion as Catholics. "Catholic before everything" is a cry too inspiring to be left by our enemies to work upon us, without their attempting to destroy its effect by a discord. Montalembert never said, "A Catholic first, a Frenchman afterwards." Though he would not have hesitated to use the words in the sense in which Mr. Gladstone says they are a truism, yet he was too wise to give a handle to his enemies, by an expression which would enable them to fix, though unjustly, odium even on a truism. No English Catholic ever attempted to improve on the great motto. We did not give the free translation of which Mr. Gladstone has made so evil a use. It was not in France that an addition was made. The motto, as used now in England, was not a translation made by an English Protestant from a French infidel. The free translation was made in England by some English Protestant, and the words were attributed to

Catholics to produce the effect above explained. The translation was, in fact, "an ingenious device" of our enemies. Montalembert's words were freely translated, or rather developed, in such a way as to be perfectly unobjectionable, in the sense in which a Catholic would use them, and at the same time contain what is called a *suggestio falsi*—a suggestion of the falsehood that, in civil matters, a Catholic would not give the laws of his country the first place. By whomsoever the device was invented, it has been adopted by Mr. Gladstone; he is responsible for it, and has never rejected it.

Before concluding these observations on the words, "A Catholic first, an Englishman afterwards," I must allude to one or two remarks of Mr. Gladstone, where he notices those words in his pamphlet. Having said that in one sense those words are a truism, he goes on to say, "but very far from a truism in the sense in which we have been led to construe them." By whom led to construe them? Certainly not by any Catholic. The words were not invented by a Catholic, as I have said. But as the words are in themselves, and properly understood, most unobjectionable, we need not at this moment unceremoniously discard them. Let them stand while we give our answer. No Catholic, either by word or by action, has ever led any one to suppose that we construe them in any other sense than that in which they are a truism. Then by whom led to construe them, we again ask? By those who have invented or adopted the phrase, in order to suggest a sense in which they are not true. How then stands the question? A grand motto of which any Christian might be proud has been put by our enemies into a special form, for the express purpose of suggesting what is false; and then we are told that it is we who have led our countrymen to construe the motto in the evil sense which by that special form is conveyed. Mr. Gladstone, continuing his comments on the free translation of Montalembert's motto, observes, "We take them to mean that the 'convert' intends, in case of any conflict between the Queen and the Pope, to follow the Pope, and let the Queen shift for herself; which, happily, she can well do." What right has Mr. Gladstone to take the words to mean anything but what a Catholic would mean by them? If he will put words into our mouths, at least he should give us the privilege of interpreting them. But he will not allow us even this. He interprets them himself, charges us with the interpretation, and founds on the interpretation a charge of intending to follow the Pope rather than the Queen in purely civil matters. If such conduct were pursued towards any other class of Englishmen than Catholics what would not be said of it? How true are the words which the author of "Norton Broadland" puts into the mouth of Lord Hillsworth!—"I must confess I am astonished at the way in which even people who know how to behave in every other relation of life, seem to forget that they are ladies and gentlemen the moment that they come in contact with Catholicity."

Is it possible that Mr. Gladstone can really imagine it is likely that there will be any conflict between the Queen and the Pope; and Mr. Gladstone must, as I said, mean a conflict in civil matters. He cannot mean in spiritual matters, for he knows that it exists, and must unfortunately exist, so long as the Queen shall remain a Protestant. And besides, Mr. Gladstone will give both the Queen and the Pope credit for placing their religion before their country in their inner hearts. He therefore means a conflict in civil matters. If Mr. Gladstone uses the word "Queen" to denominate our gracious Queen Victoria— and we hope he has not used her name in vain—then we do say that, of all the improbable things which by possibility might happen, the most improbable is any conflict between the Queen and the Pope in a civil matter. Mr. Gladstone would perhaps be delighted to catch a Catholic tripping in such a conflict, but he has not the remotest chance of catching one of us. He may as well give up his delusion, and relegate his ideal sport of catching Catholics in treason, to those queer days in future, when larks also will be caught easily, because the sky will have fallen.

But it is possible that Mr. Gladstone may have used the Queen's name only typically, to signify the laws and institutions of England, and he may think it is likely that the Pope may be in conflict with them. There is, he may be assured, nothing more unlikely. That there may be some laws on the statute-book which the Pope would like to see repealed, I think very probable; for example, the penal laws enacted by the Emancipation Act. And there may be laws which the Pope would like to see on the statute-book; for example, a law that in all public institutions Catholics shall have the same advantages for the practice of their religion as the members of the Church of England possess. But matters of this sort have not caused, and will not cause, any civil complication between England and the Pope. It is useless, therefore, to anticipate the time.

But is it possible that, by the words "conflict between the Queen and the Pope," Mr. Gladstone meant a conflict between Catholic principles and those liberal principles of the day which are opposed to Christianity? Is it in his mind that a Catholic does not discharge the duties of civil loyalty, if he opposes bills brought into Parliament for creating civil marriage, legalizing sinful divorce, and establishing a system of Godless education? Is it possible that a Catholic is in Mr. Gladstone's opinion disloyal to his country who is not loyal to him? I strongly suspect that Catholics are charged with disloyalty in these days, whenever they stand in the way of those liberal ideas which have no element of Christianity in them. English Liberalism is in these days imbibing too much of Continental Liberalism, and to this the conscience of every Catholic is and must be opposed. But I would ask, would Mr. Gladstone dare to charge a Protestant country squire with disloyalty, because he might oppose a Divorce Bill, or the Education Bill of 1870? He would not. Then he should not dare to charge us with disloyalty, because we may think proper, in the exercise of our English liberties, to oppose any bill whatever that he may choose to introduce into Parliament. Will any one dare to fetter our liberties, because the head of our Church is the Bishop of Rome? If Mr. Gladstone had any idea of frightening English Catholics into subserviency to him by holding over us the charge of disloyalty, he found himself mistaken. We have not sunk to so low a state as to quail before such a threat. But either it is true that his pamphlet meant such a threat, or his charge of disloyalty was as ridiculous a charge as one man ever made against another. Though ten years have passed since Mr. Gladstone charged us with disloyalty, we ought not to forget that the charge was made; for we may depend upon it that some one or another will repeat it whenever it may suit a party purpose. But in the midst of any persecution of public opinion excited against us by misrepresentation, we shall, with the help of God, pursue our old course. We have a glorious history to look back to. Our fathers were Catholics before everything; they fought a good fight, and kept the faith for us their children. We, let us hope, shall follow their example. "Catholics before everything" is our cry; and many hearts beat quicker at the sound. The mustering numbers increase. Fidelity and perseverance are strong powers; and, with God on our side, England may one day be as Catholic in the future as she was in the past.

One great means which the enemy of mankind has used to delude the English people has been to make them believe that Catholics are not and cannot be loyal subjects. Catholics meet this by saying that we are, to say the very least, as loyal to Queen and country as any other class of her Majesty's subjects. We are more loyal than most of those who say we are not loyal.

In the history of the English Catholics since the Reformation, one of the facts which force themselves upon the notice of the reader, is their persevering loyalty to the throne and constitution of this realm. This loyalty is proved by a continual series of acts reaching down to our own time. It is difficult to understand how any one perusing English history can fail to be struck by the prominence of Catholic loyalty. It is still more difficult to comprehend how any one, with the proof before him, can refuse to the fact its legitimate conclusion, and draw another conclusion from some fanciful theory of his own. Our love for our country and our loyalty to the Crown have been faithful through good report and through evil report. They have been tried by fire and sword. They have been stretched to the utmost; but they have not been broken. They have stood all the severest tests to which loyalty could be subjected, but they have never shown the smallest symptom of a flaw. Exclusion, confiscation, and death have done their worst, and the loyalty of English Catholics is as sound as ever.

I say, at starting, we are loyal because we are Catholics. Our religion has taught us to be loyal; our religion has made us loyal; our religion keeps us loyal. To be English and to be Catholic are the two surest marks of a loyal subject. These two qualities seem in their combination to produce the strength which is attributed to the triple cord, which is not easily broken. The word of an English Catholic that he is loyal to his sovereign and that he loves his country, is a pledge worth having. The day may not be so far off when our traducers will, by their own acts, exhibit to the world the tinsel of their own boasted loyalty in contrast to the pure gold of ours.

When we come to the proof of English Catholic loyalty, the field is so large, and the historical facts so numerous, that it becomes impossible in a short work to treat the subject as could be wished. I will, however, remind the reader of some passages in English history. Charles II. summoned his loyal subjects to meet him on the 21st of August, 1651, in the meadows which lie under the walls of Worcester. Amongst the gentlemen who met him with their troops of horse were Sir Walter Blount, Mr. Ralph Sheldon, Mr. Thomas Acton, and Mr. Hornyold of Blackmore Park. I would ask Mr. Gladstone, as head of the Liberal party in England, were those gentlemen loyal men? I hope he would answer, Yes. And yet all these men had suffered most grievously at the hands of the Stuarts only because they were Catholics, and through a bloody persecution had preserved both their loyalty and their faith.

When the battle of Worcester had been lost and won, Mr. Whitgreave of Moseley, Father Huddlestone, and the Penderells took good care of the beaten King. I would again ask Mr. Gladstone: Were they loyal men? We may presume that not even the head of the Liberal party will think less of the loyalty of the Catholics who lived at the end of the seventeenth and beginning of the eighteenth centuries, because their sympathies were not strongly enlisted on the side of William III. Without entering into any question, which is needless here as to rights *de jure* and rights *de facto* to the Crown of England, the certain fact is, that no Catholic of any note or interest did anything which William III. judged to be disloyal. And yet in William's reign some grievous penal laws were passed.

Nor can we be reproached by any one if our ancestors were not enthusiastic admirers of Queen Anne, the daughter of a Catholic, and who consented to the persecution of her Catholic subjects. But, nevertheless, Catholics were loyal to her, though neither they nor we have been able to waste much love upon her.

During the reigns of the early Georges the Jacobite sympathies of the Catholics of England were shared by them in common with the whole Tory party, and in those days there was no disloyalty in being a Jacobite. If any accusation of disloyalty is to be made against any Englishmen for their conduct in 1715 and 1745, it must be made against all who would have preferred the House of Stuart to the House of Brunswick. Now, there was a large party in England who had such a preference, and Catholics were only a small portion of that party. It would be a shabby thing to point to one section of the then Tory party, and say, "You were not loyal." It would look as if the point was not at their politics, but at their religion. And, indeed, to any one who should think that in the reigns of George I. and George II. it was treason to love a Stuart more than a Hanoverian, we may answer that the overt acts in these reigns implicated the whole Tory party, and that the Catholics as a body were not represented to the extent which is sometimes supposed. Goldsmith, who was seventeen years old in 1745, says, in his History of England, when speaking of Charles Edward's attempt, that "he was joined at Manchester by two hundred English." And Berington, writing in 1780, says, " Very few Catholics, I have observed, were engaged in the rebellion." The number must indeed have been small. And the latter author, writing about the rebellion of 1715, says of the Catholics, "The number of real insurgents was inconsiderable." But in reality the sympathy shown by English Catholics to the House of Stuart was no sign of disloyalty. The conduct of our ancestors in relation to the crown and country from the battle of Worcester to the accession of George III. was a proof of their love of both.

We may easily imagine, from what we have seen in other countries, that complications may arise which may make it difficult for a conscientious man to know what side he should take in a dynastic quarrel. A knowledge of facts and a knowledge of rights are required in the first instance. A judgment unclouded by prejudices, and a will directed by conscience and duty, are necessary for decision between conflicting claims. No bigoted admirer of William III. shall be the judge of the loyalty of Catholics during the reign of that monarch. No man whose first principle even in politics is to hate the Catholic Church, shall dictate to us what the feelings of our ancestors should have been with regard to Queen Anne and the first two of the Georges. But if any unbiassed person would learn how admirably and with what delicate regard to duty and the claims of others, a Catholic can conduct himself in political complications, let him study the history of Catholics in the times to which we have alluded.

Whatever differences of opinion, however, may be allowed as to our conduct during the events which followed close on the Revolution, this we assert, and challenge denial: as soon as the title of the House of Brunswick became undoubtedly a title *de jure* as well as *de facto*, the

English Catholics, following the dictates of that religion which is said to make them disloyal subjects, one and all transferred their hearts and their hands to the present reigning House. In giving the names of some of those who fought at Worcester, I have mentioned that of Ralph Sheldon. The Sheldons were then Catholics, and they remained so even into this century. In illustration of what has been said above, it is a curious fact that when, in 1778, the English Catholics presented to George III. an obsequiously loyal address, the secretary to the committee which drew it up was William Sheldon, a descendant of the gentleman who met Charles in the Worcester meadows. Thus this "religious, honourable, and straightforward gentleman," as Milner calls him, proved what indeed he only shared with all other Catholics, that he was then as loyal to the Protestant House of Brunswick as his fathers had been to the Catholics of the House of Stuart. What King or Queen of England is there who would not value the loyalty of such a man as that, rather than the loyalty of one who would think it expedient to support his sovereign's title to the throne, so long only as he or she should remain a Protestant? And again we ask, how is it that through such fearful trials as were inflicted by the penal laws we have preserved our allegiance to our sovereign and to our country? And again we answer, it is because we have been Catholics. It is on account of the faith which is in us that our loyalty, when weighed in the balance, has not been found wanting. Our loyalty is not a loyalty of expediency, but one of justice and of right. It is not a matter of opinion; it is founded on those laws of faith and morals by which the Church, guided by the Holy Spirit, has bound us. We do not say that we have not reasons as Englishmen, as well as reasons as Catholics, for being faithful to our country. But we say that our fidelity has its special value, from the fact that it is strengthened by the doctrines which we hold. For it cannot be denied that there is such a thing in England, and widely spread too, as a loyalty of expediency. A loyalty which is founded on the opinion that a monarchy is for us the best form of government, is a loyalty of expediency. If public opinion were to set in strongly against the throne, the throne would not stand the shock. Public opinion varies; it is "a reed shaken by the wind." It can bear no weight and strain; it cannot be trusted. It cannot hand down from father to son a principle which, however sound in its nature, is inconvenient in its practice.

In the year 1701, loyalty founded on public opinion could not stand the test of allowing a Catholic to inherit the crown of England. The Act of Settlement was passed, excluding Catholics from the throne. But loyalty founded on conscience stood every test that was applied to it.

In the year 1778, the English Catholics signed an address to the King, of which the following was the first paragraph:—

Most gracious Sovereign: we, your Majesty's dutiful and loyal subjects, the Roman Catholic peers and commoners of your Kingdom of Great Britain, most humbly hope that it cannot be offensive to the clemency of your Majesty's nature, or to the maxims of your just and wise government, that any part of your subjects should approach your royal presence, to assure your Majesty of the respectful affection which they bear to your person, and their true attachment to the civil constitution of their country; which, having been perpetuated through all changes of religious opinions and establishments, has been, at length, perfected by that revolution which has placed your Majesty's illustrious House on the throne of these kingdoms, and inseparably united your title to the crown with the laws and liberties of your people.

Such were the words of English Catholics to a Protestant

King, whose predecessors had shown but little mercy to us. Such was the first utterance of loyalty, when our great grandfathers dared for the first time to hope that they would be even listened to by their sovereign. Such was the speech of a loyalty founded upon conscience, loyalty which remained sound and true after generations of persecution. That address was even excessive in the eagerness of those who presented it. Loyalty to the King and constitution might have been fully expressed without going to the extreme length of saying that the civil constitution of the country had been *perfected* by the revolution. Perhaps our respected ancestors overlooked the fact that they were attributing perfection to an Act by which any one of their own religion was excluded from the throne.

Let us look at another contrast. If there be one principle in the English constitution more vaunted than another, it is that of civil and religious liberty. And yet loyalty to that principle would appear to be founded only on public opinion for the time being, for in 1851 it could not stand the test it was put to. The Holy Father exercised a purely spiritual act in the appointment of bishops in England. There was no law against it; the right of the Pope to act as he did had been acknowledged, and religious liberty entitled Catholics to be left in peace. But public opinion was roused by Earl Russell and the *Times* newspaper against his Holiness. Public opinion set in furiously for persecution; down fell the principle of civil and religious liberty, and a new penal law was enacted. How different on that occasion was the conduct of those whose loyalty was founded not on opinion, but on conscience informed by right and justice. The leader of the English Catholics at that time—would that, for our own sake, he could come again amongst us—would not consent to an address to Cardinal Wiseman, unless it contained an unmistakable assertion of our loyalty to the Crown. Those who heard him speak on the subject will not forget his words; they expressed towards her Majesty as enthusiastic a loyalty as might have been felt by the staunchest Jacobite to the House of Stuart. And this assertion of loyalty was sincerely made by those against whom their Queen was about to attach her sign manual to a penal law.

Mr. Gladstone once drew a distinction between those who have been Catholics from their infancy and those who embraced the faith in after life. He wrote in the *Contemporary Review* that "no one can become a *convert* without renouncing his moral and mental freedom, and placing his civil loyalty and duty at the mercy of another." And in his pamphlet he said, "that Rome requires a *convert* to forfeit his moral and mental freedom," etc. And the newspapers, especially the *Times*, have understood his meaning to be that, while he relies upon the loyalty of the old Catholic families, he suspects that of "a convert." All English Catholics repudiate the distinction. If a convert has to forfeit any principles, it is because those principles are not held by the members of the communion into which he enters. There are not, and there cannot be, two sets of principles, one for those born of Catholic parents, and another for those who joined the Church when they came to man's estate. If a convert has to forfeit his freedom, it must be because he goes amongst those who are not free; if he places his loyalty and civil duty at the mercy of another, it is because he joins a body which teaches its members to do so. And therefore no distinction can be drawn between the principles of converts and the principles of other Catholics. That a Catholic has less freedom than others, except the freedom of thinking what he likes in religious matters independent of all authority, is strictly opposed to the real truth. He has more freedom than others, and in matters of thought can wander more where he pleases, for the simple reason that he goes to sea with a rudder to his boat. Whereas others who have not that guide are driven about at the mercy of all the absurd notions of the age in which they happen to live. The charge that Catholics place their loyalty and civil duty at the mercy of another is simply a charge that we are members of a Church which has from the time of our Saviour taught its members to "give to Cæsar what belongs to Cæsar, and to God what belongs to God." So, let this be understood: a charge that a convert cannot be loyal, is a charge that a Catholic cannot be loyal. Mr. Gladstone and all others may spare their compliments to the old Catholic families. Mr. Gladstone may perhaps tell us that the facts here noticed as showing the loyalty of Catholics, prove nothing to him. Ralph Sheldon, who fought at Worcester, and William Sheldon, who wrote the loyal address to King George, he may say, lived before the Vatican Decrees, and this makes all the difference. It makes no difference at all. The Vatican Decrees have only defined what has always been the belief of the Church. Mr. Gladstone, who is famous for the fine logical distinctions which he can draw and clearly set forth, ought to be able to see the distinction between a matter of faith and a defined article of faith. He ought to understand how the faith of the Church in the first century may not be a defined article of faith until the nineteenth century. And therefore he ought to know that the Vatican Decrees have not changed, because they cannot change, the belief of the Church. Our relations with the State are precisely the same as they were before the Vatican Decrees. If Mr. Gladstone is satisfied with the loyalty and civil duty of Lord Howard of Effingham, Ralph Sheldon of Worcester, Mr. Whitgreave of Moseley, Richard Penderell, William

Sheldon, who wrote the loyal address to George III., and Mr. Langdale, who would not compliment the cardinal without proclaiming his loyalty to the Queen, he ought to be satisfied with ours. It is the same as theirs; the Vatican Decrees have made no difference. We do not see the difference; we say there is no difference to be seen; we are ready to show by our conduct that no difference really exists.

But if a serious doubt could have arisen in the mind of Mr. Gladstone, as to whether the Vatican Decrees had in any way changed the relations of English Catholics towards their sovereign and their country, why did he not go for the solution of that doubt to those who were the best able to solve it? The Catholic families of England, if not a numerous class, stand in the very first rank of English society, and some of them bear names which, amongst those which are known and honoured in our land, are the most honoured and the best known. As Mr. Gladstone tells us that he has many Catholic friends, why did he not go to them before making an assertion which before the whole country impeached their loyalty and their honour? Why did he not ask the descendants of those whose names are identified with the first beginnings of our liberties? Why did he not question those men in whose families from time immemorial, love of country and love of their religion have never been separated? Why did he not go to the present representatives of one of those long genealogies, in which even the acute eye of Mr. Gladstone would not detect either a rebel or an apostate? Why did he not question those in whose families loyalty has been proved as gold is tried by the fire? Well indeed may English Catholics feel slighted and insulted and wronged when they are charged with disloyalty by a prominent statesman; when they are accused before the whole country by the foremost man in it. We were accused in a matter peculiarly within our own knowledge. We are the accused, but we are the best witnesses. But Mr. Gladstone did not give us the benefit of his hearing what we had to say, before he made his public expostulation. He passed us over, and went for his evidence to a German professor, who gave it as his opinion that Catholics cannot be loyal. And the opinion of this man is to outweigh the evidence of history and of facts. We may exclaim with indignation that the opinion of this man is not to be taken at all. We spurn the notion that evidence of our feelings as Englishmen and as Catholics is to be taken from an apostate German priest. The idea of taking evidence of this sort would be ridiculous, and might be treated as such if it came from some men. It might be laughed at as an "ingenious device."[1] But when we see a man like Mr. Gladstone adopting the tactics of Exeter Hall, we are forced to cry out against the mischief done.

Therefore, let no Englishman delude himself with the notion that a state of things will ever be brought about when the Catholics of England will give up either their loyalty or their faith. In spite of the irreligious and revolutionary tendencies of the day, we intend, by the grace of God, to keep both.

Before beginning the history, it may be well to give a rapid sketch of the ground it will cover, when, God willing, it shall have been brought to a conclusion. Looking back to the year 1774, what a mighty change presents itself to an English Catholic! We can, perhaps, best

---

[1] Some years ago, one of the speakers in Exeter Hall—I believe he was a Protestant clergyman—in order to prove one of the usual false charges against us, read out a forged bull of one of the Popes. When he was detected, admitting the forgery, he gave himself credit for having practised an "ingenious device."

realize the change by imagining what some one dying just before 1774 would have thought if he could have seen, through the vista of years, all that has happened up to our own days. Alban Butler died in the year 1773. He was not permitted to hear even the first sound which tolled the knell of the old penal laws, and signalized the first step in the steady march of emancipation. He must have died almost without a hope for his country. He had seen the number of English Catholics gradually diminishing through the reigns of the early Georges, and to his last day on earth that number was continuing to lessen. In the year 1780, according to Berington, the number of English Catholics was not more than sixty thousand, and many missions were vacant and not likely to be filled up. When Alban Butler died, the prospect looked sad indeed. If he looked to the Catholics themselves, he could not have discerned the smallest power amongst them to obtain redress; if he looked to the Government, he could not have seen any ground for hope. Mr. Fagan, in his "Life and Times of Daniel O'Connell," remarks that the Act of 1774 was passed without any agitation whatever on the part of the Catholics themselves. It was forced upon the Parliament of Ireland in order to conciliate, in some degree at least, the Catholics of that country when the colonies were about to revolt. But it was not until 1774 that the English Government was threatened by the combined action of those colonies which afterwards formed the United States. No one, therefore, in the year 1773 could have supposed that the action of American rebels might lead, through the pressure it would exercise, to the relief of the Catholics. Standing, therefore, over the death-bed of Alban Butler, we may imagine what he would have thought had God presented to his failing eyes a vision of a hundred succeeding years. What would he have seen?

He would have seen the venerable Bishop Challoner, then in the eighty-third year of his age, living to witness this first gleam of hope afforded by the passing of the Act of 1774; and he would have seen him still living to thank God that in his extreme old age He had allowed him to see the day on which, by the Act of 1778, Catholic bishops, priests, and schoolmasters were no longer subject to perpetual imprisonment; and the old Catholic gentry could inherit the estates of their forefathers, and purchase new lands, without fear of their properties being seized by some apostate relation. He would have seen the great French Revolution bursting upon affrighted Europe, and causing the English Government again to send a message of peace to the Catholics, and give them the further relief afforded by the Acts of 1791 and 1793. Next he would have seen a sight which must have riveted his attention. His own College of St. Omer's,[1] the other colleges of the English seculars and regulars, all the convents of English ladies in France and Belgium were breaking up, and their communities were pouring into the old country amidst the sympathy and applause of their countrymen, and with the hearty welcome of a Prince Regent. He himself was liable at that moment, had he been in England, to perpetual imprisonment for being a priest; and he now sees thousands of the French clergy hospitably received, even invited to the shores of England, pensioned by the Government, and many of them scattering themselves over the country, exercising the holy ministry, loved and respected by all, and leaving a name which to this day is revered. And all this was within twenty years after the dark days on the last of which he died. At the time of Alban

---

[1] After the expulsion of the Jesuits from France in 1762, the Parliament of Paris gave the presidency of the English College of the Society at St. Omer's to the Rev. Mr. Talbot, and to him succeeded Alban Butler.

Butler's death, Milner was just twenty-one years of age. Almost in the foreground of the picture we have imagined him to behold, Butler would have seen the young man, with a mitre on his head, boldly withstanding a double foe, enemies within and enemies without the fold, a doughty champion of the Church, laying down the terms of emancipation, and, in face of statesmen who claimed a *veto* on the election of bishops, making it impossible to pass any act of relief which had his *veto* upon it. A marvellous sight this to one who knew that bishops were especially marked out for perpetual imprisonment, and who could himself remember a priest who underwent the punishment. For Alban Butler was nineteen years of age when the Franciscan Father Atkinson died in Hurst Castle after many years in prison, his sole offence being that he was a priest.[1] He would next see the whole career of the great O'Connell, the man who taught the Catholics to hold up their heads and assert their rights; who, standing at the head of millions who had been downtrodden by their oppressors until he raised the wand which made them start to their feet, fought for years a battle which ended in so glorious a victory that his name will be handed down to the end of time as the greatest champion of moral force. And then the vision would begin to expand, and the prospect would begin to brighten. For the year 1829 was a great epoch. The Emancipation Bill having passed into law, Catholics found themselves comparatively free. The freer action of the Church began—controversial meetings were held; schools were multiplied; chapels which before were hidden in back lanes were abandoned, and new ones built facing the main street; religious orders of men and women were establishing themselves; the old orders

---

[1] It is, perhaps, worthy of note that the passing of the Emancipation Act in 1829 was just one hundred years after the death of the last priest in prison.

forming larger communities, and the new ones spreading themselves over the whole land.

In contemplating this joyful scene, we may easily imagine that the eyes of that worthy servant of God, Alban Butler, would have been quick to notice the reappearance of that order of which he might well have supposed that he had seen the last. The Society of Jesus was suppressed in the year 1773, two months after Alban Butler died. But now he sees its re-establishment, he sees it in England once again; and, glancing at its progress up to our day, he sees it opening its many houses and colleges, proclaiming aloud, faithful to its old traditions, the Immaculate Conception of the great Mother of God in the very midst of the capital, taking a lead in scientific discoveries, and raising to an English virgin one of the highest and most beautiful spires that has ever been built upon British ground. And next, as the prospect widens, he sees the emigration of hundreds of thousands from Ireland into England, bringing with them the faith which had stood the test under which Englishmen had failed. He sees the necessities of this great multitude taxing the energy of both clergy and laity to supply their wants, thus bringing into full play all the vigorous life of the Church, and putting her offices in all their splendour before the English people in every large town. And distinct from this, yet harmonizing with it, he sees that great movement from the Church of England itself, which, beginning in the University of Oxford, quickly spread, bringing hundreds into the Church, affecting thousands with the Church's truths, and exerting its influence far beyond the time which he was permitted to see. Nor would he fail to discern, in this portion of the view, that it was a member of the Church who, contrasting the modern style of church buildings with the old, revived the ancient architecture of England, and with it much of the old spirit of faith. And he would see many noble edifices, representing at once all that was Roman in doctrine and all that was English in taste, standing witnesses that there is nothing antagonistic between country and religion. And he would see, too, the development of Church government keeping pace with the progress of everything else. The four vicariates are doubled, and far in the background he sees the greatest event in our history of late years—the establishment of a new hierarchy by the same authority which sent Austin into England. And a grand figure would here arrest his attention. It is that of the first Archbishop of Westminster. It is that of a cardinal too, who comes to be the first prince of the Church resident in England since the days of Pole. Butler sees this prelate arrive upon our shores in the midst of a storm of indignation. But he sees him gallantly braving the storm, vindicating his right to stand on English ground; and at length so winning his way to English hearts, that when called to his reward, well-nigh a whole city is following him to his grave. He sees the new life and vigour infused into the Church in England in consequence of the new order of things. He sees a Catholic literature rapidly forming, and the number of Catholics who distinguish themselves in the various occupations of life daily increasing; he sees many old prejudices wearing away; he sees a Catholic lord chancellor in Ireland, and Catholics wearing the ermine in Westminster Hall. We who are accustomed to pilgrimages and conversions and grand churches, we who are living in the midst of the great revival, may not notice with such intense interest the signs of the times; but to a man in 1773 what we now see would have appeared to be leading rapidly to the conversion of England.

But there is still another sight in the far background of his view. That Church of England which Alban Butler left without a sign of decay has been likened to a breakwater; and it has no doubt acted as such to the waves of infidelity. But stretching his vision up to these our days, he would have seen that work on which Englishmen have taken so much pride as the work of their own hands, gradually giving way, showing unmistakable signs of breaking up, and its condition causing great alarm to those who were trusting in it. And if a thought had crossed his mind that that work of man had in God's providence served any good purpose, he would have been amply consoled when looking to the last sight which he could behold up to our times; for he would have seen, rising above the waters, behind that crumbling barrier of human hands, the strong work of God built upon the old foundations, surely and even quickly advancing, and if not actually ready to withstand the shock, showing in its progress to completion that it would surely be ready to resist all the force that might be brought against it, when the wild waves should have completed their work on the breakwater of human hands and swept it for ever away. All this, and still more, filling up the picture, is what a man might have seen in 1773 had God pleased in His mercy to show him the future. What would he have thought had he seen it all? What he would have thought, we should think. If intense gratitude would have found vent in acts of thanks, those acts of thanks should be on our lips.

We need not disguise from ourselves that in our actual view of the state of things there is shadow as well as light; there is much to lament as well as much to rejoice at. There is a vast amount of prejudice to be yet overcome; there is even much of that persecution of public opinion against us which our Holy Father[1] has spoken of as one of

[1] Pope Pius IX.

the chief sources of suffering to the Church in these days. The evil spirit has kept alive in the minds of Englishmen that mischievous falsehood, that to become a member of the Church a man must renounce his moral and mental freedom, and place his civil loyalty and duty at the mercy of another. If the laws are equal, the administration of them is not so. Worldly interest and human respect still keep multitudes from us. But we may ask, What could God have done for us that He has not done? He might have converted England. Undoubtedly He might have done so; but if He had converted England, it would have been by a stupendous miracle, or by a succession of great miracles. If it had pleased God so to act, our gratitude to Him would have been great indeed. But it should be greater now; for if we should thank God for what He has done for our country, we owe Him double thanks for allowing our fathers and ourselves to co-operate with Him in the work. But, short of converting England by miracle, what could God have done more for us than He has done? We have seen what our state was at the beginning of the year 1774. The prospect had been gradually darkening; there was no sign of light. Unexpectedly a bright speck appears, the light increases, and gradually brightness and even splendour divide the view with shadow. We have not seen the conversion of England, but we see the Church in England brought by the hand of God to that state in which it is rapidly becoming the one strong, compact Church, with the old faith and its young life, strengthening itself daily for the new combat it will have to sustain.

Looking, therefore, back to the year 1774, as we have supposed some one to look forward from that date to our time, what more could we desire? "He hath not done in like manner to every nation."

Introduction. 39

The year 1829 will undoubtedly remain for ever a great epoch in our history. The admission of Catholics into the Legislature was the first great blow which Protestant ascendency received. England has indeed been since called an essentially Protestant country, and no doubt there are many who would still so call it. But when Catholics were admitted to an equality in the making of laws, the principle of a purely Protestant State was surrendered. In theory the majority of law-makers may be Catholics, and this is not consistent with a purely Protestant State. There is nothing in the English law to prevent the majority of the Cabinet ministers from being Catholics. Without breaking any Act of Parliament, and without violating their consciences, the fifteen judges and the vice-chancellors might all be Catholics. The making of laws and the administration of laws might be entirely in the hands of Catholics. This could not be in a State essentially Protestant. The sovereign, it is true, must be a Protestant; but Belgium was not the less a Catholic State when it had a Protestant King; nor is Saxony the less a Protestant State because it has a Catholic King. If the chancellor (the keeper of the Queen's conscience) cannot be a Catholic, the reason is not that a Catholic could not administer equity or preside over the House of Lords, but that he could not administer the ecclesiastical patronage in the hands of the Crown. The Act which enabled Lord O'Hagan to be Chancellor of Ireland is a proof of this. The general commanding-in-chief may be a Catholic. The disestablishment of the Church in Ireland was logically grounded upon this principle—that the State in the British Isles is not essentially Protestant. The disestablishment of the Church in England will, at perhaps no very distant day, be merely a corollary to the Act of 1829.

It is important that this matter should be clearly understood. It is most important that all Catholics should be thoroughly imbued with the full meaning of this principle, that England is not a purely Protestant State. What a mighty change has, under the blessing of God, taken place in the position of the Catholic Church in England during the last fifty years! This change has been effected because fifty years ago England ceased to be a Protestant State. We Catholics should never lose sight of this. It is the principle on which we demand complete equality in the administration of the law, as well as equality under the provisions of the law. It is the principle on which in these days our liberties as free men are based. The Act of 1829 was most appropriately called "the New Magna Charta." It is the sheet-anchor of our position in the British Isles. Not only by toleration, but on admitted principle, our *status* now is as different from what it was at the beginning of this century as it is possible for one thing to be different from another. The old Protestant principle, not merely of ascendency, but of the exclusion of Catholics from the framework of the State, has been exploded. In the year 1805, Mr. Pitt, speaking on Fox's motion, "That the (Catholic) petition be referred to a Committee of the whole House," said, "I cannot allow that at any time, under any circumstances, or under any possible situation of affairs, it (the relief petitioned for) ought to be discussed or entertained as a claim or question of right." And he says, immediately before these words, that "the question ought to be discussed on the ground of expediency alone."[1] Whatever we claim now, we claim as a right. Since the Act of Emancipation we are entitled to retort upon the words of the great minister, that at no time, nor under any possible situation of affairs, can we ever go back to the old principle that Catholics are not in every respect equal

[1] "Pitt's Speeches," vol. iii. p. 421.

before the law to their Protestant fellow-subjects. It is the more necessary to insist upon this, as some of the older ones amongst us, who can remember the passing of the Emancipation Act, may still retain some slight remnant of the old idea that we Catholics are a proscribed race. It is true the notion has been fast fading away; but no tinge should now remain. And it is especially important that our youth should be completely free from all suspicion that they are not on an exact equality before the law with their Protestant fellow-countrymen. For it was this sense of inequality which weakened the energy, overbore the strength, and destroyed the ambition of so many who might have used their talents to rise to the level of any others in the land. And even down to our own day, it may be the retiring shadow of the oppressor who has gone, which has kept many a young man of promise from feeling that sense of freedom which is necessary for action. For it cannot be doubted that there has been and still is, amongst the Catholics of England, a fearful waste of talent and of strength, which might be of essential service both to the Church and to the State.

Another reason why we should be anxious to instil a correct idea of our legal *status* into those whom we may have to teach is, that otherwise they may mistake the position we hold in public opinion for the position we hold before the law. By public opinion we are still a proscribed and grievously persecuted race. Our Holy Father, of happy memory, Pope Pius IX., once spoke of the persecution by public opinion as the great and continual persecution which the Church is suffering from in these days. We have our full share of this in the United Kingdom. The prejudice against us exists in as many minds, and is as much diffused as it was more than fifty years ago. And as to the virulence of the prejudice, it is perhaps as great as it was a hundred years ago, though it does not show itself in the same lawless and outrageous way. We had no reason to expect in the year 1880 the same violent proceedings against us as were taken in Scotland in 1779 and in England in 1780; but the Protestant mind and temper is such that what Lord John Russell effected in 1850 and Lord Derby in 1852 might be repeated to serve the turn of some other minister. Public opinion is as stupid and perverse as ever in misrepresenting the doctrines of Catholics, and in misrepresenting them in such a way as to excite against us the worst of passions. Hatred of the priesthood, hatred of religious, especially shown in attacks upon the vow of chastity, hatred of our spiritual obedience to the See of Peter,—so falsely asserted to be inconsistent with our allegiance,—all this most unjustifiable hatred is constantly spread abroad by the lovers of mischief. This prejudice against us is continually kept alive. I have said that prejudice against us is stupid and perverse. An instance may be given to show how prejudice afflicts, with almost judicial blindness, those of whom it has taken possession. At the general election of 1874, a man who used to defile two newspapers with every lying paragraph against the Catholic Church which he could collect, put up in the Liberal interest for an English borough. He was anxious to obtain Catholic support, and wrote a letter canvassing for votes. To excuse himself somewhat for his vile conduct, he expressed himself to this effect: "Protestants sometimes say very hard things about Catholics, and Catholics in turn say very hard things about Protestants." When Catholics write in newspapers or pamphlets or books, when they speak from a platform or in private conversation, it is a very rare thing indeed to read or hear anything beyond a temperate attack upon doctrine, or a plain statement of some historical fact. The habitual tone of our writers, the habitual tone of our speakers, is as far removed from scurrility as it can well be. The man to whom we allude must have known this well, and yet he could compare the fair and temperate remarks of Catholics upon Protestants and their religion with the foul and slanderous falsehoods which he cut in slips from foreign and home low literature, and inserted in the journals of his native city. He could class the two styles together, and hypocritically say, "Protestants sometimes say hard things about Catholics, and so do Catholics about Protestants." And Catholics are expected by the public to consider this all very fair.[1] Prejudice is also shown in the evident dislike to see Catholics appointed to some of the more important offices in the State, and those connected with royalty.[2] It is shown also in the interpretation of the law. Even where the intention of the Legislature is known to create equal advantages, if a loophole be left in the clause through which Protestant administrators of the law can escape from the duty of treating Catholics with equality, they will too frequently take advantage of it. As an example of this, a case may be mentioned which actually occurred in an English town. The Act of Parliament authorizes a priest to instruct in their religion Catholics in workhouses; but the Act does not expressly provide that he shall have any place to do it in. A Protestant clergyman, who was chairman of the board of guardians, decided that the priest should not be allowed the use of a separate room in which he might

---

[1] The reader will have some satisfaction in knowing that this man was not on this occasion returned to Parliament, though he would have been if the Catholics who voted for his opponent had voted for him.

[2] When Lord Ripon was appointed Viceroy of India, there was a general howl of disapprobation amongst Protestants, which the *Times* systematically kept up. Whatever his lordship did was, in the opinion of that journal, wrong; and when success followed, it was not the result of wise and prudent measures, but of chance.

instruct his people; but that he must content himself with seeing each one of his people separately, in whatever part of the house the person might be, provided his so doing did not interfere with any regulation of the place. And he based his decision on this principle, that the Established Church alone had the right to assemble the people together, and that a Catholic priest had only the right of what he called "cottage visitation"—that is, the right of visiting their people separately wherever they might be, as at their own homes.[1]

The administration of the law according to the prejudice of those who have to administer it, is the cause of great practical persecution. We have seen enough of this in the case of prison chaplains; we see it in the workhouses, where, from the governor to the porter, the poor are often practically at the mercy of one who may be a fair-minded man or an unfair bigot. And oftentimes where the officer of the law may be inclined to carry out its letter, no equity is admitted in its application; and so it happens that the old saying is verified, and *summum jus* administered by a beadle may be *summa injuria* to a poor Catholic dying without the sacraments. As there is a hesitation in appointing Catholics to high offices, and a positive refusal to return them to Parliament, so, and throughout the whole land, the vast majority of Protestants will not, if they can with any sort of convenience avoid it, employ a Catholic tradesman.[2] This persecution by public opinion, this universal prejudice against us, is so rife and so vigorous

---

[1] This case is mentioned merely to illustrate the action of prejudice. But it may be noted that, as the Catholic Union of Great Britain was established not merely to present addresses to the Holy Father at appropriate times, but to attend to the general interests of British Catholics, such unfairness in the administration of the law as that mentioned in the text, and which no doubt frequently occurs, might very properly be taken up.

[2] This prejudice may be slightly diminishing.

that Cardinal Newman, in his "Lectures on the present position of Catholics in England," calls it "the life of the Protestant view of the Catholic Church." But still, great as are the effects of this prejudice, we must never forget that in almost every case it is by prejudice only, and not by the law, that we are made to suffer.

When we consider our history since the Reformation; when we remember the great and persevering efforts which were made with all the determination of the English character to root out our religion from the land, down to the reign of George III., and even in the beginning of his reign; when we reflect on the still abiding hatred of our religion, and the prejudice against us;—we cannot but wonder at that marvellous blessing from Heaven which during the last fifty years has made our new life, under the clauses of the Emancipation Act, fructify with a rapid growth into the grand revival of the Church which we now witness in our native land. To stand on anything approaching to an equality before the law with our Protestant fellow-subjects, would itself alone have been thought by our grandfathers too much to be hoped for. What, then, should be our thanks to God when we think of what has been done for England? The English Catholic must indeed have a cold temperament who, looking "on this picture and on that," cannot "out of the abundance of his heart" exclaim, "My heart and my flesh have rejoiced in the living God."[1]

In taking a rapid view of the progress of the Church since the year 1829, the first effect of the great Act was the greater sense of security, superadded to that which had been caused by the Relief Acts of 1778[2] and 1791.

[1] Psalm lxxxiii. 2.
[2] I do not remember to have seen in the year 1878, in any Catholic periodical, even a notice that that year was the centenary of the first Act passed for the relief of English Catholics.

In consequence of this, Catholics ventured in many ways upon a much more open display of their religion. It was felt, too, that Protestants held out the hand of fellowship to them, much more freely and cordially than they had ever done before. The spirit of liberality entered the door which the Emancipation Act had opened. The period between 1829 and 1846[1] was probably the time when public opinion yielded most to the spirit of toleration, and when English Catholics felt most at ease with their Protestant fellow-subjects. The next great benefit was that we had defenders of our own religion in the House of Commons, and this was shown at first in a remarkable way. Down to this time the tone of many members of Parliament, in speaking of Catholics and their religion, had been offensive and oftentimes grossly insulting. "Papists" were considered fair game for any honourable gentleman who was naturally inclined to indulge in abuse, and very few spoke of us with respect. Our great emancipator completely put this down, and the manner of speaking of us became entirely changed.[2] Though the inveterate hatred against us still caused the spirit of exclusion to operate, and prevented for some time the appointment of Catholics to offices which they were entitled to hold, prejudice at last gave way, and practice began to assimilate itself to theory.

It was not until the year 1834 that O'Loghlen was appointed Solicitor-General of Ireland, and, as M'Cullogh Torrens says, "for the first time since the Revolution the Catholics saw one of their communion recognized as worthy

---

[1] In the year 1846 the Bill for the Endowment of Maynooth College raised a storm of bigotry.

[2] The author has often heard testimony to what O'Connell did in this respect, from a Catholic who well remembered the times long before the Emancipation Bill passed, and who was in general not well affected to O'Connell himself.

Introduction. 47

of public trust and honour, as a law adviser of the Crown."[1] In 1836, O'Loghlen was appointed a baron of the Irish Exchequer. This was the first appointment of a Catholic judge since the Revolution. But this appointment once made, others, as we know, followed, and in this matter there is now little or nothing to complain of.

Since Emancipation and in consequence of it, many Acts of Parliament have passed in favour of Catholics; some to repeal old penal laws, and others of more practical use, to place us in several important matters on an equality with our Protestant fellow-countrymen.

Besides the improvement in our position, which has been caused by Acts of Parliament, and by the appointments and orders of the Executive, there is that wonderful change which the providence of God has wrought in the Church in England, by making use of so many active agencies in our own body, and in persons external to it. These active agencies may be classed under three heads. The first may include all that has been done to assert and insist upon our rights; to perfect Church government; to provide Christian education; to multiply churches, building them worthy of the God who is adored in them; to add splendour to the services of Religion; to increase the numbers of Religious Orders and Houses; and to give to our people all those incentives to devotion, contained in so many Catholic practices which were unknown to us in the days of the penal laws. I propose to treat of all these matters in detail; for the present, it will be sufficient to say that I may class under this head all those delightful memories which will for ever hang around the names of O'Connell, Wiseman, Newman, Gentili, Faber, Spencer, Pugin, Lucas, and Langdale.

The two other heads under which may be included the

[1] "Memoirs of Lord Melbourne," vol. ii. p. 26.

great active agencies which have been at work in advancing the progress of the Church in England are—first, the great movement which began at Oxford in the year 1833, for then was thrown the stone which caused the ripple whose ever-widening circles are still moving onward to the far-distant shore—and secondly, the providential influx to England of the faithful Irish, whose numbers and whose faith have enabled us to put the Church on a footing which otherwise it could never have held.

Every movement in the Church in England which has begun during the last fifty years has progressed, except one. That one is the organization of the laity for the defence of Catholic rights and the promotion of Catholic interests. There has been more than one organization of the kind, and they did good work in their day. But for many years past there has been no permanent association which has effectually advocated the Catholic cause. There should be such an institution. There should be an association to do now what the Catholic Institute did in years gone by, an association well known by its good service to all Catholics of the empire; an association to which we could all refer for advice and assistance, and which from its head-quarters in London could bring to bear upon ministers and members of Parliament that influence which can only be exerted by a representative body, whose members, from their numbers and station, can make themselves respectfully and oftentimes efficaciously heard. Let us hope for better days.

For the rest, after fifty years, we find ourselves in one other important matter in a far different position to that in which we were. We English Catholics are fast becoming a greater power in the State. The last few years have produced very clear evidence of this. We are much more thought of and spoken of; Catholic affairs are much more noticed, and made known through the newspapers ; our political action is brought more into calculation ;—in fact, everything concerning us attracts more attention, and we are looked upon more as of the State, and as exercising influence over its destinies. The sense of our obligation to discharge every duty, both civil and religious, should be augmenting in proportion.

In conclusion, there is no English Catholic who can remember the passing of the Emancipation Act who will not, when his days are numbered, thank God that he has been allowed to see all that great and increasing mercy has done for England during the last fifty years.

CHAPTER I.

THE ACTS OF 1771 AND 1774.

The Acts of 1771—The unsuccessful bills of 1774—The Act of 1774 introduced—Prejudice against Catholics—Preamble of Act of 1774—Address of the Irish Catholics to the King—Relief granted by the Act of 1774—Tom Moore, Mr. Fagan, Charles Butler, and George Canning on the Act of 1774—Suggestions of disloyalty in the Act of 1774—The power and influence of Ireland—Fear the great motive of relief—Combination amongst Catholics.

THE first indication of any kind of desire on the part of the Legislature to relax the tyranny which Government exercised over Catholics, occurred in the year 1771. I will give the short account of it in the words of Mr. Sheil. After mentioning that the Speaker of the Irish House of Commons had received an address from the Catholics for transmission to the lord lieutenant, he says, "This was the first instance in which the political existence of the Irish Catholics was acknowledged, through the medium of their Committee. This recognition, however, was not followed by any immediate relaxation of the penal code. Twelve years elapsed before any legislative measure was introduced which indicated a more favourable disposition towards the Catholic community, if, indeed, the 11 and 12 George III. (1771) can be considered as having conferred any boon upon that people. The statute was entitled, 'An Act for the reclaiming of unprofitable bogs,' and it enabled 'Papists' to take fifty acres of unprofitable bog for sixty-one years, with half an acre of arable land adjoining, provided that it should not be within one mile of a town."

"The first step," continues Mr. Sheil, "had been taken in the progress of concession, and every day the might of numbers, even destitute of all territorial possession, pressed more and more upon the Government."[1]

In the year 1774, an Act was passed in the Irish Parliament which served as an immediate prelude to the Acts which began the repeal of the penal laws. This Act permitted the Irish Catholics to testify their loyalty to George III. by taking a prescribed oath. The Rev. Thomas England, in his "Life of Father Arthur O'Leary," writes that the Act was said to have had its origin in the following occurrence. The Earl of Bristol, Bishop of Derry, was travelling in France; and being at Toulouse, he was invited to dinner by the superiors of the Irish college in that city. At this dinner the earl bishop expressed his regret that his kind and learned hosts should be obliged to spend the best part of their lives in a foreign land. But to this expression of regret he added, that he could not understand why his countrymen should refuse to the sovereign of their native country that allegiance which they gave to the monarch in whose dominions they were living. This observation drew forth from the hosts a denial of its truth. A long talk ensued, the result of which was that when the Bishop of Derry left the college, he was convinced of the loyalty of the Irish Catholics, and of the falsehood of the many gross charges that were made against them. On his return to Ireland, the bishop spread as widely as he could the statement that the Catholics were ready to testify in any reasonable way their loyalty to King George; and he did this with such effect that it

[1] Sheil, "Legal and Political Sketches," vol. ii. p. 161.

was the origin of the bill which terminated in the Act of 1774. The friendly conduct of the bishop may have helped towards a more willing acceptance by the Protestants, of the small favour that was given to the Catholics by the Act we are speaking of. But there can be no doubt that the real origin of this first overture to the Catholics was the same that caused all further concessions to us, namely, fear on the part of the English Government. The Americans were beginning to show in a most decided manner their determination to resist, even by physical force, the imposition of taxes upon them by the British Parliament. The Government at home had determined to levy by force what the colonists would not peaceably yield. A great conflict was foreseen. It became, therefore, a matter of policy to conciliate Ireland, in order to promote union at home, draw off the sympathy of the Irish from the Americans, and make the Irish more inclined to enlist in the regiments which it would be necessary to send across the Atlantic. Sir Robert Peel once said in the House of Commons, that when foreign affairs showed a menacing aspect, and England was likely to be involved in questions threatening war, he was always glad to be able to send a message of peace to Ireland. And so thought the English Government when the Americans commenced their revolt. They sent a message of peace to Ireland.

But it was not without some difficulty that the Government procured the passing of the Act of 1774 through the Irish Parliament. It is well known that down to the year 1782, the Irish Parliament was, in practice at least, entirely dependent on the English Government. The English minister could generally pass what bills he liked in Ireland. Two bills of small relief were introduced into the Irish Parliament in the beginning of the session of 1774, but they did not proceed. Their introduction was in consequence of instructions received by the lord lieutenant, Lord Harcourt, from Lord North. Lord North was anxious to conciliate the Irish Catholics, in order to unite the subjects of the King in Great Britain and Ireland, and because he saw that some of the maxims of government, especially the one which was loudly proclaimed in America, "no representation, no taxation," applied rather awkwardly to the state of things on the other side of St. George's Channel. These bills were given up on the advice of Lord Harcourt. At length, however, the British minister, says Mr. Plowden, sent positive orders that some Act of the Legislature should be passed in that session of conciliatory tendency to the Catholics. Accordingly a bill was brought in, and passed both Houses without opposition. This was the bill of 1774, remarkable as being the first conciliatory measure since the Revolution. When passed into an Act, it was entituled, "An Act to enable his Majesty's subjects, of whatever persuasion, to testify their allegiance to him."[1]

It will be well worth the reader's while to study this Act, and especially its preamble. The wording of the Act is well calculated to show us the thoughts and sentiments of Protestants about Catholics, and particularly of English Protestants about the Irish Catholics. We shall also very clearly see the reckless manner in which assertions and insinuations can be made, when those who govern tyrannically wish to blind themselves or others to the real motives which prompt their actions. Considering the subject in this way will not be a useless reminder of old grievances. It will not be the mere act (to use a common expression) of ripping up old sores. We shall learn a useful lesson for the present, by analyzing the thoughts

[1] 13 and 14 George III. c. 35 (Irish Statutes).

and motives of those who have preceded us. The difference of our position before the law, and before public opinion, was noticed in the introduction. The Legislature has done a great deal to relieve us from persecution by the law, but in consequence of the prejudice against us in the minds of a large majority of Englishmen, we are still grievously oppressed by public opinion. This prejudice against us, existing at the present day, is the prejudice which has been handed down from father to son, since the time when, in the sixteenth century, the first reformers succeeded in poisoning the minds of the English. In the reign of Elizabeth and the three first Stuarts this prejudice produced a bloody persecution. In the reigns of William III., Anne, and the early Georges, this prejudice, though it did not prompt the shedding of blood, yet it led to the most searching and grinding laws, enacted for the express purpose of destroying, if possible, the very existence of the Church in the British Isles. In the reign of George III., the necessity of uniting the people against the common enemy, and the milder views of our religion taken by several influential statesmen, caused a relaxation of the penal laws. But still the prejudice against us was so great that we Catholics were not even acknowledged as forming part of the State. We were looked upon as strangers, and as dangerous strangers. The Acts passed in our favour were regarded both by those who enacted them and those who benefited by them, as gratuitous acts of cautious mercy.

A hundred and six years ago, a priest had only been a few months safe from arrest, and the property of a Catholic gentleman had only been a few months safe in his own hands. It is only fifty-six years since that same prejudice gave way to the extent, and a great extent, no doubt, of establishing our right to be considered as a portion of the

State. But was prejudice extinct? Far from it. Even Lord Grey, who was always "our friend," who had, along with Lord Grenville, broken up a Ministry because he could not pass a Relief Act, Lord Grey, the Reformer of 1832, the champion of "civil and religious liberty," even Lord Grey, to the last hour of his days of office, could not be prevailed upon to appoint a Catholic to a legal office in Ireland. Down to the first administration of Lord Melbourne in the year 1834, "Catholic emancipation" had been, to use the phrase of M'Cullagh Torrens, "an empty name and mocking unreality."[1] In other words, the prejudice against us had prevented the carrying out of that law for which two great parties in the State had fought for many years. And so down to our own days prejudice prevents the impartial administration of the law, and the practical application to Catholics of several admitted principles of the British Constitution. In the introduction were given some instances to illustrate the action of prejudice. Many more in different matters might have been added. But its influence is well known to all.[2] It lives and acts. It is an heirloom of evil in thousands of English families; and it is kept with the greatest care. It is an evil plant which is constantly cropping up. It cannot be eradicated. Its existence cannot be ignored, for

---

[1] "Memoirs of Lord Melbourne," vol. vii. pp. 1, 2.

[2] When Lord Bury became a Catholic, the following paragraph appeared in a provincial newspaper :—" Lord Bury's secession to the Church of Rome disposes altogether of his chance of becoming Lord Redesdale's successor as Chairman of Committee, a post on which Lord Bury is said to have set his heart." How far the facts stated in this paragraph are true, I do not know. But it shows only too well the action of prejudice. A man becomes a Catholic, and it is immediately concluded that, however well he may be fitted for an office, all chance of obtaining it is for ever gone. This may not be quite so true as it was five or six years ago. There are now two Catholics judges on the English bench, and there has been a Catholic Viceroy of India. But the question of religion still enters unfairly into consideration when an appointment has to be made.

it poisons the air. We should know its properties, in order to be on our guard against its influence. We must judge of it by its fruits. We must not be content with looking at the fruits it now bears. We must look back to its history, and see what it has borne. The venom is still in the root, its produce is always bad; and sometimes it fructifies to the injury, and even the ruin, of many.

It is, therefore, worth while to consider attentively the Irish Act of 1774. The oath prescribed by this Act was, I believe, the first proposed to Catholics which was not condemned at Rome; it could be conscientiously taken without explaining the words in such a way as to explain away their meaning, and it was the model on which the oaths to be taken under future Relief Acts were formed. The preamble of the Act was as follows:[1]—"Whereas many of his Majesty's subjects in this kingdom" (that is, Ireland) " are desirous to testify their loyalty and allegiance to his Majesty, and their abhorrence of certain doctrines imputed to them, and to remove jealousies which hereby have for a length of time subsisted between them and others his Majesty's loyal subjects; but on account of their religious tenets are, by the laws now in being, prevented from giving public assurances of such allegiance, and of their real principles, and good will, and affection towards their fellow-subjects: in order, therefore, to give such persons an opportunity of testifying their allegiance to his Majesty, and good will towards the present constitution of this kingdom, and to promote peace and industry among the inhabitants thereof, be it enacted," etc. I must digress for a moment to observe, that shortly after the passing of this Act the Irish Catholics determined to address the King, in order that they might be assured that their grievances were personally known to his Majesty. The

[1] This Act may be found in the " Pamphleteer," vol. xx. p. 454.

address was written for them by Edmund Burke, the staunch friend of the Catholics; and probably as great a friend as it was possible for a Protestant to be, and whose wisdom, experience, and exertions in the management of our affairs have been handed down to posterity in the grateful testimony of the illustrious Milner.[1]

This address was intrusted by Lord Fingall, Mr. Preston, and Mr. Dermott, to Lord Buckinghamshire; and through him it was presented to the King. This first address of the Irish to the King is a more dignified and less timorous production than the first address of the English Catholics to his Majesty in the year 1778. It puts the state of the Irish Catholics before the King in a forcible way, reminds him of the breach of the treaty made with William III.; and though the tone of the whole is submissive, there are indications of a latent spirit which might remind a sovereign that submission has its bounds. There is one unfortunate expression in it. If the address is correctly printed in Sir H. Parnell's pamphlet on the penal laws, Mr. Burke puts into the mouths of the Catholics the following words:—" We respect from the bottom of our hearts that legislation under which we suffer." It may be supposed that the idea intended to be conveyed was, that the Irish Catholics respected the authority of the King, Lords, and Commons of Ireland. That they could have any respect for the actual legislation, that is, for the penal laws themselves, is quite impossible. As the address of the English Catholics in 1778 will be given to the reader in the course of this history, it will be sufficient to say here that if it is a little too obsequious, it must be remembered that those who presented the English address spoke for only between fifty and sixty thousand people, "enough," as Mr. Burke said, "to torment, but not enough

[1] " Letters to a Prebendary," end of Letter vii.

to fear;"[1] but the representatives of the Irish Catholics had at their backs a number which was rapidly approaching two millions.

As this address of the Irish Catholics was presented to the King after the passing of the Act of 1774, it was not from the address that the Legislature learned, as the preamble to this Act recites, that the Irish Catholics were desirous of testifying their loyalty to the King, and their abhorrence of the false doctrines imputed to them. That there was such a desire, if the object of it would obtain them justice, we may easily believe; and no doubt many men in Ireland had openly expressed such a desire. But it must be kept in mind that the real meaning of the words of the preamble is, that the Government were desirous that in the fast-approaching crisis they should have an expression of loyalty from Ireland, in order that they might deal with the Americans without being troubled with more than ordinary anxiety about home affairs.

Another thing well worthy of remark in the preamble of the Act, is the distinct acknowledgment, made in the most authentic and solemn manner—that is, in an Act of Parliament—that Catholics were suffering solely on account of their religion. The words are, "on account of their religious tenets, they are, by the laws now in being, prevented from giving public assurances of their allegiance." The defence which was universally set up to justify the penal laws was, that Catholics were not loyal subjects, and therefore it was necessary to bind them in fetters. This is the defence still urged by our fellow-subjects to justify the past. We have heard it all our lives. We are told that it is not on account of our doctrines, but on account of our politics, because we are always for giving to the Pope what belongs to Cæsar. But in that Act we have

[1] Speech at Bristol in 1780.

it clearly told us, that we suffer on account of our religious tenets. What a refinement of tyranny do those words of the Act express! We were persecuted because they said we were not loyal; and then they forbade us, on account of our "religious tenets," to open our mouths to disprove the charge. In the year 1759, an Irish judge told a Catholic gentleman, from the bench, that "a Catholic could not breathe without the command of Government." We could not breathe a word even to declare our allegiance, while we were persecuted for being disloyal. Tyranny, with its cruelty and proverbial inconsistency, surely never went beyond this mark.

Another portion of the preamble worthy of notice is that in which it is said that the Irish are desirous "to remove jealousies, which hereby have for a length of time subsisted between them and others his Majesty's faithful subjects." The word "hereby" refers to the effect which certain doctrines imputed to Catholics had upon others. That is, the Irish Catholics are made to say that they desire to remove the jealousies of the Irish Protestants and of the English by testifying their allegiance and abjuring certain doctrines. Thus the preamble of the Act makes the Catholics acknowledge that the jealousy of the Protestants was caused by a suspicion of Catholic loyalty, and a fear that certain doctrines held by Catholics might prove injurious to the State. So far as the English and Irish Protestants entertained suspicions of Catholic loyalty, it must never be forgotten that that jealousy was not the suspicion which a good Government might have cause to feel of the loyalty of ungrateful and rebellious people; but it was the suspicion which must always haunt a tyrant, that his victim may one day turn upon his tormentor. The Irish Protestants dreaded any development of Catholic strength; they suspected that a desire of revenge on the part of the Catholics would be, at least for the time, the predominant passion. This was the suspicion. The jealousy was not caused by any well-grounded fear that the Irish Catholics were disloyal to the reigning House or to the British Constitution. It was caused by the fear with which the tyrant noticed the smallest accession of strength to the arm of his victim. Nor was there on the part of those Englishmen who knew Ireland well, any suspicion of the loyalty of the Irish. But there was in England then, as there is in England now, a rooted jealousy of Ireland, lest she should become free and prosperous. There are two things in Ireland which are hateful to the great bulk of the English—its religion, and its capability for prosperity arising from its internal resources, and from the fitness which, on account of its position with regard to America, it possesses of being the *dépôt* of the western trade. Ireland free and prosperous implied an increase of the influence of the Catholic religion, and a diminution of wealth in England. It is true that England could easily afford to let Ireland take some portion of her trade; but the love of money amongst the English merchants has always been greater than their love of fair play. The English are, however, very sensitive of their reputation for liberality; it was therefore necessary to make it believed on the Continent that there was some honest ground for doubting the loyalty of the Catholics. Hence hypocritical words were put into the mouths of the Irish, who were made to parade before the world their desire to remove excusable jealousy by testifying their loyalty. Hence, too, the pompous words of a preamble are employed to proclaim to every one, what every one knew, that there was nothing in the Catholic religion opposed to fidelity to the powers that be.

The last words of the preamble must not be lost sight

of. In these words it is asserted that one object of the bill was to promote peace and industry amongst the inhabitants of Ireland. This was the great boast of the English statesmen. These were the words that, trumpet-tongued, were to send forth the praise of English and of Protestant liberality on the four winds of heaven. But what was the truth? The peace and prosperity of Ireland had been ruined by the grinding power of the penal laws; and by this Act not one of those penal laws was to be repealed.

We now come to consider the material clause of the Act, which is as follows:—"Be it enacted by the King's most excellent Majesty, by and with the advice and consent of the Lords spiritual and temporal, and Commons, in the present Parliament assembled, and by the authority of the same, that from and after the 1st day of June, 1774, it shall and may be lawful for any person professing the Popish religion to go before the Judges of his Majesty's Court of King's Bench, any Justice of the Peace for the county in which he does or shall reside, or before any magistrate of any city or town corporate, wherein he does or shall reside, and there take and subscribe the oath of allegiance and declaration hereinafter mentioned; which oath and declaration such Judges of the King's Bench, Justices of the Peace, and magistrates are required to administer."

Such was the Act of 1774. The oath which it prescribed was similar to the oaths prescribed in all subsequent Relief Acts, the only important difference being that it contained a special abjuration of allegiance "unto the person taking unto himself the style and title of Prince of Wales, in the lifetime of his father, and who, since his death, is said to have assumed the style and title of King of Great Britain and Ireland, by the name of Charles III."

What, then, was the relief granted by this Act? All the penal laws remaining still in force, an Irish Catholic was to be considered a good subject if he took the oath. Looking from our point of view, the relaxation looks small indeed. But still, though not a single law was repealed, the Act afforded practical relief, and opened the door to subsequent Acts of Emancipation. It gave relief because it meant that many of the penal laws against the Catholics, especially those laws which most galled them in private life, should not be enforced against those who, by taking the oath, entitled themselves to be considered as good subjects. The Act was a sort of charter of breathing-time to those who had been "groaning in fetters;" it released from apprehension "the children of the slain." For three or four years previous to 1774, Catholics had not been pursued with the unrelenting cruelty of former years. The word of God had gone forth to the persecutors of His Church: "Thus far shall you go, and no farther." Before the passing of this Act, the waters had reached their highest mark; when it had passed, the ebb-tide of persecution set in. This Act was, therefore, most important in its consequences. It was followed by the English Acts of 1778, 1791, and 1803, and by the Irish Acts of 1778, and the most important Act up to that time of 1793.[1]

It will be interesting, and it will tend to illustrate the state of Catholics previous to the year 1774, to give the remarks which have been made by some well-known men on the Irish Act of that year.

The poet Moore, after having alluded to the great boon which the Irish Catholics received in being allowed to

---

[1] The immense importance of the Irish Act of 1793 consisted in this, that it gave the franchise to the Irish. It was the possession of this right which enabled O'Connell to carry the Clare election. We English Catholics did not obtain the franchise until the Act of 1829.

cultivate a few acres of bog, writes as follows :—" The next great benefit bestowed upon the Catholics was the allowing them to take the oath of allegiance; and this kind permission to the victim to come and swear eternal fidelity to his tormentor, though as insulting a piece of mockery as can well be imagined, was received with the warmest gratitude by the Catholics, because it, at least, acknowledged their existence as subjects, and put an end to that lively fiction of the law which would have returned *non est inventus* of two million of people."[1] Mr. Fagan, in his " Life and Times of Daniel O'Connell," says—

" Up to 1774, the laws, to use the expression of a zealous Lord Chancellor of former days, 'did not presume a Papist to exist in the kingdom; nor could they breathe without the command of Government.'[2] At that time the American colonies were beginning to proclaim their wrongs, and were struggling successfully against the arbitrary dictation of England. The British Government, conscious they had no hold on the affections or gratitude of the people of Ireland, deemed it prudent to recognize the Irish Catholics as subjects, without at the same time admitting them to the slightest privilege under the laws. They were then for the first time permitted, forsooth, to swear allegiance to the sovereign and become subjects of the Crown; and yet even this paltry enactment, which was deemed an act of grace by the helot Catholics of that day, was not passed without the positive demand of the English Government, so deeply prejudiced at that time were the Irish Parliament and the Protestant party against the great mass of the community. This Act of condescension was passed from dread of American contagion and without Catholic agitation."

Mr. Charles Butler observes that the Act "did not enjoin them" (the Catholics) "to take the oath under any

---

[1] "Memoirs of Captain Rock."
[2] The "former days," mentioned by Mr. Fagan, were not so very far removed from the year 1774. That absurdly tyrannical *dictum* of the chancellor was delivered in the year 1759. *Vide* England's "Life of O'Leary," p. 50, quoting Plowden's "Historical Review," vol. i. p. 322.

penalties, or accompany the taking of it with any advantages."[1]

Mr. Plowden, as cited by Mitchell, says of the Act, that it gratified the Catholics, inasmuch as it was a formal recognition that they were subjects, and to this recognition they looked up as to the corner-stone of their future emancipation.[2]

One of the most interesting passages relating to the Act of 1774, occurs in a speech made by Mr. Canning in the House of Commons on the 22nd of June, 1812:

"Let us look," he says, "at the state of the Catholic in the year 1760, at the accession of his present Majesty, when the system in Ireland had received the finishing hand, and before any remedial or alleviating measures had been applied to it. We find him cut off from all the relations of social life: we find the law interfering between the parent and child, between the husband and the wife, stimulating the wife to treachery against her husband, and the son to disobedience towards his parent; establishing a line of separation in the nuptial bed, and offering an individual inheritance as the tempting prize for filial disobedience. I am sure that no man will now venture to say that this is a state in which, consistently with the spirit of British legislation, any class of his Majesty's subjects ought to be placed; yet this is the state to which those who admire the penal code in its perfection must refer; and it is to this state that we should return, if we were to reject as innovation every amelioration that has been made in that code since the period of its maturity. But it belongs to this system, in a degree beyond other systems of unnatural violence, that no sooner had it arrived at its maturity, than it

---

[1] "Historical Memoirs," vol. iii. p. 486.

[2] Mitchell's "History of Ireland," vol. i. p. 188. It was in defence of the oath prescribed by this Act that Father Arthur O'Leary wrote one of his celebrated "Tracts." The defence was, as all Father O'Leary's writings were, exceedingly clever. Of its literary merits I need not speak, as they are well known. But the tract contained a somewhat forced display of learning, some very objectionable propositions, and some flippant and disrespectful remarks against Cardinal Bellarmine.

began to decay; other systems have had a period during which they grew, a period during which they flourished, and in which they flourished for some time before their vigour began to decline; but in this, ripeness and decay were nearly coincident. After the greater part of two centuries had been spent in bringing it to maturity, this code existed in perfection only about fourteen years. From the beginning of his present Majesty's reign, to the year 1774, when the first relaxing statute was enacted, is the short period at which it was at once complete and stationary. That, therefore, is the period at which those must look who would admire it in all the fulness of its glory. Every step taken in respect to it since 1774 has been in the spirit, so much deprecated, of irreverent innovation."[1]

In the history of this Act, and from the perusal of the Act itself, we distinctly see the spirit which animated the lawgivers, and which can be traced down to our own days, in every Act of Relief, and in all the dealings of our Protestant fellow-countrymen with us as Catholics. The reason given for passing the Act is stated to be, that Catholics were desirous of testifying their loyalty. The real reason which prompted the introduction of the Act at that time was, that the Government were anxious that Catholics should profess their loyalty at that particular juncture of affairs. The object of the Act, as professed in the preamble, was to promote peace and industry amongst the Irish; the real object was, that soldiers might be more easily enlisted to recruit the British ranks. There is a certain tone of condescension to weakness, and a self-complacent air of doing a favour to inferiors which pervades the whole. There is an insinuation of disloyalty, and, what is more insulting, an insinuation that Catholics were conscious themselves that there was something in their religion which might excuse a suspicion of disloyalty. The Act seems to say, which in fact it practically did say

[1] *Vide* "Canning's Speeches," Therry's edition, vol. iii. p. 293.

to the Catholics, "Though you cannot be admitted to citizenship, you may as strangers be allowed to say that you love your rulers." False insinuations, patronizing insolence, hypocritical assertion of benevolent motives, are not these the very pest which is too often so revolting to Catholics even to this day, when, in pursuance of our rights, we are brought into contact with the governing powers and with public opinion?

Peace and industry amongst the Irish! Peace and industry lead to prosperity. Prosperity creates power. Power in Ireland means power in the Catholic portion of the inhabitants of the United Kingdom; an increase of power means an increase of influence to the principles of the Catholic religion, and in the action of the Catholic Church. Is this what the English wish to bring about? No! But it is what every English Catholic should desire. One of the greatest misfortunes of the Catholics of the United Kingdom, one of the defects in our state which we have most to lament, is that the legitimate influence of our religion in State affairs is not what it might be. We do not covet, nor do we want, the influence which a wealthy Church can exercise. God forbid! We are poor, and we are blessed in our poverty. But we do feel the want of, and desire to have, that influence which always has weight in affairs, when any special interest is backed by the numbers, the wealth, and the social position of the laity. We Catholics, who have the Deposit of Faith, know well that secret which others will not be told of, or will refuse to understand—that the better Catholics we are the better subjects we are; that an increase of devotion to God means an increase of devotion to Queen and country. We, therefore, cannot for a moment excuse the faintest suspicion that an increase of power amongst us would be a source of danger to the common country, or should be a cause of the smallest anxiety to our rulers. On the contrary, seeing what power, properly managed, has done for us, seeing what the legitimate action of wholesome fear has effected, the influence of the Catholic Church as a strong power, would be a great and most useful safeguard to the liberties of all. If all our just demands were supported by that power which forced emancipation in 1829, they would be obtained, and obtained by lawful means, and within the constitution. It is a narrow-minded, shortsighted policy which fosters dissensions, and keeps up divisions amongst the Catholics of the British Isles. Such dissensions and divisions produce a weakness which make a weak point in the State. It is neither wise nor prudent to lessen a power which, when exercised, forces the Legislature to remove the causes of reasonable discontent. *Divide et impera* may be a very good principle when we have an enemy to conquer, but it is the very worst principle of household government. A united Catholic people in the British Isles would support the throne, and would be a security against that bad government which leaves a people with something to resent.

But whatever course may be followed by the majority of Englishmen, it is clearly the duty of English Catholics, not only to keep up a good understanding with our Irish fellow-subjects, but to interest ourselves in their affairs, and to value the power and influence of Ireland. For the power and influence of Ireland is the power and influence of the Catholic Church in the United Kingdom. What should we have been had it not been for the Irish? In what state before the law should we now be if it had not been for the power and influence of Ireland? Should we have been emancipated at all? And if emancipated, should we have had those chains struck off which kept us out of Parliament, and out of office, without being weighted with other newly forged chains, which would have fettered the action of the Church? Some concessions, some *concordat*, would no doubt have accompanied the Act which gave relief. We might perhaps have been safe from "securities" and vetoes during the life of the illustrious Milner; but even he could not have obtained us emancipation. Every new light that is thrown on the history of the great Act by memoirs and biographies and the publication of correspondence, shows that emancipation could not have been obtained by any other means than it was—by the moral force of the Irish people, led by O'Connell. The orator Grattan, alluding in the House of Commons to Lord Avonmore's irresistible argument in favour of emancipation, said of it, in one of his daring flights of imagery, that "it was the march of an elephant, it was the wave of the Atlantic, a column of water three thousand miles deep."[1] How grandly these words apply to the triumphant progress of O'Connell, at the head of the Irish people! "It was the march of an elephant, it was the wave of the Atlantic, a column of water three thousand miles deep." "Securities," concordats, vetoes, were trampled down and crushed beneath the heavy tread; the reluctance, the delays, the doubts and hesitations of King, Lords, and Commons were overwhelmed in the advance. Canning once said in the House, "Are we to give everything to the Catholics, and are they to give us nothing in return?" But now there was not even a whisper of concessions which had been publicly advocated for years. The public looked on with amazement. The conquering power was pressing on so near and with such force that there was no time for delay. The discussions in the Cabinet had to be cut short. The final instructions for the framing of the bill became a question of hours and almost minutes, and it was

[1] "Grattan's Speeches," edited by Madden, p. 319.

immediately drawn by one vigorous hand, which left nothing in the draft on which Catholics would be likely to make a stand.¹ And so emancipation passed.

The world may never again see another O'Connell, but the Catholics of the United Kingdom possess the same elements of power which O'Connell wielded. Were we to use that power, as all others in the State would if they had special interests to protect, we should be in a far better position than we are. We should be a united people, exercising a legitimate influence, and that influence would be one of good, both to the altar and the throne.

As it is desirable that Catholics should thoroughly understand their position in the United Kingdom, and, amongst other things, the motives from which concessions to them have sprung, it may be well, at the very outset, to fix steadily in the mind the truth that fear has been the prevailing motive of all Acts of Relief.² The chief motive for the reception of the address from the Irish Catholics

---

[1] Lord Lyndhurst. The above account of the precipitance with which the final draught of the Emancipation Act was written, was often told to me by the late Mr. George Eyston, who was living in London at the time, and who always had an accurate knowledge of matters which concerned Catholics. He told me that the law-stationer who made the fair copy of the draught told him that the bill came into his office, in Lord Lyndhurst's handwriting. Sir Robert Peel's account of the last days of the bill before its introduction into Parliament ("Memoirs," vol. i. p. 351) does not give an impression of the same precipitance. But still, I do not think that there is a positive discrepancy in the two accounts.

[2] It is, unfortunately, necessary in these days to add a note to this sentence. It is a shameful thing that an author should be obliged to do so. The sentence was written before certain miscreants, whose acts would increase the disgrace of the most cruel monsters who have been a curse to the world, began, in the sacred name of liberty, to use means diabolically wicked to create fear in the minds of their rulers. The fear alluded to in the text is that fear which is caused either by acts done within constitutional rights or, as in the cases of the revolt of the States and the French Revolution, by the political acts of other people, which bring about a state of things which alters circumstances and which naturally causes a pressure upon those who have to govern. Fear caused in this way is a very different thing from that which is caused by the grossest violation of the laws of God and man.

by the Speaker of the Irish House of Commons above alluded to was, that it was a loyal address upon the alarm of the invasion of Conflans in the year 1759. The threatening attitude of the colonists produced, as we have seen, the Irish Act of 1774. In the month of February, 1778, the French solemnly acknowledged the independence of the United States, and concluded with them a defensive treaty, which England treated as a declaration of war. In the following month of May, the first Act relieving the English Catholics was brought into Parliament, and passed without opposition; and the first Act which repealed any of the penal laws against the Catholics of Ireland was passed about the same time in College Green. The next Relief Act was that passed in Ireland, 1782, to conciliate the Catholics in presence of the armed volunteers, and a threatened invasion from France. In the year 1790, the alarm of the French Revolution sounding through Europe, an Act was passed to explain and amend a previous Relief Act, which had not produced the effect intended; but, as Sir Henry Parnell observes, "This common act of justice was not, in any degree, the result of an inclination on the part of the Government to treat the Catholics with more than customary liberality."[1] The state of affairs in France threatening still more to involve other European nations, naturally caused a desire on the part of the English Government to promote as far as possible the union of all Englishmen; and an Act giving substantial relief to English Catholics was passed at Westminster in the year 1791. On the 21st of January, 1793, Louis XVI. was executed, and on the following 1st of February, the National Convention declared war against England. Irish soldiers were immediately wanted. In addition to this, a conspiracy with republican tendencies was known to

---

[1] Sir Henry Parnell on the penal laws.

be forming, which professed to embrace all Irishmen, but in reality was confined to the Protestants and Presbyterians of the North. It was most important, therefore, to conciliate the Catholics; accordingly, to use the words of Moore, the very same Parliament which in 1792 rejected with scorn the whole petition of the Catholics, in the very next year precipitately granted more than they asked for; and the Relief Act of 1793 was passed.[1] Finally, all the world knows that the Emancipation Act of 1829 was passed, as Wellington and Peel both avowed, to prevent a civil war in Ireland.

It cannot be denied that other causes besides fear operated in a certain degree to produce concessions to Catholic claims. The spirit of animosity against us had lessened in the breasts of many; the principle of religious liberty, as it is called, had taken deep root in some master minds, as in those of Burke, Fox, and Canning; and party feeling found the Catholic question a convenient one to bring to the front. But all these motives only brought the Protestant feeling of the country up to a certain point. The history of the Relief Bills clearly shows, that not one of them would have been passed at the time it was passed, if fear of something worse than concessions to Catholics had not driven our oppressors to action. Since the passing of the Emancipation Act, it cannot be said that any one of the many Acts for our relief has been caused by the fear of French invasion, or of a revolution in Ireland. But the most substantial of those Acts which have passed of late years, have been promoted for reasons which may be resolved into fear of another kind, namely, in order to gain or in order not to lose the Catholic vote. Public opinion in England in regard to the concessions enumerated above, and the actual force of the different motives which brought

[1] " Memoirs of Captain Rock," pp. 330, 336.

about those concessions, may be well illustrated by the present state of public opinion, and the motives which now operate, to incline our countrymen to act justly to us. There is no county and only one borough in England which returns a Catholic member to Parliament. It would be almost universally admitted that in theory a candidate should not be rejected on account of his religious opinions; but in practice, no matter how much more eligible a Catholic might be than his Protestant rival, he would poll but few votes, simply on account of his religion. If it were possible that some great evil to the county or borough might ensue from the rejection of the better man, the fear of that evil, and that fear alone, would ensure his return.[1]

There is no doubt something discouraging in the thought that fear is the chief motive which urges the majority to do us justice. But as we have so many things to encourage us, we must not allow too much influence to that discouraging thought. And even in this very motive of fear, which sometimes forces justice to be done, we can bring good out of evil. For we learn from it that we Catholics have a power which, if prudently used, is good both for defence and for attack. When fear operates as a motive to give us what is our due, it is because there is something in us to be afraid of. It is a good thing for us to know this; and it is a still better thing for us to understand it, and the use we can make of the knowledge. If we were governed by a mob, if a succession of pamphlets like those which Mr. Gladstone wrote against us a few years ago, had succeeded in renewing in the year 1880 the No-Popery riots of 1780, then indeed fear would be all on our side, and we should be overborne and trodden

---

[1] It is thought by some that there are certain towns and divisions of counties which would return a Catholic, if those who could offer themselves as candidates under favourable circumstances would do so. There is perhaps some truth in this with regard to a very limited number of places.

down by numbers. But so long as opposition to the Catholic Church is to be kept within the bounds of the Englishman's favourite axiom, "civil and religious liberty;" so long as we can act with the same freedom as others act, and receive the same fair play as is given to all others;— we have a right to expect that the same motives will operate in the dealings of our countrymen with us, as would operate in their dealings with any other body of the same number and importance as ourselves. Due weight is always given to numbers and importance; and the effect which that weight has is often nothing more than that wholesome fear, which prevents a majority from becoming tyrannical, and a minister from being a tyrant. If the Catholics of the United Kingdom had been a united body from the time that a common interest should have bound them together, their numbers and importance would not have been, by fits and starts, a motive for fear; but they would have been continually in action, and our position in the State would have answered much more accurately to the great principles of English liberty than at present it can be said to do.

Any one who has read the details of that history of which, in the first part of this chapter, I have only given a sketch, must be struck with the great power which the Catholics of the United Kingdom can exercise when they choose to do so. When the Catholics of Ireland are united, their power is simply overwhelming. This was proved in the year 1829. And even English Catholics have within themselves the means of exerting a much greater influence than we do. If we were to act as others who have a special interest to attend to, we should in reality be a very considerable power in the State. When political parties wish to preserve their traditions, or to carry a certain measure, and to keep their followers together; when particular trades wish to protect some special interest (like the Licensed Victuallers at the general election of 1874);—they form what is called an organization. They know well that without this they will be weak, but that with it they will be strong. How is it that we do not act in the same way? We have special interests to protect, and interests, too, of greater importance than an enlargement of the county franchise, or the selling of beer. Yet we have no systematic organization; and this organization is absolutely necessary in order that our interests may be attended to, and that the power we have within us may, as far as possible, be properly directed. I will conclude this chapter by alluding to one matter in which want of organization causes us a great loss of power. There can hardly be any doubt that the first duty which any body of Catholics, banded together for the general good, should turn their attention to at the present moment, would be the registration of voters; for one great element of our power is in the votes of Catholics in many of the cities and boroughs of Great Britain. Registration cannot be effectually carried out, in many places, unless there be some central motive power to excite action and watch the progress of the work. The Catholic Union a few years ago began this work gallantly. But of late years I understand that its efforts have relaxed. It patronizes the work, I believe, but it does not superintend it and push it, as it began by doing. This is a great pity, from whatsoever cause it may arise.[1]

The fact is that, in the use of political power, most emphatically we want "educating." Who will educate us? Who will lead us? Who will begin by teaching us how to

---

[1] English Catholics ought not to be too squeamish about the way in which the Irish may vote in our large towns. In any matters vitally affecting the interests of our religion, the overwhelming majority of the Catholics in England, whatever may be their nationality, will always be found on the right side.

learn and put in practice a great and most useful lesson taught by the late Sir Robert Peel. It was either during the administration of Lord Grey, immediately after the passing of the Reform Bill, or at the second advent of Lord Melbourne to power, that Sir Robert, anxious above everything to restore the fallen fortunes of the Tory party, had one word only for his followers: "Register, register, register." And so we should say to the Catholics of Great Britain now, "Register, register, register." There is indeed plenty of work for an organization of Catholics to attend to, but the most pressing duty is to attend to the registration. It should be a boast of British Catholics, that to the best of our power we use our liberties as Britons in defence of our religion as Catholics. Are there no young men fired with the desire to serve their religion and their country? Are there none who, under the advice and approving eye of their clergy and their elders, will give themselves to the work? Let them not think that by increasing the power of the Catholics in England they will create a giant who will do them any mischief; such an idea is merely "a thing devised by the enemy." On the contrary, they will do a great service both to religion and to the land they love so well. They can act without fear, for they will have the blessing of God on their labours, and under that blessing, the guardian angels of England will bring their work to a prosperous end.

CHAPTER II.

STATE OF CATHOLICS PREVIOUS TO ACT OF 1778.

State of Catholics previous to the Act of 1778—and Lord Mansfield's charge to the jury at the trial of Mr. Webb.

BEFORE giving the reader the history of the English Relief Act of 1778, it will be well to recall, as far as we can, the state in which English Catholics were at that period. It must be remembered that only three and thirty years had then passed since the last attempt of the Stuart family to regain the throne. Many Catholic families, as well as many Protestant families of the Tory party, were known to have sympathized with Charles Edward Stuart in 1745. But although there were many Catholics in the Highland army which invaded England, a very few of the English made any attempt to assist the Prince. Charles Edward was still alive in 1778; and although, during the thirty years which followed his gallant enterprise, the British Catholics had gradually, but effectually and for ever, transferred their allegiance to the House of Hanover, yet strong political motives, as well as religious hatred, prompted our Protestant fellow-countrymen to keep us down. But as years went by, it became evident that the dynasty which began its career from the Revolution of 1688 had nothing to fear from internal enemies.

It is difficult for us to realize the state in which our

ancestors lived up to the year 1778. There were then very few Catholics in England except the English Catholics. Burke, in his celebrated speech at Bristol, previous to the election of 1780, estimated the number of Irish at that time in London to be four or five thousand. Supposing that there were half that number in Liverpool (though it is not probable that there was half), the rest scattered over England would not have reached anything approaching to one thousand. The English Catholics consisted of several, in almost every county, of what we call the old English Catholic families; of a large number of Catholics of the middle and poorer classes in Lancashire and the north of Staffordshire; and of here and there over the rest of England some few in the humbler walks of life, whose families, like their Lancashire brethren, had never lost the faith. There were not very many converts in those days. Conversion had always to be done secretly, and in many cases it was accompanied with considerable danger to all who engaged in it. Later on in the century ridiculous stories were told by malicious fanatics of the great number of converts. "Two thousand of the common people," it was said, "chiefly servant-maids, were converted by the French clergy in one part of London in the space of two years." "That is to say," writes Father O'Leary, in his address to the Lords spiritual and temporal of the Parliament of Great Britain, "more than all the Catholic clergy of England have converted since the reign of Elizabeth."[1] If this be true, the number of converts at the time we are writing about must have been very small.[2]

The total number of Catholics in England in the year

[1] "Life and Writings of the Rev. Arthur O'Leary," by the Rev. M. B. Buckley, p. 383.
[2] Dr. England, however, in his "Life of Father O'Leary," p. 295, says that "some very distinguished individuals were led by his doctrinal instructions to embrace the Catholic creed."

1778 was probably about sixty thousand. Joseph Berington, writing in 1780, says, "From the best information I can procure, their number does not at this day exceed sixty thousand, and this even I suspect to be far beyond the mark." Burke, in his speech at Bristol in 1780, says, "The Catholics of England are but a handful of people, enough to torment, but not enough to fear, perhaps not so many of both sexes and of all ages as fifty thousand." Sheridan, in his speech against Sir H. Mildmay's Convent Bill in the year 1800, says, "It had been said that in the time of James II. there was but one Catholic in this country to a hundred Protestants, and that the number was the same or nearly the same now." This proportion would give over seventy thousand in the year 1778.

The English Catholic county gentlemen lived for the most part in great retirement, taking little or no part in county matters. Those who wished to mix in general society kept their religion as much in the background as possible, and many endeavoured to conceal it altogether. An instance may be given of a country squire and a most sincere Catholic, who when in London used to associate with Fox and Sheridan, but who, being anxious when he came into his property to make his appearance at the county assizes, went into court, and hearing the grand jury, when they had finished their work, announce to the judge that they had made all due search for Papists, left the court, and could not be induced to attend again during a long life. The Catholic gentlemen of that day had been almost all educated in one of the English colleges established abroad, and they were sent chiefly to St. Omer's and Douay. The education at those places, so dear to English Catholics, was of a very superior kind; Douay and St. Omer's will be lasting evidence of what English Catholics can do to educate themselves. To pass over the long list of accomplished divines and scholars which those colleges produced long before the time we are writing about, we may fairly say that schools which gave to the world such men as Alban Butler, Challoner, O'Connell, and Milner have made their mark in the history of the Church. Those who can remember to have met in their boyhood many of the Catholic gentlemen who had been brought up at St. Omer's and Douay, must remember also their polished and courtly manners, their taste for literature, and that patriotic and independent tone of mind which they preserved, while living in their country seats under the ban of their own country. The English-Catholic ladies of that period had been chiefly educated in those convents abroad, the establishment of which began in the days of Elizabeth. Those who have seen the lists of names preserved in any of those communities which returned to England at the time of the French Revolution, have observed how many young ladies of old English families remained in the houses they were brought up in, to serve God in the religious state. And many Catholic families still remaining, scattered over England, have to thank God that those revered communities sent back to England every year, young maidens who in after life formed as grand a class of Christian mothers as the world has ever seen. We can remember some of them still. What strong faith, what matronly bearing, what a deep sense of the responsibility they felt was upon them, to be the guardians of religion and morals in the Catholic families of England, and that with them rested in great measure the charge of handing down truth and virtue to their posterity. When we daily thank God for the great increase He has given to our English Church in the numerous conversions of later years and our own days, let us not omit the acts of a grateful heart, when we remember the days of old; when we think of the preservation of our religion in times when there were few conversions; when we see the effects of continuous mercy in those many old families still remaining, the chief support of religion in our native land.[1]

Nor must we forget the steadfast faith and the sterling worth of those whose names are not so well known, though as much honoured, who in Lancashire and other parts handed down the truth to their children. Though in 1778 the English Catholics were but a handful, it was proved in after years that the few were enough to be the foundation of the new Church when the better days began. As we pursue our history we shall see how the old stock prepared the way for the great increase which arose, when converts by hundreds returned to the fold, and the Irish by thousands came to help us in the work of restoration.

The Catholic families, for the most part, lived a quiet and unmolested life in the country. But there were exceptions. The author was told by the late Charles Thomas Clifford that his grandfather, Lord Arundell, had four horses taken out of his carriage by a Protestant, who offered him £5 each for them.[2] Mr. Butler tells us that "during the first part of the reign of George III., Catholics suffered a considerable degree of persecution. So lately as in the year 1782, two very poor Catholic labourers and their wives were summoned before one of his Majesty's justices of the peace in the county of York, and fined one shilling each, for not repairing to church,

---

[1] There were only two convents in England at this time: one at York, and which is still there, and another of the same order in the neighbourhood of London. They had great difficulties to contend with, and a hard struggle for existence.

[2] Such was the law. It was not that a Catholic could not have a horse worth £5, but any one could take the horse at the price of £5. An Irish gentleman about this time, on being offered £5 each for his carriage horses, went up to them as they were being harnessed and shot them all.

and the constable raised it by distraining, in the house of one of them, an oak table and a plate-shelf; in the house of the other, a shelf and two dozen of delf plates, one pewter dish, with some pewter plates, one oak table, and an armchair. The sale was publicly called at the market day, and the goods were sold by auction at their respective houses."[1] Young men were cautioned, when travelling, not to let their religion be known, for fear of personal abuse. If a more tolerant Protestant ventured to ask a Catholic to his house, he privately apologized to his guests for introducing "a Papist" among them. It is often remarked amongst Catholics, that what would be considered as ungentlemanly if said or done to a Protestant, is not so in regard to a Catholic in any matter connected with religion. Instances of this conduct occasionally happen even now; at the time of which we are writing, it was the normal standard of Protestant manners. We will again quote Mr. Butler on this subject; and it may be remembered that Butler was not at all inclined to take an unfavourable view of the conduct of Protestants towards Catholics. He says, "No person, who was not alive in those times, can imagine the depression and humiliation under which the general body of Roman Catholics then laboured. Often in early life has the writer heard the ancestors of the Catholic youth of that period tell them, that they could form no idea of the sufferings of the Catholics in the beginning of the last century. He, in his turn, can now aver, that the present Catholic youth can form no idea of the lamentable state of the Catholics, so lately as in the reign of George II. and the first years of George III. They cannot picture to themselves the harsh, the contemptuous, and the

---

[1] "Historical Memoirs," vol. iii. p. 277. At this time Mr. Butler was thirty-two years of age.

distressing expressions which at that time a Catholic daily heard, even from persons of humanity and good breeding." Mr. Butler then gives an instance which shows to what an extent Protestant bigotry could change the courtesy of a gentleman into the rudeness of a churl. "At a court ball," continues Butler, "a Roman Catholic young lady of very high rank, distinguished by character, by beauty, and by the misfortunes of her family, was treated with marked slight by the lord chamberlain. 'It is very hard,' she exclaimed, 'to be so treated; after all, I was invited!' and burst into tears. They were noticed by Queen Caroline; and, when her Majesty learnt the cause, there was not a kind, a generous, or a soothing excuse which she did not make to her. While this compassionate gentleness showed the amiable mind of the Queen, the unfeeling rudeness of the chamberlain as strongly showed the temper of the times."[1]

The eastern counties of England are well known for their bigotry in matters of religion. A manuscript at Bury St. Edmund's, written between 1830 and 1840, says that a man was still living who could bear witness to the fact that it was only by stealth they could attend the chapel, which was a room in a house; and that Catholics dared not to appear in public, and, indeed, to practise their religion at all. A Catholic gentleman, who was born in the middle of the last century, making his will in the present century, in leaving money to the poor, gave it to the Protestant rector for distribution in order that the lawyer who drew up the will might not know that he was a Catholic.

[1] "Historical Memoirs," vol. iii. pp. 277, 278. It may be remarked that there are several instances which show that when George III. and his two sons, the Prince of Wales and the Duke of York, were brought into personal relations with Catholics, they always behaved with great consideration and kindness.

The instances I have given will give the reader some idea of the state in which the grandfathers lived of men now living who would not like to be called very old. It is a pity that there is not more in print to throw light on the state in which Catholics were living about the time at which the Relief Act of 1778 passed. There exist, no doubt, in most old Catholic families many manuscripts and documents, a compilation from which would be a most interesting volume. In concluding this mention of the state of the Catholic laity, it must be noticed that many Catholics had been successful in trade. There is a somewhat curious passage touching this subject in Edmund Burke's celebrated speech at Bristol in the year 1780. Speaking of the desire of some fanatics to repeal the Act of 1778, he says, " Had we listened to the counsels of fanaticism and folly, we might have wounded ourselves very deeply. You are apprised that the Catholics of England consist mostly of your best manufacturers. Had the Legislature chosen, instead of returning their declarations of duty with correspondent good-will, to drive them to despair, there is a country at their very door to which they would be invited. . . . And thus bigotry would have repeopled the cities of Flanders. . . . But I trust we shall be saved this last of disgraces."[1]

The clergy in many parts of England lived in continual fear. About the year 1760, the year of the accession of George III., an infamous scoundrel, named Payne, sought to obtain, and in some instances succeeded in obtaining, the fine of one hundred pounds on the conviction of priests for saying Mass, and against whom he had informed. The Rev. Mr. Malony was tried and condemned at Croydon

---

[1] The author has frequently tried to ascertain who and what manufacturers these were to whom Mr. Burke refers, but he has never met with any satisfactory explanation.

in the year 1767, for the exercise of his priestly functions. Burke, in his speech at Bristol, from which I have already quoted, says of this trial, " It is but six or seven years since a clergyman of the name of Malony, a man of morals, neither guilty nor accused of anything noxious to the State, was condemned to perpetual imprisonment for exercising the functions of his religion, and after lying in gaol two or three years, was relieved by the mercy of Government from perpetual imprisonment on condition of perpetual banishment." In 1768, the Rev. James Webb was tried in the Court of Queen's Bench for saying Mass, but was acquitted. He owed his acquittal to Lord Mansfield, as we shall see later on. In 1769, the Honourable James Talbot was tried for his life at the Old Bailey, and, as Mr. Butler tells us, only escaped conviction from the want of evidence. Other priests were prosecuted. Mr. Butler made inquiries "in 1780 respecting the execution of the penal laws against the Catholics, and found that the single house of Dynely and Ashmall in Gray's Inn had defended more than twenty priests under such prosecutions, and that, greatly to their honour, they had generally defended them gratuitously." Mr. Talbot was tried more than once. I believe the last time was in the year 1771. From the accounts I have seen, it does not seem clear whether the last of his trials was for saying Mass or for exercising his functions as a bishop.[1] However this may be, Bishop James Talbot was the last ecclesiastic tried under the penal laws for the exercise of his office, and, I believe, the last priest tried for saying Mass—an honour of which I have no doubt his collateral descendants are justly proud.[2]

[1] Mr., or, as we should now say, Dr. James Talbot, was coadjutor bishop to the venerable Challoner.

[2] Bishop Talbot was the great uncle of Earl John of Shrewsbury, whom many still remember, and whose name will be inseparably connected with the revival of religion in England, and the returning beauty of God's House.

Dr. Oliver narrates how two Fathers of the Society of Jesus were, in the year 1767, dogged from Ostend by a Protestant clergyman, and put to trouble at custom-houses and other places, and how one of these fathers was afterwards threatened with the penal laws by another Protestant clergyman for having instructed a young woman who applied to him, desiring to be received into the Catholic Church.[1] It was a common thing for priests to adopt feigned names, in order to escape detection. When living at Norwich, Alban Butler went by the name of Mr. Cross. There is an interesting story connected with this. Alban Butler lived in the palace of the Duke of Norfolk, to whom he was at that time chaplain. A large case of books arrived at the palace of the Protestant Bishop of Norwich, addressed, "The Rev. Mr. Cross, the Palace, Norwich." The bishop opened the case. Butler was told of its arrival, and applied to the bishop for his goods. His lordship refused, on the ground that they were popish books. Butler, however, had an influential friend where the bishop would have least imagined that a friend of a popish priest could be found. After the battle of Fontenoy, a large number of English prisoners of war were sent to Douay, where Butler then resided. The learned author of the "Lives of the Saints" devoted all his time to the care, temporal as well as spiritual, of the British soldiers. For this service he received the personal thanks of the Duke of Cumberland, who told Alban Butler that he should be most happy, if he should ever be able, to make some return in England for what Butler had done for his soldiers in France. When the Bishop of Norwich refused to give up the case of books, Butler wrote to the Duke of Cumberland. The duke kept his word. A short time after, the books were forwarded to "Mr. Cross."

[1] *Collectanea S.J.*, p. 79, under the head of "Forrester."

The doors of Catholic chapels were in those days bolted and secured before Mass began, in order to keep out spies. About the year 1835, a man was still alive who remembered having been refused admission to the chapel at Old Oscott, which was then only a small country mission, on Christmas Day, because they did not know who he was. All manner of precaution was taken to conceal the existence, if possible, of Catholics. At the beginning of the baptismal register kept at the Church of the Holy Apostles in Norwich there is written on a flyleaf as follows:—"A Register of Baptisms copied from Mr. Angier, beginning from September 1775, no one being kept before by reason of the Penal Laws." "The Laity's Directory" for the year 1777 has no name of publisher or printer, or place where printed or sold. It has not the name of any one priest or chapel or school. There is no advertisement in it—nothing, in short, which could identify a single priest or chapel, or even any one lay Catholic.[1]

The short account I have given of the state of Catholics in England about the time of the first Relief Act, the reader will find but a poor description. It will have produced some effect, however, if it shall have induced a few people to put in writing, for the use of some future historian, those interesting traditions which are handed down in many Catholic families about "the days of the penal laws."

For a few years preceding the first Relief Act, there were several indications of a desire on the part of some Protestants to relax the severity with which Catholics had been treated. Though George III. obstinately opposed

---

[1] An interesting account of the state of English Catholics about the year 1775, and of the reception of a gentleman and his wife into the Catholic Church by Dr. Challoner, may be seen in a little book well worth reading, entitled "A Hundred Years Ago," published by Washbourne in the year 1877.

the final emancipation, yet it must be remembered that the Act of 1778, which gave some little relief, and the Act of 1791, which gave great relief, were both passed in the King's reign. And he himself showed personal kindness to Catholics. Butler attributes this disposition on the part of the King to the kindness which had been shown to his father Prince Frederick of Wales, by the Duke of Norfolk, at whose house, in St. James's Square, George III. was born. Indeed, Butler looks upon the friendly relations which existed between the royal and the Norfolk families as the first symptom of the return of brighter days.

About this time, also, the Protestant relative of a wealthy Catholic lady having commenced proceedings to enforce the infamous Act which gave power to the nearest Protestant relative to seize the property of a Catholic, an Act of Parliament was passed to prevent his taking the mean advantage, and to secure the lady in the possession of her land.[1]

Lord Mansfield, when lord chief justice, put every obstacle he could in the way of the conviction of priests who were tried for saying Mass on the information of the infamous Payne. An Act of William III., as we shall see later on, punished with perpetual imprisonment any *priest convicted of saying Mass.* Payne and his associates used to go in disguise to where they knew Mass was being said, and then swear at the trial that they had seen the priest say Mass. The only evidence, therefore, that the accused was really a priest was that it was sworn he had said Mass. Two things, however, had to be proved—one, that the accused was a priest; the other, that he had said Mass. The counsel for the prosecution argued that it was only necessary to prove that he had said Mass, for if he had

---

[1] Lord Camden, in the House of Lords, had the honour of introducing this bill into Parliament.

said Mass he must be a priest, for no one but a priest could say Mass. Lord Mansfield laid it down in his charge to the jury, that each of the two facts—namely, that the accused was a priest, and that he had said Mass—must be supported by independent proof; that the jury must be first satisfied that he was a priest without regarding the fact that he had said Mass. His lordship further observed, that if the jury were to convict a man of being a priest on the ground that it had been sworn he had said Mass, they would run a great risk of convicting an innocent person. He said a man must be better acquainted with the ceremonies of the Mass than most Protestants were, in order to be able to swear that what he had seen was the Mass, and not any other ceremony. And supposing the ceremony to have been correctly performed, even that would not prove the man going through it to be a priest, as it was well known (and Lord Mansfield mentioned a particular case which had actually occurred) that the Mass had been so well imitated by an impostor, that even Catholics themselves had been taken in. His lordship concluded by repeating to the jury that they must have some positive proof that the accused was a priest, such as his ordination papers, or something equally authentic; that that proof neither he, the lord chief justice, nor the jury would ever be able to get. In this way Lord Mansfield obtained the acquittal of Mr. Webb, whose trial we have mentioned above. For this justice to Catholics, Lord Mansfield had his house pillaged, and his own life endangered two years afterwards during the Gordon riots. The degree of persecution varied in different parts of England, according to the cupidity or spite of the informers: in London it was rife, in some parts of the country there was little or none. The present chapel at Mawley was opened by Dr. Thomas Talbot, vicar-apostolic of the Midland District, only three or four years after his brother, Dr. James Talbot, had been tried for his life in London.[1]

In the introduction it was observed that the present state of the Church in Great Britain has arisen from three sources—from the descendants of those who had never lost the faith, from the converts of later days, and from the providential arrival of large numbers of our Irish fellow-Catholics. It is not a little remarkable that all these three sources sprang from suffering and sorrow. It was in extreme suffering that our Catholic ancestors kept the faith. When their chains were struck off, it was from suffering they arose, to begin again that glorious work of the Church in England, which will one day, let us hope, join a glorious future to a glorious past. It was in suffering and sorrow that the converts of the last fifty years broke through their own trammels and entered the Catholic Church. The loss of friends, the loss of wealth, the loss of position in life, the snapping of the dearest ties, the blighting of the fondest hopes,—these were the sufferings and sorrow which followed hundreds—perhaps thousands—who were ready to make any sacrifice to obey the call of God. It was suffering and sorrow that compelled thousands and tens of thousands to leave the land of their birth, and in

---

[1] The centenary of the opening of this chapel was celebrated a few years ago, during the lifetime of that fine old English baronet, the late Sir Edward Blount.

A descendant of Lord Mansfield told my informant that it was a tradition in the Mansfield family, that on one of the occasions when Bishop James Talbot was tried for saying Mass, the following dialogue occurred:—Lord Mansfield: "You say this man is a priest?" Informer: "Yes; I saw him say Mass. He had vestments on." Lord Mansfield: "Do not the Catholics say that the Mass essentially consists in certain words?" Informer: "Yes." Lord Mansfield: "Did you hear those words?" Informer: "No; they are said secretly." Lord Mansfield: "How, then, can you swear he said them?" Informer: "Oh, he had vestments on." Lord Mansfield: "If I were to put vestments on, would you say I was a priest?"

suffering and sorrow they came to repeople our land with the children of God. The seed of the early spring was sown in tears. Without doubt it seems to have had the blessing of God upon it. If the Catholics of England prove faithful to their stewardship, the older ones amongst us may go to rest in firmest hope, that ere long an abundant harvest will be reaped in joy.

CHAPTER III.

THE ACT OF 1778.

Edmund Burke on the Act of William III.—Address of English Catholics to George III.—Remarks on the address—Debates on the bill of 1778—Sir George Savile, Mr. Dunning, Attorney-General Thurlow, Lord Beauchamp, and Henry Dundas on the bill—Second reading of the bill—A specimen of bigotry—A liberal speaker—The bill passes the Commons—Second reading of the bill in the Lords—Speech of a bishop—and of two future prime ministers—Lord Shelbourne on the trial of Mr. Malony—The bill of 1778 passes the Lords—Relief given by the Act.

IN the last chapter I endeavoured to give the reader some idea of the state in which our Catholic ancestors were living at the time of the first Relief Act, in the year 1778. I will now give an account of the Act itself.[1] It was intituled, "An Act for relieving his Majesty's subjects professing the Popish religion from certain penalties and disabilities, imposed on them by an Act made in the eleventh and twelfth years of the reign of King William III., intituled 'An Act for the further preventing the growth of Popery.'" This Act of William III. deserves the same epithet of "ferocious" which Edmund Burke gave to the Acts passed against the Irish Catholics in the reign of Queen Anne. It enacted that whoever after March 25, 1700, should "apprehend a Popish bishop, priest, or Jesuit, and convict him of saying Mass, or exercising his functions within the realm," should "receive of the sheriff

[1] 18 Geo. III. cap. 60.

of the county for every such conviction the sum of £100, to to be paid within four months, upon tendering the judge's certificate of the conviction." If the sheriff made default in payment, he was to forfeit £200. It further enacted that "every Popish bishop, priest, or Jesuit who should say Mass, or exercise his function; every Papist keeping school, educating or boarding youth for that purpose," should suffer perpetual imprisonment. It enacted that "persons educated in, or professing the Popish religion who" should "not within six months after they attained the age of eighteen, take the oaths of allegiance and supremacy, and make the Declaration in 30 Car. II."[1] should "be disabled (but not their heirs or posterity) to inherit or take any lands, tenements, or hereditaments within this kingdom. And during such persons' lives, until they should take the said oath, the next of kin being a Protestant," should "enjoy his lands," etc., without being accountable for the profits, but should not commit waste. It further enacted that after April 10, 1700, "every Papist" should be disabled "to purchase lands in this kingdom, or any profits out of the same." Whoever should convict a person of sending his child or ward "beyond the sea to be educated in Papacy," was to receive as a reward the whole penalty of £100, inflicted by the Statute III. of James I. Finally, if the "Popish parents" of Protestant children should refuse them a fitting maintenance, in order to compel them to change their religion, the Act gave the lord chancellor power to order as he should think proper.

We saw in the last chapter that two clauses of this Act had been recently acted on: the clause against ecclesiastics exercising their functions, and the clause giving power to

---

[1] This was the declaration commonly called the "Declaration against Popery." The Act 30 Charles II. cap 2, was the Act which disabled Catholic peers from sitting and voting in the House of Lords.

the next of kin, being a Protestant, to seize the lands of his Catholic relation. The Act had therefore been by no means a dead letter, and the Act of 1778, which repealed a portion of it, was a substantial relief.

Before proceeding to the Relief Act itself, it will be interesting and instructive to mention the circumstances under which the Act of William was introduced into Parliament and passed the Legislature. These circumstances may be best described in the words of Edmund Burke. Addressing the electors of Bristol, after having alluded to the very penal nature of the Act, he proceeded as follows :—" Does any one who hears me, approve this scheme of things, or think there is common justice, common sense, or common honesty in any part of it? If any does, let him say it, and I am ready to discuss the point with temper and candour. But instead of approving, I perceive a virtuous indignation beginning to rise in your minds on the mere cold stating of the statute. But what will you feel when you know from history how this statute passed, and what were the motives, and what the mode of making it? A party in this nation, enemies to the system of revolution, were in opposition to the Government of King William. They knew that our glorious deliverer was an enemy to all persecution.[1] They knew that he came . . . out of a country where a third of the people are contented Catholics under a Protestant Government. He came with a part of his army, composed of those very Catholics, to overset the power of a popish prince.

"The party I speak of (like some amongst us who

---

[1] The reader will remember that, in speaking of Burke in a former page, it was said that he was perhaps as great a friend of Catholics as a Protestant could well be. He was a Protestant Whig of the old school. For his signal services to the Catholic cause, we must excuse the epithet "glorious" which he applies to William the usurper, and allow the great orator to indulge in the delusion that the object of his admiration was an enemy to all persecution.

would disparage the best friends of their country), resolved to make the King either violate his principles of toleration, or incur the odium of protecting Papists. They therefore brought in this bill, and made it purposely wicked and absurd, that it might be rejected. The then Court party, discovering their game, turned the tables on them, and returned their bill to them stuffed with still greater absurdities, that its loss might lie upon its original authors. They, finding their own ball thrown back to them, kicked it back again to their adversaries. And thus this Act, loaded with the double injustice of two parties, neither of whom intended to pass what they hoped the other would be persuaded to reject, went through the Legislature, contrary to the real wish of all parts of it, and of all the parties that composed it. In this manner these insolent and profligate factions, as if they were playing with balls and counters, made a sport of the fortunes and the liberties of their fellow-creatures. Other acts of persecution have been acts of malice. This was a subversion of justice from wantonness and petulance. Look into the history of Bishop Burnet. He is a witness without exception."[1]

It ought to be a matter of surprise how such a "ferocious" Act as this, brought into Parliament from such unworthy motives, and so recklessly passed into a law, could ever have been allowed to be enforced. The account I have given in the words of Burke clearly shows the supreme contempt which the Protestants had for the Catholics in England. We were in so degraded a position, that it was looked upon as good political sport to use us as any one pleased, and put us to the torture to gain the ends of Whigs and Tories. This contempt was the effect of the intense hatred which the English had for the Catholic Church, acting on the small minority of the faithful, which

[1] Speech to the electors of Bristol in 1780 (*vide* Burke's works).

gross oppression had left in the land. This hatred and contempt continued, and permitted the execution of a savage law, which had its origin in the jealousies of Protestant parties.

In 1778, there was a disposition to relax the more ferocious parts of the penal law. It was also expedient to gain the good-will of Catholics, at a time when America and France were banded together against England. The expediency of conciliation operated more in regard to the Irish Catholics, though it was not without its effects in regard also to the Catholics of England. The opportune moment was seized by the English Catholics, and they determined to address the Throne. A committee was formed, of which Lord Petre, Sir John Throckmorton, and Mr. William Sheldon were the most active members, Sheldon was appointed secretary to the committee; he was the principal actor on the part of the Catholics, and managed the affair with great prudence and success. We shall see later, on the authority of Dr. Milner, in what his prudence chiefly consisted, and to what he owed his great success. The reader will be interested in reading the address which was drawn up by the committee, and presented to George III. It was as follows:—

> " To the King's most excellent Majesty. The humble address of the Roman Catholic Peers and Commoners of Great Britain.
>
> " Most Gracious Sovereign,
>
> " We, your Majesty's most dutiful and loyal subjects, the Roman Catholic Peers and Commoners of your kingdom of Great Britain, most humbly hope that it cannot be offensive to the clemency of your Majesty's nature, or to the maxims of your just and wise Government, that any part of your subjects should approach your royal presence, to assure your Majesty of the respectful affection which they bear to your person, and their true attachment to the civil constitution of their country, which,

having been perpetuated through all changes of religious opinions and establishments, has been at length perfected by that revolution which has placed your Majesty's illustrious house on the throne of these kingdoms, and inseparately united your title to the crown, with the law and liberties of your people.

"Our exclusion from many of the benefits of that Constitution has not diminished our reverence to it. We behold with satisfaction the felicity of our fellow-subjects, and we partake of the general prosperity which results from an institution so full of wisdom. We have patiently submitted to such restrictions and discouragements as the Legislature thought expedient. We have thankfully received such relaxations of the rigour of the laws as the mildness of an enlightened age and the benignity of your Majesty's Government have gradually produced, and we submissively wait, without presuming to suggest either time or measure, for such other indulgence as those happy causes cannot fail in their own season to effect.

"We beg to assure your Majesty that our dissent from the legal establishment in matters of religion, is purely conscientious; that we hold no opinions adverse to your Majesty's Government or repugnant to the duties of good citizens. And we trust that this has been shown more decisively, by our irreproachable conduct for many years past, under circumstances of discountenance and displeasure, than it can be manifested by any declaration whatever.

"In a time of public danger, when your Majesty's subjects can have but one interest, and ought to have but one wish and one sentiment, we humbly hope it will not be deemed improper to assure your Majesty of our unalterable attachment to the cause and welfare of this our common country, and our utter detestation of the designs and views of any foreign power against the dignity of your Majesty's crown, the safety and tranquility of your Majesty's subjects.[1]

"The delicacy of our situation is such, that we do not presume to point out the particular means by which we may be allowed to testify our zeal to your Majesty, and our wishes to serve our

---

[1] In February of this year, 1778, an offensive and defensive alliance was formed between France and the United States.

country; but we entreat leave faithfully to assure your Majesty, that we shall be perfectly ready, on every occasion, to give such proofs of our fidelity and the purity of our intentions as your Majesty's wisdom and the sense of the nation shall at any time deem expedient."

This address was signed by the Duke of Norfolk, the Earls of Surrey and Shrewsbury, by Lord Linton for the Scotch, by Lords Stourton, Petre, Arundell, Dormer, Teynham, and Clifford, and by one hundred and sixty-three commoners.

There is a timidity, not to say obsequiousness, about this address which cannot fail to strike the reader. No fault, however, can on this account be found with those who composed or with those who signed it. English Catholics had been beaten down by brute force into a condition in which no language but that of submission would have been prudent and useful. We were not considered as belonging to the State at all. Anything like a claim on our part to equality with our Protestant fellow-subjects would have caused us to be laughed at or rejected with indignation. Any such demand from us would have been looked upon much the same as a claim of some unwelcome stranger in a house to share in the rents of his host. After a hundred years of gradual relief, and with the liberty we now enjoy, he would be a foolish man amongst us who should complain of the too-submissive style of the address. Still, it is open to some remark. In the first paragraph there is unnecessary praise of the revolution which placed William III. on the throne. In the second paragraph, the word "expedient" is rather suggestive of the idea that we thought the Legislature had some excuse for the ferocious laws which were enacted against the members of the Catholic Church. No Catholic, under any circumstances, should ever admit that Protestants have the smallest reason for asserting that our loyalty is to be suspected because we are Catholics. And yet Protestants do assert this, even to this day. We know that our religion, so far from tempting us to be disloyal, is a strong motive to the staunch loyalty of which we boast. And yet we have frequently to listen to the charge of at least a tendency to be disloyal, from Protestants of all parties, and sometimes even from men whose own loyalty is evidently of so superficial a kind that we should think it a disgrace that our loyalty should be compared with theirs. The allusion in the second paragraph to "relaxation in the rigour of the laws," merely referred to a relaxation in the administration and execution of existing laws, and not to any repeal of the penal laws. This Act of 1778 was the first legislative relaxation.

The time had at length arrived when in the decrees of Providence the chains were to be loosened which had bound our fathers in fetters. The seed of the martyrs, which had been trodden underfoot, was now to spring up and blossom and bear fruit. A disposition to treat us with less severity existed in the minds of many. It was advisable to unite the people, in face of an American and European war. It was, therefore, to use the words of the preamble of the Act, "expedient to repeal certain provisions," made in the Act of William III., "for further preventing the growth of Papacy." Mark the word "expedient." Catholics were relieved in 1778, as they have been relieved at various times since that year, not because our right to redress was admitted, but because it was expedient. As it was expedient to relieve us in 1778, so it was expedient in 1791; and it was expedient, it was most expedient, to prevent a civil war in 1829. It was expedient in 1846 to include Catholics in the education grant, lest the House of Commons should otherwise have rejected the whole grant. Lord John Russell felt that it was very expedient then to put Catholics on an equality with others. When the Irish Church was to be disestablished, it was expedient to repeal the Ecclesiastical Titles Act; otherwise the Irish Protestant Bishops would have fallen under penalties which had been enacted to scourge only Catholics. I will not now multiply instances, though many might be cited. For the present, it is sufficient to say that when the united action of Catholics shall make it expedient to grant to the Irish what they want and what they reasonably demand, then, but not till then, will their undoubted rights be obtained.

The bill for our relief was introduced into the House of Commons on the 14th of May, 1778,[1] by Sir George Savile, and the motion for leave to bring in the bill was seconded by Mr. Dunning.

A short account of the debates on this bill in the two Houses of Parliament cannot fail to interest the reader. Sir George Savile, on moving for leave to bring in the bill, began by saying that "one of his principal views in proposing this repeal was to vindicate the honour and to assert the principles of the Protestant religion, to which all persecution was, or ought to be, wholly adverse." As we Catholics ought to have a great respect for the memory of Sir George, on account of his having been the very first member of Parliament to propose a repeal of penal laws, it is with great satisfaction that we must notice in the above sentence the words, "or ought to be." If he had not uttered them, we should have had to accuse him of a ridiculous paradox. Sir George Savile also said that "the Act" (that is, the Act of William) "had not been regularly put in execution, but sometimes it had; and he understood

[1] 18 Geo. III. cap. 60.

that several lived under great terror, and some under actual contribution, in consequence of the powers given by it. As an inducement to the repeal of those penalties, which were directed with such a violence of severity against Papists, he stated the peaceable and loyal behaviour of that part of the people under a government which, though not rigorous in enforcing, yet suffered such intolerable penalties and disqualifications to stand against them on the statutes. A late loyal and excellent address, which they had presented to the Throne, stood high among the instances which Sir George pointed out, of the safety and the good consequences which were likely to attend this liberal procedure of Parliament."

"Mr. Dunning," the solicitor-general, "seconded the motion." Speaking of the clauses of the Act of William, he said, "Some of them had now ceased to be necessary, and others were at all times a disgrace to humanity. The imprisonment of a popish priest for life, only for officiating in the services of his religion, was horrible in its nature, and must, to an Englishman, be ever held as infinitely worse than death. Such a law, in times of so great liberality as the present, and when so little was to be apprehended from these people, called loudly for repeal; and he begged to remind the House, that even then they would not be left at liberty to exercise their functions, but would still, under the restriction of former laws, be liable to a year's imprisonment, and to the punishment of a heavy fine." Mr. Dunning concluded, according to the report, by saying, "With respect to the encouragement held out by it" (that is, by the Act) "to those children who were base enough to lay their hands on the estates of their parents, or which debarred a man from the honest acquisition of property, it needed only to be mentioned in order to excite the indignation of the House." "Mr. Attorney-

General Thurlow declared he had no intention of opposing the bill." He spoke very strongly against that part of the Act of William which punished a parent for sending his child to be educated abroad : " To remedy so glaring an evil required," he said, " little hesitation ; but to repeal the penalties against popish priests exercising their functions freely, required some consideration. The House was first to determine how far they thought it safe to allow the free preaching and teaching of that religion. When this point had been settled, Acts would be framed accordingly." This last sentence of Thurlow's helps us to understand the difference in the position of Catholics in England between the times when the Queen's grandfather had been reigning for eighteen years, and the days of her present Majesty, whom may God long preserve.

Lord Beauchamp next spoke, and made some observations which it is half cheering, half sad to read even after the lapse of a hundred and seven years. He "expressed his satisfaction that the motion was not likely to meet one dissentient voice ; and it gave him the more pleasure at this time, as he thought the commercial advantages that Parliament now meant to bestow on Ireland, would be of very little use to that country unless they were accompanied by a repeal of their penal laws, which so long depressed three-fourths of the people there ; and this bill, he hoped, would, when passed, be an example to the Irish Parliament, in whose power it was to give that relief to their brethren ; and he was sorry to say he thought, though their faith was in some degree pledged for the effect of some such measure, that nothing had yet been done for that people. They had begged to have a test of loyalty and obedience to the Government given them—that test was made and taken by a large and respectable number of Roman Catholics, yet nothing had yet been granted them in return for that test:[1] nay, more; when a bill had been brought into the Irish Parliament to allow Papists to take building leases in corporate towns, that most reasonable indulgence was ungenerously refused them. Something," he said, "might be suggested in excuse with relation to the late disturbance in the south-west part of Ireland, but he assured the House he never knew a Roman Catholic of property in that country who did not express the greatest abhorrence of those violences; and he was convinced that it was want of employment, want of industry, and want of reward for labour, that caused them: and he concluded with a declaration that he did not think the little indulgence which was now proposed to be given the Roman Catholics of this kingdom should be accompanied by any test, as he was sure that any member who read over the Act of King William, would think that in repealing it he was not so much employed in conferring favours on the Catholics as in rescuing the statutes from disgrace." If the statesmen who have governed Ireland since the year 1778 had possessed the sense and wisdom implied in Lord Beauchamp's speech, and had acted accordingly, no two people in the world would have been more united than the English and Irish. Mr. Henry Dundas, who was then lord advocate, and afterwards became Lord Melville, "informed the House that the Acts intended to be repealed were made before the union of England and Scotland, and therefore the repeal would not extend to Scotland, as a statute had taken place in their own Parliament, nearly in the same terms, and which he would bring in a motion to repeal." These few words of Mr. Dundas are worthy of being recorded, as the announcement which he then made, that he contemplated the repeal of the Scotch Act, was

[1] This test was the one provided by the Irish Act of 1774, as recorded in the first chapter.

the origin of the riots in Scotland in the following year, 1779, and of the celebrated Gordon riots in London in the year 1780.

After Mr. Serjeant Adair had said a few words in support of the motion, it was agreed to *nem. con.*[1]

"On the 18th of May, the bill being brought in and read a first time, Sir G. Savile moved the second reading." Only two speeches are reported in Hansard. They are both characteristic as showing how differently men looked upon the penal laws, and in what opposite views Catholics were regarded. They are, therefore, well worthy of the reader's attention.

"Mr. Ambler thought that the whole system of our penal laws should be revised: infinite and well-grounded were the objections against them, and whatever might have been the cause for which they had been enacted, he was satisfied that none existed now. A committee ought to be appointed to examine into the penal code, and see what parts of it ought to be repealed; but as that must necessarily take up a great deal of time, being a business of very great importance, and the session being so far advanced, he thought it would be proper to defer the further consideration of the bill to next year. He insinuated, however, that some restraint should be laid on the Catholics. He had no objection to giving them security for the quiet possession of their estates—those who now enjoyed any might be confirmed in them, and their heirs, as Catholics, declared capable of succeeding to them without being obliged to conform, in order to secure themselves from informations, or against the mean attacks of Protestant relations on their property—but he wished

---

[1] The report of the debates in both Houses is taken from Hansard's "Parliamentary History," vol. 19, pp. 1137-44. The expression "a statute *had taken place*" in Mr. Dundas' speech shows the loose style of reporting in those days.

that the bar which Parliament had formerly thought proper to lay in the way of any future acquisition of landed property might not be removed: let them enjoy what they have, but let them not increase their possessions." These bigoted and tyrannical words called up a Mr. Turner, who said that "he detested the cruel policy that reduced men, by nature free, to a state of slavery. Religion," he said, "had always been an engine in the hands of power to enslave mankind; he wished to see all his fellow-subjects free, Catholics and Dissenters alike, and a universal toleration established by law. The Catholics of this country were amiable, worthy citizens; they lived on their estates, improved them, spent the produce of them at home, and daily exercised the most voluntary and generous acts of charity among those who resided on or near their estates. Their charities knew no bounds; and by all their actions he declared they had manifested a behaviour highly worthy both of good citizens and good Christians."

"The bill was read a second time, and afterwards passed the Commons without opposition."

On the 25th of May the bill came on for the second reading in the House of Lords. The Bishop of Peterborough (Dr. John Hinchcliffe) said, "As a friend to civil and religious liberty, I am free, my lords, to own that I think there ought to be neither penalty nor restraint on the intercourse between God and a man's own conscience. I cannot, therefore, but disapprove of all laws which are calculated to oppress men for their religious persuasion; and to tempt any one with views of interest to trespass on his duty and natural affection, by depriving his father of his estate or supplanting his brethren, is a policy, in my opinion, inconsistent with reason, justice, and humanity. At the same time, my lords, permit me to say, I am not so ignorant of the genius of popery as not to know it is a very difficult matter to consider its religious principles altogether distinct from that political superstructure which has been raised upon them, and to the support of which, I cannot but fear, that should occasion offer, they might still be made too subservient."

What the political superstructure was in the mind of the bishop I cannot pretend to say. His lordship could not have meant the sympathies of any Catholics with the House of Stuart, for, in the first place, thirty-two years after the battle of Culloden, the title of George III., *de jure* as well as *de facto*, was admitted by all; and, in the second place, Jacobite tendencies had shown themselves quite as strongly amongst Protestant Tories as amongst Catholic Tories, and the Anglican religion quite as much as the Catholic Church would have been open to the charge of bearing an objectionable superstructure. Perhaps the good bishop did not know exactly what he meant. In the course of his speech the Bishop of Peterborough said he wished the bill "had been brought in sooner in the session, that it might not appear to be hurried through both Houses; but," he added, "there might be particular circumstances which might make delay inconvenient." These particular circumstances were the alliance, offensive and defensive, between France and the United States, which, as we have seen, England regarded as a declaration of war. After the Bishop of Peterborough, "the Marquis of Rockingham, who was afterwards prime minister, said a few words, to show that the repeal of these clauses would but relieve a very dutiful and loyal part of the King's subjects from hardships which it was disgraceful for any government to inflict."[1] The Earl of Shelburne, who

---

[1] Four years afterwards, that is, in 1782, Lord Rockingham became prime minister on the resignation of Lord North.

also became a prime minister on the death of Lord Rockingham, made an interesting speech. According to Hansard, he "followed the noble marquis" (that is, Rockingham) "upon the same grounds, wishing that restraints similar to those now about to be repealed had not reduced three-fourths of the people of Ireland to a state of wretchedness, tending equally to alienate their affections from this Government, and to prevent an influx of wealth from that country to this. He wished that, with a liberal toleration of religion, there should be given to a people who had demeaned themselves so well, a security and free disposal of their property. Further than this he would not venture to hint at or approve; and as the present bill did not go beyond that, or indeed so far, he wished it should neither meet with opposition or delay. He went a little into the history of the penal clauses, which the Act was intended to repeal, and observed, that when they were first proposed in Parliament nobody approved of them, yet nobody had spirit enough to oppose them. He adverted to the case of a Mr. Malony, a priest of the Roman Catholic persuasion, who had been apprehended and brought to trial by the lowest and most despicable of mankind, a common informing constable of the city of London.[1] He was convicted of being a popish priest, and the court were reluctantly obliged to condemn him (shocking as the idea was) to perpetual imprisonment. His lordship was then in office, and although every method was taken by the privy council to give a legal discharge to the prisoner, neither the laws then in force would allow of it, nor dared the King himself to grant him a pardon. He, however, with his colleagues in office, were so perfectly persuaded of the impolicy and inhumanity

---

[1] This was the Mr. Malony whose trial and conviction at Croydon was alluded to in Chapter II.

of the law, that they ventured to give him his liberty at every hazard."

"The bill was read a second time, and afterwards passed without opposition."

Lord North, who was prime minister at this time, either did not speak in this debate, or, having spoken, his speech is not reported in Hansard. His mind was perhaps too full of the American war to give much attention to the rights, as British subjects, of a few English Catholics.

The bill having passed into an Act, it is time to give the reader a short account of its details. It repealed only those clauses of the Act of William which related to the prosecution of Catholic "bishops, priests, and Jesuits;" which subjected any Catholic keeping a school to perpetual imprisonment; and which disabled any Catholic from taking real property by descent or purchase, and gave such property to the nearest Protestant next of kin. It will be observed that the relief given by these clauses was precisely the relief which was most necessary at the time: the clauses of the Act of William which were repealed were those under which Catholics had lately suffered. And if it be said that there were still left on the statute-book other laws which made it criminal to exercise ecclesiastical functions and to keep Catholic schools, the answer is, that those unrepealed statutes did not work the same grievance as did the Act of William; for under the latter any informer could prosecute, whereas under the former, either the informer was not entitled to a reward, or the prosecution could only be by the attorney-general. It will also be noticed that the Act of 1778 did not repeal the whole of the Act of William III. It left untouched the clause which forbade a parent or guardian to send a child beyond the sea to be educated in the Catholic religion, and which, on conviction, gave to the informer a reward of £100. To this penalty, therefore, all Catholics subjected themselves who continued to send their sons and daughters to Douay, St. Omer's, Liege, Bruges, and the other English colleges and convents which were not dissolved until the time of the French Revolution. The Act of 1778 also left unrepealed the clause which enabled the lord chancellor to order a maintenance for the Protestant child of a Catholic parent. As Mr. Butler remarks, every pain, penalty, and disability inflicted by other Acts remained, after the passing of this Act, in all their force against us. But, as Butler continues to observe, "though the legal benefits which the Catholics derived from this Act were limited, the advantages which they derived from it in other respects were both substantial and extensive. It shook the general prejudice against them to its centre; it disposed their neighbours to think of them with kindness; it led the public to view the pretensions to further relief with a favourable eye; and it restored to them a thousand indescribable charities in the ordinary intercourse of social life, which they had seldom experienced. No Catholic, who recollects the passing of the bill, "will ever forget the general anxiety of the body, while it was in its progress through the Parliament, or the smile and friendly greeting with which his Protestant neighbour met him the day after it had passed into a law."[1] The same author also says that "in consequence of this Act, Catholics mixed more with their Protestant brethren, and, becoming better known to them, dissipated their anti-Catholic prejudices. Still, to a certain extent,

'Manserunt veteris vestigia ruris.'

The effect of a defamation of two centuries could not be undone in a moment."[2] Many moments have passed

[1] "Historical Memoirs," vol. iii. p. 294, edition of 1822.   [2] Ibid., p. 353.

since 1778; several Relief Acts have been passed; many things have been done to restore our rights to us; still the effects of a defamation of now three centuries is continually checking complete justice, and is for ever drowning the voice of the Holy Spirit calling upon the English people to return to the Church.

The manner in which this Act was received by our ancestors will perhaps best appear in the two following pastorals of the English Vicars Apostolic, which cannot fail to be interesting to the reader:—

"To all the Catholic clergy, both secular and regular, residing in the Southern District of England.

"DEAR BRETHREN,—The great Apostle St. Paul, writing to his beloved disciple Timothy,[1] and in him instructing all Christian pastors of souls, desires first of all, that supplications, prayers, intercessions, and thanksgivings (Eucharists) should be made for all men, for kings and all that are in high station and authority; that we may lead a quiet and peaceable life in all goodness and chastity. For this is good, saith the Apostle, and acceptable in the sight of God our Saviour. It is a duty we owe to our princes by His Divine ordinance, and the very principal part of that honour, which we are to give them, which is so much insisted upon in the Word of God.[2] Wherefore, dear brethren, that both you and we may religiously comply with the most indisputable precept of God's own law, we take this occasion of addressing these lines to you in this public manner, requiring that all and every one of you should offer up your most ardent prayers to the Almighty, for our most gracious Sovereign King George III. and his Royal Consort Queen Charlotte, and all their royal family, and also that in your respective congregations (when you shall be able to meet, without danger to yourselves or your flocks from the many grievous penal laws which stand out against the Catholics of this kingdom) you shall recommend the rest of the faithful to offer up also their prayers for the same intentions: this being a duty

---

[1] 1 Tim. ii. 2.
[2] Romans xiii.; 1 St. Peter ii. 13, *seq.*

which by the law of God all Christian people owe to their respective sovereigns.

"Given at London this 4th of June, 1778.
+ RICHARD DEBOREN. V.A.[1]
+ JAMES BIRTH.[2]

"Published and signed also for the Midland District.
+ JOHN PHILOMEL. V.A.[3]
+ THOMAS ACONEN.[4]

"Published and signed also for the Northern District by
+ WILLIAM TRACHON. V. A."[5]

"To the Catholic clergy, secular and regular, residing in the Western District of England.

"DEAR BRETHREN,—The duty of praying for sovereign princes is fully recommended by the two great Apostles SS. Peter and Paul; and it has been the constant practice of the Christians from the first ages of the Church, as all ecclesiastical records testify. Moreover, the Roman Catholics of this kingdom have at this present time a further inducement to the same, arising from the extraordinary favour newly granted to them by the Act of Parliament. On these motives, therefore, we think it necessary to require that you offer up your fervent prayers to the Almighty for our most gracious Sovereign King George III., his Royal Consort Queen Charlotte, and all the royal family, and that you recommend the same to your respective flocks. We ordain that on all Sundays to the last Collect be added, *Et famulos tuos*, etc., as in the London District. Let a memorial of the King by name be made every day in the Canon. Lastly, after the Divine Service in the morning on Sundays add Psalm xix., and the prayer as in the London District. The great humanity of Government towards us suggests a propriety of behaviour on our part, in using the present indulgence with caution, prudence, and moderation. We, therefore, strongly recommend to you that line of conduct, and to be careful in avoiding what may tend to raise disputes or give offence. + CHARLES RAMATEN.V.A."[6]

BATH, July 3, 1778.

[1] Dr. Challoner.   [2] Dr. James Talbot.
[3] Dr. Hornyold.   [4] Dr. Thomas Talbot.   [5] Dr. Walton.
[6] Dr. Walmesley, O.S.B. He was a learned mathematician, and had a great reputation both in England and on the Continent. His assistance and advice were made use of by the English Government, when the change was made from the old style to the new style.

CHAPTER IV.

REMARKS SUGGESTED BY THE ACT OF 1778.

IT has been noticed that Catholics were relieved not because relief was an act of justice, but because it was expedient to pass the Act. We English Catholics, who love our country at the same time that we love our religion, are naturally inclined to look favourably on the actions of our countrymen, and to judge well of their motives. To attribute bad or inferior motives where it would be rash judgment to do so, would be as foolish as it would be wrong. Such conduct on our part would not escape observation, and it would help to defeat one just object we have, namely, to amalgamate as much as possible with our fellow-countrymen, whenever we can do so without sacrificing religious principle. Our wish is to be thoroughly English, as well as thoroughly Catholic; in the same manner, it is the wish of the Irish to be thoroughly Irish, as well as thoroughly Catholic. It is our desire, therefore, to be just to all; and it is our inclination to look rather at the bright side than at the dark side of what is said about us, or done in our regard. Still, we must not ignore the existence of the dark side. If we Catholics of England are to act with credit to ourselves, we must understand our position. We must know what is thought of our religion, and of our actions as Catholics. We must not shrink from admitting those motives which evidently prompt the treatment which we receive. When we obtain relief, when we are given an instalment of our due, is it because those who favour us love our religion? is it because they love justice in the abstract, and, having no very defined faith themselves, allow equal liberty to all? or, on the contrary, when Parliament passes an Act for our benefit, is the chief motive of action expediency—that it is expedient to grant what we ask? Is there a general desire in the nation to allow no difference between Catholics and Protestants, merely on account of the difference in our religion? When men talk of wishing to put us in every respect on an equality with others, do they regard us as forming part of the family, and therefore as strictly entitled to share in all the rights of children? or do they not rather look upon us as favoured strangers admitted to equal rights with the family? Do those who are friendly to us still look upon the Church and Catholics as simply tolerated in England, or do they admit that the Church has as much right to stand upon English ground as Protestantism has? Are we Catholics considered to be debarred from any civil right whatever because we are Catholics? Then, again, what are our relations with the different parties in the State? Can any one party be said to be favourably disposed to us, or at least so well disposed to us that we can afford to be off our guard? Can we be as certain of the intention of any one party to support the principle of perfect equality, as the reformers in Great Britain were certain of the support of the Whigs in the year 1832? Are we as sure of the advocacy of any one great statesman as Mr. Cobden was sure of the advocacy of Sir Robert Peel in 1846? If we can rely on any party or on any man, on which party is it, or on which man? Is there any large section of the Tory party which hates our religion, and would keep us down as much as possible? Is there any portion of the Whig party which has drifted so far down into continental Liberalism that their detestation of Catholic principles makes them, so far as they have power, more dangerous to us, and more opposed to our liberties, than two houses full of Inglises and Eldons? On the answer to these questions depends our position as it is regarded by those who make the laws. On our position as it is in itself and as it is regarded by others, depends our attitude in the State, and our course of action in all political questions.

There can be no doubt that we are not in all matters as free and as equal to others as we ought to be. The Catholic interest and the Protestant interest in Great Britain are not twin sisters; they are not related one to the other: they are opposed to each other. Hence we must always be expecting an attack, and be ready for defence. It follows, also, that we must be ready ourselves to attack whenever an opportunity shall arise. An attack of the Catholic interest upon the Protestant interest is merely a use by Catholics of those constitutional means which we have by law in common with others, in order to obtain equal rights, many of them being rights which in theory we possess, but which in practice we do not. If we cannot obtain our rights because it is just that we should have them, we must, as far as we can, make it expedient to our adversaries to grant them. The difference between giving us relief because it is just and giving us relief because it is expedient, is clearly to be noticed at the very commencement of the Relief Acts. The word "expedient" in the preamble to the Act of 1778 was meant in its strict sense. It implied, and was intended to imply, that we had not a strict right to relief, but that under the circumstances it was a proper thing to relieve us. If Parliament considered that it was a gross injustice to us that an apostate in a family should be able to seize the inheritance from his elder brother, why were those cases excepted from the operation of the Act in which an action had been commenced, especially as a private Act had lately been passed, to prevent in one instance the prosecution of the monstrous claim? Again, if it was considered unjust that a priest or a schoolmaster should be imprisoned for exercising their offices, why did the Legislature repeal the Act which subjected them to imprisonment for life, and leave unrepealed the Act under which they might be imprisoned for a year? Mr. Dunning used this argument with the House to induce it to pass the bill—that priests and schoolmasters would still remain punishable by law. And the reader will remember, in the report of Mr. Dunning's speech, the following words:—"He begged to remind the House, that even then" (that is, after the passing of the Act) "they" (priests and schoolmasters) "would not be left at liberty to exercise their functions; but would still, under the restriction of former laws, be liable to a year's imprisonment, and to the punishment of a heavy fine."[1] The words of Mr. Pitt in 1805, which have already been quoted, and which may be taken as expressing the ideas of a large majority of both Houses, leave no doubt that the motive for relieving us was because it was expedient, and not because it was our right.[2] The sentiments of the members of the Houses of Lords and Commons towards us no doubt represented the sentiments of the vast majority of Englishmen. The state of the law and the state of feeling towards us after the passing of the Act of

---

[1] Annual Register for 1778. Butler's "Historical Memoirs," vol. iii. p. 292.

[2] Mr. Pitt said that he could not allow that the question of relief should be discussed as a claim of right, but on the ground of expediency alone.

1778, account for the caution and prudence enjoined upon Catholics in the pastoral letters of the bishops. It is true, as we have heard from Mr. Butler, that many sincere friends of the Catholic cause were rejoiced at their relief. But the great majority of the people continued to look upon Catholics with distrust and disfavour. As it was then, so it is now. There may be some who, having themselves an attraction to the Church, regard us with favour. There may be some of the Liberal party who, from a broad sense of justice, look upon us as Burke and Fox did. But making allowance for the modifications in opinion which a hundred years have produced, hatred of the Church, and the manner in which Catholics are regarded, are pretty much the same as they were a hundred years ago. At any rate, our position is such that we have distinct interests to be guarded, definite points to be defended, and undoubted rights to be gained. We should, therefore, be always prepared. A thoroughly good understanding between clergy and laity, and the hearty co-operation of both, are, in the first place, absolutely necessary in order that we may keep the ground we have gained, and advance towards the enjoyment of all our rights. And this brings us to the next reflection which is suggested by the Act of 1778.

Dr. Milner, speaking of the Act of 1778, says, "What rendered it more remarkable was, that it took place without opposition in Parliament, or dissension among the Catholics themselves. The latter circumstance was chiefly owing to the proper conduct of the Catholic leaders, in timely submitting the religious part of the bill to the judgment of their prelates; and to the religious, honourable, and straightforward conduct of William Sheldon, Esq., a gentleman of ancient family, who acted as secretary on the occasion."[1] The committee formed at this time to watch

[1] "Supplementary Memoirs of English Catholics," p. 42.

for the Catholics the bill of 1778 was, I believe, the first committee which conducted our affairs in relation to the Government. From the few words I have just quoted from Dr. Milner, it would appear that the action of that committee was precisely what the action of every Catholic committee should be. The special interests which we have arise from the fact that we are a minority of Catholics living in the midst of a large majority of Protestants, who possess almost exclusively the legislative and executive power of the country. Our special interests, therefore, are always connected with our religion. From this it follows that our clergy, and especially our bishops, form an essential part of that council, if I may use the expression, which has to decide what course of action we should follow in any matter affecting us as Catholics. When matters of doctrine are in question, the bishops and clergy are the sole judges, subject, of course, to the supreme authority of the Holy Father. The laity have no right to decide what we can take and what we can give, nor to make any compromise, nor to effect any arrangement with any party in the State, nor with Government in any matter in which doctrine is concerned. As all our Catholic affairs touch religion in some way, the bishops and clergy must have a voice not only in those matters in which they are supreme, but also in all subsidiary questions. There are, however, some matters which can most properly be left chiefly, if not entirely, to the laity. This arises from the fact that matters which we should call matters of religion, are treated by English statesmen as merely matters of politics. For example, we should say that it is a matter of religion that instruction in the Catechism should form an essential part of education. If we make a claim grounded on this principle, the Ministry upon whom we make the claim will look upon it as a question of politics, and consider whether it will be politic to grant what we ask. We have, therefore, in our relations with the Government, to manage matters of religion in the same way as we, in common with others, should manage any other question of politics. If, for instance, we wished to obtain a repeal of those clauses of the Emancipation Act which make it penal for men to take the vows of religion, we should have to take the same means, or some of them at least, as Englishmen would take to obtain a repeal of the corn laws. Bills, motions, and questions in Parliament, deputations to ministers, the organization of committees, the calling of public meetings, the preparation of petitions and declarations and addresses, and all the details of the ordinary working of what we call an *agitation*,—all these things are the proper work of the laity, subject of course to the approval, in those matters where it is necessary or advisable, of our bishops and clergy. It is the duty, in other words, of the Catholic laity, subject to that supervision which they understand so well, to take advantage of all the means which English liberty places at their disposal, to obtain our rights in those matters which concern our special interests. The Catholic laity should keep in mind two things: first, that they are the laity; secondly, that they are Englishmen. If they remember that they are laymen, they will not encroach on the dominion of the clergy, by deciding matters which only Churchmen should decide; and they will at the same time show by their activity that they understand their duties as laymen, and do not consider religion merely as a matter of interest to the clergy, but as the most precious gift they possess, to be kept and guarded as carefully as any of the liberties which they enjoy as Englishmen. And they must remember that they are Englishmen, in order that they may act as Englishmen; work as Englishmen are wont to

work when they have an object to obtain; and show that
energy and perseverance in prosecuting a cause, that open,
straightforward, bold course of action, that rejection of
unnecessary secrecy, and that love of wholesome publicity,
which are so characteristic of our race. An imaginary
instance will show what I mean.[1] Let us suppose that
any society or committee which might deal with Catholic
interests were to consider, after due deliberation, that the
time was come when we should try to erase from the
statute-book that foul blot which stains the great Emancipation Act—the clauses against Religious Orders. The
committee, we will suppose, comes to the decision that
the time has come. They send two or three of their
members to the Home Office or to the Premier, or perhaps
one member of the committee offers to go alone, to test
the feeling of the authorities. The deputation (I will
suppose that it consists of two or three persons) seeks and
obtains an interview with the minister, and opens the
matter to him. "Take care what you are about, gentlemen," he says; "take care what you are about. For
goodness sake don't moot that question. You'll have
Newdegate up, with a motion against the nunneries, or
asking for a royal commission to inquire as to the number
of Jesuits in England." The wily minister, who naturally
dislikes anything which will cause an outcry against what
he does, succeeds in dejecting the members of the deputation; and then, not to alienate them too much from his
party, he adds some words of comfort: "Wait a little,
gentlemen; wait a little. The time is not ripe yet for
meddling with the Emancipation Act: your best plan is
to be quiet and bide your time; we shall not be hard on

---

[1] A case which has not occurred, and which I am afraid is not likely to occur, is purposely taken, in order that it may not be supposed I am condemning a course which may have been taken in any particular matter.

your friends in the mean time." The deputation goes back to the committee, and the word henceforth is, "Hush, hush! we must not bring forward this question just yet." The minister may have said a very true thing when he said that the country was not prepared for the change proposed by the deputation. And no doubt, after five years from that time, he would say the same thing with equal truth, and again after another lustrum. But whose fault is it that the country is not prepared to purify the Emancipation Act, or to allow some other right to us which might be more easily obtained than a repeal of the penal laws against Religious Orders? It is our own fault, because we have not prepared the country by continually keeping up our protest and our claim, and letting every one know that we cannot submit to oppression, when by energy and perseverance we can get rid of the grievance. No doubt prudence will sometimes suggest secrecy; but secrecy in the prosecution of a claim which an Englishman demands as a right, must be the secrecy of prudence, and not that secrecy which is only meant to conceal action, for fear it should be criticized as not sufficiently energetic. It must be the secrecy of wisdom, and not the secrecy of pusillanimity. All that is done to obtain what we want should be done by a body of men, clergy and laity, well known to represent the Catholics of England. No one person, no two or three unauthorized and unknown persons, should undertake to settle a matter which can only be settled well when it is conducted as Englishmen are accustomed to conduct their affairs.

The committee which managed on the Catholic side the bill of 1778, acted in the most Catholic and the most English way. The bishops settled the religious part of the bill, and then left the laymen to do their work. It is not a little remarkable that the conduct of Mr. Sheldon in this affair earned for him the praise of both the two doughty antagonists, Dr. Milner and Mr. Charles Butler. And we must remember that at that time Catholics were obliged to act with the greatest caution. Even after the passing of the Act, it was not always and in every place safe to appear publicly either for religious or for civil purposes. At that time there was a dormant hatred of us in the country, which only two years afterwards broke out in the Gordon riots. If Catholics in those days could act in a religious, straightforward, and manly way, surely we can do so now. A certain amount of reserve and secrecy might have been naturally expected of those who could hardly be said to have emerged from their hiding-places. But now, after all the liberty we have obtained, we are expected to act as others act: nothing is looked for in our conduct which would be the sign of an oppressed people, or of people who have not a title to every right which others enjoy.

On the co-operation of clergy and laity depends in great measure the true spirit of the Church amongst the Catholics of England. If the laity were to act without the clergy, they might soon fall into heresy and schism. If the clergy were to act without the laity, they would be giving Catholic laymen no opportunity of learning how to use their liberties as Englishmen in defence of their religion as Catholics. If laymen were to be excluded from what we may call Catholic politics, or not allowed all proper freedom of action, they would cease to take an interest in Catholic questions, and would end in ceasing to take an interest in more vital matters connected with religion. For want of understanding their position as lay-Catholics in England, for want of knowledge, for want of practice, they would, some day, awake to a sense of their exclusion, mistake their real office in the Church, and, to the scandal of all, meddle with matters which they should leave alone. Whatever faults might now be found in the action of English Catholic laymen, of this I feel sure—that never were Catholic men less inclined to interfere with the rights of the clergy than the English Catholic laity of our day.

CHAPTER V.

THE IRISH RELIEF ACT AND THE GORDON RIOTS.

The Irish Act—The riots in Scotland—Scotch and English bigotry—Compensation to the Scotch Catholics—Petition for compensation—Debate on the petition—Lord George Gordon—The Gordon riots—Services of Catholic priests not appreciated—Human respect and bad manners—Inconsistency of statesmen—Conduct of Dissenters—The Wesleyan Methodists.

AT the same time that the Act for the Relief of English Catholics was passed in 1778, another Act was passed for the benefit of the Catholics in Ireland. The nature of the relief given by this latter Act may be stated in the words of Mr. Butler. It "enabled Roman Catholics who should take the oath of allegiance prescribed by the former Act, to hold leases for nine hundred and ninety-nine years, or determinable upon any lives, not exceeding five. The lands of Catholics were made devisable and transferable, and Catholics were rendered capable of holding and enjoying those which might descend or be devised or transferred to them."[1]

It will be observed that this Act did not extend to Irish Catholics the same relief which was given to the clergy under the English Act. But this relief, and more than this, was given to the Irish by an Act passed in 1782, in which were contained provisions which discharged from

[1] "Historical Memoirs," vol. iii. p. 487.

all penalties such Ecclesiastics as should register their names and abodes in the manner it prescribed. Another Act of the same year allowed Catholics to teach schools.[1] English Catholic priests and schoolmasters were not relieved from all penalties until the year 1791.

The Act of 1778 did not extend to Scotland; "and thereby hangs a tale." It was proposed, as we have seen, to extend the bill to Scotland; but the Presbyterians rose up against the very notion of relief to Papists; the press and the pulpit stormed against concession; the great majority of the synods passed strong resolutions against the proposed measure; a solemn fast was proclaimed in Glasgow, and on the 18th of October, 1778, the Sunday following the fast, a mob attacked a small house where a few Catholics were assembled, and dispersed the worshippers by pelting them with mud and stones. The spirit of John Knox, evoked by the modern Pharisees, stalked the land. The fierce spirit of bigotry gained strength after the cowardly act of the 18th of October, and on the 9th of February, 1779, the fanatics plundered and burnt to the ground the house of a Mr. Bagnal, in which the Catholics had met occasionally for Mass, after their old place of refuge had been destroyed. At this point the magistrates interfered, and order was restored. The Annual Register for the year 1779 tells us that "the magistrates and principal inhabitants of Glasgow, being equally ashamed and concerned that the character and government of so extensively commercial a city should suffer under the imputation and disgrace of such an act of outrage and persecution, seemed willing, so far as it could be done, to obliterate every trace of it from the memory. Bagnal was accordingly speedily acquainted that he should be reimbursed for every part of his losses to the uttermost

[1] Butler, ibid.

farthing; and several of the principal inhabitants, including respectable names among the Protestant clergy, acquired no small honour by the attention and kindness which the wife and family of the sufferer experienced from them, during the immediate pressure of their terror and distress."[1]

But it was not in Glasgow alone that the fanatics vented their rage against us on account of the proposed Relief Act. Edinburgh was also the scene of the most disgraceful proceedings. Bishop Hay had opened a chapel, which was merely a room in a house in Leith Wynd. The following circular was scattered about the city:—

"MEN AND BRETHREN,—Whoever shall find this letter, will take it as a warning to meet at Leith Wynd, on Wednesday next, in the evening, to pull down that pillar of Popery lately erected there. A PROTESTANT.

"Edinburgh, *January* 29, 1779.

"P.S.—Please to read this carefully, keep it clean, and drop it somewhere else."[2]

The Protestants obeyed the summons, and, in their eagerness for persecution, anticipated the day and met on Tuesday evening. They attacked, plundered, and burnt down the house. On the following day the mob broke into and plundered another house in Blackfriars' Wynd, where a priest rented and used a small room as a chapel. On the evening of the same day they were proceeding to execute their vengeance upon Dr. Robertson, the famous historian, who had supported the cause of the Catholics. But at this time the Duke of Buccleuch arrived at the head of the fencibles, who, with the aid of some dragoons,

---

[1] Mr. Bagnal had introduced from Staffordshire into Glasgow the manufacture of stoneware.

[2] Walsh's "History of the Catholic Church in Scotland," p. 522.

prevented any further pillage and restored order in the city.

Although the Gordon riots, as the reader will soon see, were much more serious than the riots in Scotland, yet the animosity of the Scotch against the Church was, and still is, much stronger and deeper than that of the English. By many English Protestants the Church is hated more on political than on religious grounds, though in the minds of the majority there is no doubt a great revulsion from the Church's teaching. But in Scotland the predominating sentiment is undoubtedly a fierce and, if I may be allowed the expression, a fiendish hatred of the dogmas of the Christian Church. Hence the riots in Glasgow and Edinburgh were purely directed against the Catholics; it was the property of Catholics only which was destroyed: whereas in London the destruction of Catholic property immediately developed into general licence. Mr. Wilkes, speaking in the House of Commons in the year 1779, on the bill for the relief of Protestant Dissenters, said that "the progress of knowledge in almost every nation had softened the rigour of their laws respecting religious worship, or at least had, in a degree, suspended their execution, Scotland alone excepted."[1]

It has been noticed that the magistrates and principal inhabitants of Glasgow assured Mr. Bagnal that he should be reimbursed for the losses he had sustained. It would appear, however, that there was some difficulty in obtaining compensation, for on the 18th of March Edmund Burke said in the House, that he had a petition to present "from several of His Majesty's Roman Catholic subjects of North Britain." Before the petition was brought up, "Lord North, by his Majesty's command, acquainted the House that his Majesty, having been informed of the

[1] "Parliamentary History," vol. 20, p. 320.

contents of the said petition, recommends it to the consideration of the House."[1] Then the Petition was brought up and read: it was a very long one. It is given at full length in Hansard, and it bears marks which seem to me to show that Burke himself had a good deal to do with its composition. The substance of the petition was a request for compensation, and future protection. The petitioners approach the House with "the most profound respect and deference," and they ask for reimbursement "most humbly, and with the most profound submission." It gives a graphic account of the way in which the Scotch people were excited to commit the outrages. It is extremely humble and forgiving: "We are far, very far," they say, "from entertaining a resentment against any one whatsoever, or from desiring that any person should be called to account, much less should be punished, for the injury done to us; we forgive from the bottom of our hearts; and should any person be taken into custody, or prosecuted on our account, if we were worthy to be heard, we should presume to petition in the most earnest manner for his pardon." The petitioners also say that, "considering the present flame which is raised against" them, they "cheerfully lay aside all thoughts of asking any relaxation of the severe laws" against them at that time. The portion of the petition in which they ask for protection is worth recording, as showing the condition in which we Catholics of Great Britain, at least in Scotland, were a hundred years ago. The words of the petition are as follows:—

"We most humbly beg leave to assure this honourable House that this our earnest request for protection is not made without the strongest reason, for the same unprovoked enemies who have hitherto persecuted us in so cruel a manner, far from being

[1] "Parl. Hist.," vol. 20, p. 322.

satisfied with their late success, have made it a ground for further violence. Those who never threatened us without executing their menaces, have published and dispersed a sort of manifesto, calling upon all orders of people strictly to enforce the execution of the most sanguinary laws upon us, denying the authority of Parliament to repeal those laws, or any other laws made before the Union, threatening the magistrates with the same violence which they have employed against your petitioners, if they do not cause them to be executed; representing those means of banishing and putting to death your petitioners as their rights and privileges, and proposing associations against buying or selling, borrowing or lending, or having any of the ordinary intercourse of society with those of our religion, and threatening to proceed against all who shall refuse to join them in those measures, as if they were Papists; and they have, in their late violent attempts against some of the most respectable characters in the established Church of Scotland, shown how far they are capable of acting against such as discover any degree of moderation in their sentiments: in a word, nothing can be more deplorable and (without the effectual aid of the Legislature) more hopeless than our condition."

Such were the terms in which loyal British subjects had to address their own House of Representatives. Perhaps no portion of the petition shows more completely the abject condition of the Scotch Catholics than those words in which they say, "if we were worthy to be heard." This needs no comment. The reader should notice the recommendation to the House from the King to consider the petition. With only superficial knowledge, a Catholic might be inclined to look unfavourably upon George III., merely because he opposed the final Emancipation Bill; but, as a matter of fact, he was the first to begin and to develop our emancipation, and, up to the point of admitting Catholics into Parliament, he was to us by far the most liberal sovereign, indeed, the only liberal sovereign, who had governed England up to that time.

The petition having been read, Burke proposed that it

should be referred to a committee. He probably made a long speech; but as the report of it in Hansard is very short and contains an amusing incident, I will give it in full.

"He showed the absurdity of the arguments used by the Scotch in justifying their violent conduct, and exposed the supineness of Government upon the attacks of the Scotch rioters on the peace and property of his Majesty's subjects in that part of the empire. He hoped that Government was not dead, but only asleep. At this moment he looked directly at Lord North, who was asleep, and said, in the Scripture phrase, "Brother Lazarus is not dead, but sleepeth." The laugh upon this occasion was not more loud on one side of the House than on the other. Even the noble lord alluded to seemed to enjoy the allusion as heartily as the rest of the House, as soon as he was sufficiently awake to understand the cause of the joke." [1]

As the remainder of the debate as reported is not long, and as it possesses some interest, the reader will probably like to see it.

"Lord Beauchamp was for granting the request of the petitioners.

"Lord George Gordon spoke against the expediency of giving toleration to the Roman Catholics of Scotland, equal to that allowed to the same sect in England and Ireland.

"Mr. Fox said the Roman Catholics of Scotland were not only entitled to compensation for their losses, but that it became the honour and humanity, as well as the dignity, of Parliament to repeal the penal laws against them, and not be deterred by little insurrections in a small corner of their empire from doing an act of common justice.

"Lord North declared that he thought compensation should be made, and would be most ready at any time to give his support to such a measure, if he were not decidedly of opinion that voluntary compensation was infinitely more eligible than that which was compulsory. He had been well informed that due

[1] "Parl. Hist.," vol. 20, pp. 226, 227.

recompense was intended to be made by the magistrates of the district in which the mischiefs were committed; he thought it prudent to defer any further proceeding in the business till the result of their measures should be known; he therefore thought it best to move the previous question."

"The previous question was then put, and carried without a division; after which the petition was ordered to lie upon the table."[1] The speech of Lord George Gordon on this occasion was, as far as appears from Hansard, the first which he made in the House of Commons against concessions to Catholics. He made his second speech on the same subject on the 5th of May. The sentiments and expressions which he uttered on this occasion ought to have warned the House that he was a dangerous fanatic. Some of his phrases were certainly treasonable. He concluded his speech with two motions: one, that the petition presented by Burke on the 18th of March should be "thrown over the table;" the other, "that all further proceedings on the said petition be postponed to this day three months."[2] No member could be found to second the motions, and consequently the Speaker refused to put the questions.

From a passage in Lord George Gordon's speech, it would appear that previous to the presentation of the petition by Burke, the celebrated Dr. George Hay, V.A., of the Lowland District of Scotland, and to whom Lord George gives his proper title of "Lord Bishop of Daulis," had circulated two editions of a memorial amongst the members of the House of Commons.

But the comparatively liberal feelings expressed by many of the members of Parliament was no index of the sentiments of the English people. For the flame which had been kindled in Scotland spread to England. "Then

[1] "Parl. Hist.," vol. 20, p. 327.   [2] Ibid., p. 623.

VOL. I.   K

of a sudden," to use the words of Lord Stanhope, "like a meteor rising from the foulest marshes, appeared those fearful riots, to which the most rank intolerance gave origin, and Lord George Gordon a name. Then the midnight sky of London was reddened with incendiary fires, and her streets resounded to the cry of an infuriated mob; then our best and wisest statesmen had to tremble, not only for their lives, but for their hearths and homes; then for once in our annals the powers of government and order seemed to quail and succumb before the populace of the capital in arms."[1]

Lord George Gordon gave notice at a public meeting that on Friday, the 2nd of June, he would present a petition to the House of Commons against concession, and for a repeal of the Act of 1778. He invited the petitioners to meet him on that day in S. George's Fields, which they accordingly did to the number of over sixty thousand. They marched to Westminster, and maltreated on their way to the Houses every member who was not known to be opposed to the Catholics; and to such an extent did they carry their brutal conduct, that many of the peers appeared in the House of Lords with their clothes torn and covered with mud and filth. The authorities did not interfere. A certain madness seems to have seized upon the mob at the very commencement of the riots, giving to their conduct the appearance of diabolical possession; for they accused of being Catholics several members of Parliament who were well known to be staunch Protestants. About nine o'clock in the evening the Foot Guards appeared upon the scene; but it was only to enable the House of Commons to divide. The House adjourned. The rioters rushed off to the two chapels of Warwick Street and Lincoln's-Inn-Fields, both of which they burned

[1] "History of England," A.D. 1780.

to the ground, some soldiers coming up too late to prevent the mischief. On Saturday evening there was a renewal of the rioting, but it did not lead to anything serious. But on Sunday evening, owing to the weak conduct of Kennet, the lord mayor, the fanatics again assembled and pillaged Moorfields Chapel and the dwelling-houses of several Catholics in the neighbourhood, making a bonfire in the street of all the church and domestic furniture they could lay their hands on. On Monday afternoon a Privy Council was held, but nothing further was done to stop the rioting than to offer a reward of £500 for information as to the men who had fired the chapels of the ambassadors. In consequence of the little notice taken of the disturbances by the authorities, the mob determined to continue them. On Monday evening they destroyed the chapels in Wapping and East Smithfield, and pillaged the house of Sir George Savile, who had, as we have seen, introduced and carried through the bill which resulted in the first Relief Act of 1778. At this period of the riots the life of Burke was threatened, and this great philosopher and orator, than whom, Mr. Butler says, the Catholics never had a more able or more sincere advocate, was obliged with his family to take refuge with his military friend, General Burgoyne.

On Tuesday the two Houses met under the protection of the Guards; but the riots were continued in various parts of the town. Lord North's house was attacked, and saved by a party of soldiers. Newgate prison was attacked, taken, and burned to the ground, all the prisoners gaining their liberty.[1] Clerkenwell gaol was also attacked, broken into, and all its inmates released. The houses of three magistrates were attacked and gutted. At midnight a fierce gang broke into the house of Lord Mansfield, in

[1] Some of the rioters of Friday evening had been committed to Newgate, hence the fury of the mob against the prison.

Bloomsbury Square. The lord chief justice was particularly obnoxious to the rioters, on account of his charge to the jury at the trial of Mr. Webb. The family had barely time to escape: pictures, furniture, the books of a valuable library, manuscripts, and everything else the house contained, were thrown out of the windows, piled up in the square, and burned. Several other prisons were attacked and the prisoners released. The mob had found wine in Lord Mansfield's house; and they proceeded to attack a distillery belonging to Mr. Langdale, who was a Catholic. The horrors of drunkenness and its effects were now added to the fury of fanaticism. "It might be said," observes Lord Stanhope, "with but slight exaggeration, that for two days the rabble held dominion in the town. It might be said, in the eloquent words of Gibbon, an eye-witness to these proceedings, that 'forty thousand Puritans, such as they might be in the time of Cromwell, have started out of their graves.'" Thus things went on until Wednesday evening.

One remarkable circumstance of these riots was the absence of all effectual means to suppress them. The means, indeed, were present, but they were not used. At the pillage of Moorfields Chapel, the lord mayor and the military stood looking on; the latter, indeed, with loaded muskets, but joining in the cheers and huzzas of the mob.[1] In the same way, at the pillage of Lord Mansfield's house, Lord Stanhope says, "Strange as it may appear, all these outrages were committed in the hearing, and almost in the sight, of a detachment of Foot Guards, which had arrived at nearly the commencement of the fray. But they had been restrained by the doubts which then prevailed, whether the troops had any legal right to fire upon the

[1] "A Dispassionate Inquiry into the Cause of the Late Riots in London," pp. 14, 15.

mob, unless a magistrate were present first, to read forth at full length all the provisions of the Riot Act. When a gentleman, a friend of Lord Mansfield, went to the officer in command, requiring him to enter the house and defend it, the officer replied that the justices of the peace had all run away, and that consequently he could or would do nothing. When at length a magistrate was caught and made to mumble through the clauses, the soldiers did advance and fire two volleys. It was then too late." In fact, the King, the chief magistrate, was deserted by his subordinates; his servants, both civil and military, refused to act. The members of the House of Brunswick are remarkable for their personal courage. George III. was no exception in this respect, and he showed himself equal to the crisis. Rising from a council, at which Wedderburn alone supported him, the King exclaimed, " There shall be, at all events, one magistrate in the kingdom who will do his duty." His Majesty issued a proclamation, warning all peaceably disposed persons to keep within doors, and ordering the military to act without waiting for directions from the civil magistrates. The rioting was going on; but on that Wednesday night "two hundred persons were shot dead in the streets, and two hundred and fifty were lying wounded in the hospitals, of whom seventy or eighty within a short time expired."[1] The next morning, Thursday, the 8th of June, the Gordon riots were at an end.

Another circumstance well worthy of the remembrance of all, and especially interesting to Catholics, was the conduct of our clergy and laity during those six fearful days. This matter is so well and chivalrously expressed by Mr. Burke in the speech to the electors of Bristol, from which I have in the course of this history so often quoted, that

[1] Lord Stanhope's " History of England."

the reader will willingly pardon a somewhat long extract. Speaking of the riots, the orator said, "There was one circumstance (justice will not suffer me to pass it over) which, if anything could enforce the reasons I have given, would fully justify the Act of Relief, and render a repeal, or anything like a repeal, unnatural, impossible. It was the behaviour of the persecuted Roman Catholics under the acts of violence and brutal insolence which they suffered. I suppose there are not in London less than four or five thousand of that persuasion from my country, who do a great deal of the most laborious work in the metropolis, and they chiefly inhabit those quarters which were the principal theatre of the fury of the bigoted multitude. They are known to be men of strong arms and quick feelings, and more remarkable for a determined resolution than clear ideas or much foresight. But though provoked by everything that can stir the blood of men, their houses and chapels in flames, and with the most atrocious profanations of everything they hold sacred before their eyes, not a hand was moved to retaliate, or even to defend. Had such a conflict once begun, the rage of their persecutors would have redoubled. Thus, fury increasing by the reverberation of outrages, house being fired for house, and church for chapel, I am convinced that no power under heaven could have prevented a general conflagration; and at this day London would have been a tale. But I am well informed, and the thing speaks it, that their clergy exerted their whole influence to keep their people in such a state of forbearance and quiet as, when I look back, fills me with astonishment; but not with astonishment only. Their merits on that occasion ought not to be forgotten; nor will they, when Englishmen come to recollect themselves. I am sure it were far more proper to have called them forth and given them the thanks of both Houses of Parliament, than to have suffered those worthy clergymen and excellent citizens to be hunted into holes and corners, whilst we are making low-minded inquisitions into the number of their people ; as if a tolerating principle was never to prevail, unless we were very sure that only a few could possibly take advantage of it. But, indeed, we are not yet well recovered of our fright. Our reason, I trust, will return with our security ; and this unfortunate temper will pass over like a cloud."

But the cloud did not completely pass by. It became less black and dense, and the lightnings which it discharged were not so destructive. Even to this day the atmosphere over our heads is not clear. The tolerating principle does not wholly prevail ; our Protestant fellow-countrymen have not completely recovered from their fright. Our priests have never been called up to receive the thanks of both Houses of Parliament ; but they have been frequently called up to hear the false witness which is still from time to time borne against them, that they are not loyal· During the last hundred years, Catholic priests have preached nothing but loyalty, when instructing their flocks in their duty to the State. In the year 1848, the preaching of the Catholic priests was to some practical purpose, when it prevented a rebellion in Ireland which might have taken the whole power of England to quell. Is the teaching of the Catholic priests in the matter of loyalty of no use even at the present day? Would any minister of state be answerable for peace in the British Isles, if he did not feel assured that Catholic priests are the trustiest guardians of the loyalty of the people and the truest supporters of the throne? And yet we have still to hear from those very ministers themselves, charges which show that the merits of our clergy are forgotten as soon as earned. It is only a few years since a foremost statesman in England wrote a series of pamphlets for the express purpose of raising a cry over the whole country, that priests and their flocks were not loyal. There never was amongst any people a greater delusion, there never was a greater falsehood uttered, than that the Catholic clergy and laity of England are not loyal. If any occasion were to arise on which the loyalty of the English people would be tested, her Majesty would find that "popish bishops, priests, and Jesuits" would be the staunchest supporters of her throne. They have always been so, and they will always be so. This we always proclaim. Our voices may be drowned in the din of those who hate our faith, but we shall persevere in the cry; and history will be our witness to the truth.

The Gordon riots were the most violent and destructive eruption of a volcano which is not yet extinct. It broke out with violence in 1807; with diminished violence in 1829; also when, in 1846, Sir Robert Peel made permanent the grant to Maynooth; and again, with somewhat fiercer energy, when his Holiness Pope Pius IX. replaced us in the hierarchies of the Church. It may burst forth again. We can never be secure, so long as the great mass of the English people entertain the same idea of the Church, and the same hatred of her doctrines, as they do at present. The ignorance of the British people of everything belonging to the Catholic religion, their mischievous delusions regarding it, and their intense bigotry against it, are far too valuable instruments in the power of the enemy of mankind, not to be made use of when God shall permit him to do so. What greater enemies can the Church have than ignorance, delusion, and bigotry? And are the enemies of the Church accustomed to let her rest in peace? Amongst the few there is more accurate knowledge, juster views, and less bigotry; but in the mass, covered over with a thin layer of toleration, the old fire exists. Can we, then, afford to slumber as if there were no danger? Can we exult as if the fire were at last burned out? We must thank God for the security we enjoy; but we must at the same time resign ourselves to the thought that, while the disposition of the people remains as it is, what has happened before may happen again. The number of Catholics may increase, but opposition will increase in proportion. England may, in God's good providence, be again a Catholic country; but it will be through many, many tribulations. In the mean time, we are British subjects, entitled to all the liberties and rights of Britons. These liberties and rights must subserve the greatest of causes: they cannot do this unless we allow ourselves to be the instruments in the hands of God. We cannot co-operate with Him in the manner we may and ought, unless we co-operate amongst ourselves. Union, co-operation, and organization—these are the means which we must oppose to the union, co-operation, and organization of our enemies. Religion is a cause common to English, Irish, and Scotch Catholics. Any one who should contribute, even in a small degree, to promote union amongst us, would be a benefactor to the best of causes, and deserve the thanks of all.[1]

Mr. Burke's praise of the conduct of the Catholic clergy during the Gordon riots has given occasion to speak of their loyalty, and the little credit they got for it. It cannot be doubted that the firm adherence of our

[1] I am conscious of having given a very meagre account of the Gordon Riots. The best historical account is, perhaps, that of Lord Stanhope: it is certainly better than that in the Annual Register. The best impression of the horrors of the time will be made by the perusal of "Barnaby Rudge." By reading also Lord Stanhope's history, the reader will be able to separate the true facts from romance in Mr. Dickens's novel. Since the above was written, the Rev. A. Mills's very interesting "History of the Riots in London in the year 1780" has appeared, and to which the reader is referred.

clergy to the cause of law and order is a mainstay of peace, and of the present order of things in the British Isles. We need not speculate as to what would happen if the clergy, especially in Ireland, were as disloyal as they are often said to be. The certain result is so well known, that the conviction that the result will not happen because the cause does not exist, must form one of the greatest consolations of a British minister. Anything which disturbs the even course of political life: a display threatening physical force; a serious riot, especially if it be occasioned by some question of general interest; still more, anything looking like a tendency to rebellion —any one of these things is what a minister most cordially dislikes. What he is most inclined to favour is that which favours law and order, and tends to keep people quiet. Why, then, are Catholic priests constantly held up to the public, and spoken of as not being loyal, and as teaching disloyalty to their people? Why are they not acknowledged and treated as promoters of law and order? Why are they not praised and favoured as the great supporters of the public peace? Some years ago a well-known member of the House of Commons, of great influence with his party, and who is still alive and in Parliament, though a very old man, said in private conversation, that no good would ever be done in Ireland until the influence of the priests should have been destroyed; the fact being, that the destruction of the influence of the priests in Ireland would probably lead to the greatest of England's troubles during the present century. Why should he have said what he did? When a man is inclined to do good, he should be allowed freedom to speak and act. The preaching and teaching of a Catholic priest is calculated to promote the very state of things which a minister likes best. Why, then, should the late

Lord Derby, the leader of the Conservatives, have said in the House of Lords that he was for "keeping the dog muzzled"? Why, we may again ask, should Lord John Russell, in 1850, have spoken and written of the establishment of the hierarchy in terms so unnecessarily offensive as to evoke the warning voice of Dr. Murray, the very man whom the minister trusted as the great promoter of peace in Ireland? Many other instances might without much trouble be collected, to show how the language of needless insult is used against the Catholic clergy, by those who in their hearts know that they are the great supporters of peace and order. How are we to account for this? A motive with some is that intense hatred of the Church which can only be accounted for when we attribute it to the same source as that which is constantly tempting men to heresy and schism. Hatred affects the intelligence, and destroys the action of sound common sense. Fanaticism in a man who is half mad produces a Lord George Gordon; fanaticism in a sane man impels him to act against his better judgment, though he may stop short of burning down Moorfields Chapel, opening the doors of Newgate, and attacking the Bank of England. We have no sufficient reason, however, for attributing this diabolical hatred of the Church to the majority of those ministers who of late years have had charge of public affairs. There is another motive, and one more generally diffused, always in active operation, and as strong, if not so violent in its action, as the one to which I have alluded. This motive is human respect; the fear of acting against public opinion. Men who would admit the principle that a country can be best governed by doing justice to all, are afraid to do justice to Catholics, for fear of what the public will say of their acts. Where they would do nothing opposed to their principles as Protestant ministers by granting relief to Catholics, men will refuse that relief, lest it should be said they are, to use the cant phrase, "favouring the growth of Popery." This human respect is a motive of action amongst Protestants in every class and station. If a member of the House of Commons, whether a minister or a private member, has to speak in favour of some demand for equal government on behalf of Catholics, he generally thinks it necessary to use some hard and offensive words against the Church. A Duke of Argyll, for instance, cannot protest in the House of Lords that he is in favour of an equal administration of the poor law without telling their lordships that he hates the Catholic system. A duke may hate the Catholic Church without publicly announcing it; and, judging from his words and actions, no one would suppose the present Duke of Argyll to be favourably inclined to the Church, though he should not use the word "hate" when speaking of our religion. But those who know how to measure their words by the standard of good manners still find it necessary to guard against all suspicion of a leaning to the Church, by protesting against any inference of the kind from the fact that they advocate our claims. An English Protestant cannot speak well of Catholics without its being supposed that he is going to become one. It is the knowledge that this conclusion will be drawn which shuts the mouth of many a man who would utter words of peace, and not of affliction. To such an absurd length is this disposition to judge rashly in this matter carried by the English people, that a writer cannot treat an historical subject with truthfulness, if it relates to Catholics, without laying himself open to grave suspicion, if not to censure. Many of us can remember, and all may know by reading Foster's "Life of Dickens," that after the publication of "Barnaby Rudge," it was at once said that the popular novelist was going to become a Catholic, and this merely because he had founded an interesting story on the Gordon riots. It has been already noticed how a member of Parliament or a tradesman would lose his seat or his business by becoming a Catholic; and so, a man in either of those classes would considerably endanger his future prospects, only by being a prominent advocate of our claims. We have not alone to complain that public opinion is against us, but also of that human respect, which causes public opinion to produce such an effect on those who have to make and administer the laws. Against this we ought loudly and perseveringly to express our sense of the wrong which it causes us to suffer. In God's good time, some minister will perhaps arise who will defy public opinion in this matter, who will not look unfavourably on a man because he is a Catholic, nor on a question because it is a Catholic question; and who will not allow the frown or the clamour of the public to bully him into partiality and injustice. When such a man of moral courage and influence shall arise amongst us, we shall see that the tyranny of the multitude has as much cowardice in it as the tyranny of a single individual; the advance of bigotry will recede before bold action; and even the generation in which he shall live will applaud the conduct of the man who will have united the people of the British Isles more firmly than they have ever been, during the last three hundred years. It is sad to look back upon the last fifty years, and see the effects of human respect in the conduct of those who have ruled England as ministers of the Sovereign. Great good has been prevented, and great wrong has been done in England itself. But when we look to Ireland, it is lamentable to see the effects of that policy which yields to public opinion against the better judgment of legislators, and which has not only been unjust, but foolish and impolitic in the extreme. We often hear it said that Ireland is a chief difficulty of an English minister. But why is Ireland a chief difficulty? It is because the Irish are not content under the government of their rulers. And why are they not content? Because, being Irish and Catholic, they are governed by a public opinion which is English and Protestant. No statesman has yet had sufficient impartiality or sufficient moral courage to govern Ireland as a Catholic nation. Hatred of the Church in some, human respect in others, has well-nigh spoilt all they have done. Of what avail is it to be the advocate of equality; of what use is it to make, for instance, an "appropriation clause" a party question, and then write a letter denouncing "the mummeries of superstition?"[1] Such a man could never give peace and content to Catholic Ireland. To have disestablished the Irish Protestant Church is a great boon to Ireland, no doubt; but if that boon is followed by a series of pamphlets, to prove that Catholics cannot be loyal to the Queen because they believe the Holy Father to be infallible in spiritual matters—the man who can do both these things in succession will never content a Catholic country. No man, and no set of men, will ever succeed in governing well the Catholics of the Queen's dominions, of whom it may be said, "In quorum manibus iniquitates sunt: dextera eorum repleta est muneribus."[2]

If from the year 1829, the year of the Emancipation Act, our public men had not been under the influence of English public opinion, if they had governed Ireland as a Catholic country according to Irish and Catholic opinion, instead of English and Protestant opinion, the

---

[1] Lord John Russell's Durham Letter.
[2] "In whose hands are iniquities: their right hand is full of gifts" (Psalm xxv.).

Irish would have been well contented to be ruled by an Imperial Parliament, and would never have asked for a separate Government for themselves; the words, "tithe massacre," "wholesale evictions," "agrarian outrages," would never have soiled the pages of England's history; the repeal agitation of 1843, the abortive rising in 1848, the Fenian insurrection of 1868, the Home Rule movement, and the non-payment of rent scheme, would never have been heard of. Why should a London rabble be able to compel a chancellor of the exchequer to withdraw a threatened tax, while the call of a whole nation cannot obtain its rights in the great question of education? The reason is the same in both cases. English public opinion decides, and has its own way. What would the English think if they were governed by men wholly under the influence of what Irish Catholics would say to their measures? Would they be content? Then, how can we expect the Irish to be content? Let a bold English minister, in his government of Ireland, brave English public opinion consistently and perseveringly, and the result would be the defeat of an unholy and cowardly tyranny on this side, and peace and content on the other side, of St. George's Channel.

Nor can we English Catholics acquit ourselves of all blame in this matter: we must to a certain extent share reproach. The English public opinion which rules the destinies of Ireland is not, if I may use the expression, a simple substance. It is a compound of two ingredients. It is made up of what is English and what is Protestant. It is a combination of national prejudice and religious hate. Of prejudice against Ireland because it is Catholic, of course we English Catholics have none, and therefore we are perfectly free from that element of prejudice which is the most noxious and the most deadly. But are we so free from the other portion of the compound? Is there no unreasonable national prejudice in our minds? Is there not rather a sufficient quantity of it to prevent us from steadily opposing as we ought, however small our numbers may be, the more oppressive influence which religious combined with national prejudice exercises in the affairs of Ireland? It ought to be our boast not only that we never join in any cry against Ireland, but that we continually protest against the Sister Isle being governed by English opinion. Our voice, though weak in comparison with that of the majority of the English people, has still some strength in it; it is quite strong enough to be heard; it is loud enough to prevent complete unison in the chorus; it is sufficient to attract attention; and will be accepted as a protest, if overpowered as a vote. It has been noticed in a former chapter that it is our duty to value the power and influence of Ireland, for they are the power and influence of the Church in the United Kingdom. If we do not sufficiently value our strength in Ireland, let us consider whether our indifference to so great a power is not the effect of national prejudice with which we, as well as our fellow-countrymen, are affected.

Another reflection suggested by the Gordon riots is upon the conduct of the Presbyterians and the Dissenters. Dr. Aikin writes that "the liberal spirit displayed in the relief granted in the last session" (the session of 1778) "to the Roman Catholics, encouraged the Dissenters to apply for a further exemption to their ministers and schoolmasters, from the penalties to which they still by law remained liable. A bill for the purpose was moved in the House of Commons by Sir Henry Hoghton, and seconded by Mr. Frederic Montague; and the opposition to it was so inconsiderable, that a motion by the representative of the University of Oxford, for putting it off for four months, was supported by only sixteen votes against seventy-seven. It passed without difficulty through the Lords, and received the royal assent in the course of the session."[1] And Lord Stanhope, in his account of the Gordon riots, alluding to this relief granted to the Dissenters, says, "It had been hoped, in the course of last year" (1779), "that some indulgence to the Protestant Dissenters might be the best means to lessen or divert their rancour against the Roman Catholics, and to convince them that no exclusive favour was intended to these last. With such views, nearly the same measure of relief from subscription which the Lords had rejected by a large majority in 1772, and again in 1773, passed their House in 1779, when transmitted from the Commons, and, it is said, without debate. The indulgence was accepted, but the rancour was not removed. This plainly appeared from the great popular support with which even the wildest projects of Lord George Gordon were received."[2]

The rancour which, according to Lord Stanhope, the British Parliament was anxious to allay, had shown itself in the riots in Edinburgh and Glasgow; it had also assumed a threatening form in the formation of the "Protestant Association," which had been got up for the express purpose of opposing any further relief to Catholics, and of obtaining, if possible, the repeal of the Act of 1778. For the origin of the Protestant Association, I will quote Dr. Milner, who was in his twenty-seventh year at the time it was formed, who received threatening letters in 1780, and was, as he tells us, indebted for protection to a strong military guard. Speaking of the Act of 1778, he says, "Which, however small in itself, was as great

---

[1] "Annals of George III.," vol. i. p. 234.
[2] "History of England," A.D. 1780.

as the temper of the times would bear. For now the *green-eyed monster* of religious jealousy, who had so long slept over his unresisting prey, at the first appearance of its escape from his cruel fangs, began to rouse himself to all his native fury. The pulpits of the lower sort, particularly those of John Wesley and his associates, resounded, and the presses of the metropolis groaned, with hypocritical lamentations on the pretended increase of Popery, and the fatal consequences to be apprehended from the late indulgence granted to its professors; a religion which, it was asserted, had slain its thousands by its cruelty, and its tens of thousands by its ignorance. By these and other inflammatory harangues, a society was collected together at the beginning of the ensuing year, 1779, under the title of *The Protestant Association*, professedly instituted on the plan of similar associations in the last century, and particularly on that of the 'Solemn League and Covenant,' which produced the murder of the King, and the subversion of the Constitution. The pretext which was held out to the public . . . was the preservation of the civil constitution and the Protestant religion, by petitioning Parliament for a repeal of the late Act. . . . In the course of the same year, *an appeal from the Protestant Association to the people of England* was published and dispersed all over the kingdom, inviting the people to form similar associations in the different counties. . . . At a general meeting towards the close of that year," 1779, "it was unanimously resolved, that, 'on account of the noble zeal for the Protestant interest, which had distinguished the parliamentary conduct of Lord George Gordon, he should be requested to become the President of the Association.' The 2nd of June, in the year 1780, will be ever memorable in the history of this country, for the presentation of the grand petition of the London

Associators to the House of Commons by Lord George Gordon."[1]

In the early part of the year 1780, John Wesley wrote a "Defence of the Protestant Association," an inflammatory production, in which, amongst other things, he said that "an open toleration of the popish religion is inconsistent with the safety of a free people, and a Protestant Government; *and that every convert to Popery was by principle an enemy to the Constitution of this country.*"[2] Wesley, about the same time, also wrote a letter to one of the newspapers to prove by a series of ridiculous syllogisms, that "no Government, not Roman Catholic, ought to tolerate men of the Roman Catholic persuasion." To prove that the Act of 1778 meant the toleration of Catholics, he says that Catholics understood it as such, and that this was shown by their preaching openly, building chapels at Bath and elsewhere, raising seminaries, and making converts. This letter and the defence of the Protestant Association were so incentive to violence, that Milner calls Wesley "the chief author of the riots in 1780."[3]

We need not wonder, then, that the Wesleyan Methodists have always been amon·st the most bitter enemies of the Church. Their founder was not only an enthusiast, but a firebrand. One of his first principles was, No toleration to Catholics; he inculcated it in his followers, and he urged it by actual persecution. Hatred of the Church

---

[1] "Letters to a Prebendary," end of letter vii.
[2] The words I have put in italics will remind the reader of Mr. Gladstone's words in 1874: "No one can become a convert without renouncing his moral and mental freedom, and placing his civil loyalty and duty at the mercy of another." So much progress has Protestant intelligence made in a hundred years!
[3] "Inquiry into certain vulgar opinions about Ireland," note at the end of letter iii. Wesley was ably answered by the witty and eloquent O'Leary; but his defence of the Church was no protection against the excited passions of the multitude.

may be said to be almost as much of the essence of Methodism, as hatred of Christianity is of the essence of Mohammedism. Hence there are very few converts amongst the Methodists. The anti-Catholic riots of 1779 and 1780 were, as we have seen, the work almost entirely of Presbyterians and Dissenters; and Presbyterians and Dissenters are to this day the most obstinate maintainers of heresy, and the most determined haters of God's Church. This is shown in England by an extreme unwillingness on the part of Dissenters, especially of the Methodists, to listen to the voice of truth; and it is shown in Scotland, amongst the Presbyterians, by the instinctive horror which they seem to have of everything Catholic, I might almost say of everything Christian, and the rudeness with which they show it by word, look, and gesture. In the Church of England, as a Church, it is impossible, indeed, for a Catholic to see anything respectable; but amongst the members of the Church of England there are many who not only lead blameless lives, but are gradually preparing themselves to receive the truth. It would seem as if God were in these days offering a very great grace to thousands in the Church of England. We should help them by our prayers.

CHAPTER VI.

THE ACT OF 1791.

The Committee of Five—Letters of the Committee to the Catholics of England and to the Vicars Apostolic—The Committee and Milner—The Committee of Ten—The Protestation—The oath proposed by the Committee—The bishops condemn the oath—The schismatical protest—Milner attacks the Committee—Milner defeats the Committee—The passing of the bill of 1791—Relief given by the bill of 1791—Religious Orders under the Act of 1791—Further relief given by the Act.

THE next act which was passed for the relief of English Catholics was in the year 1791. But during the interval between the Act of 1778 and that of 1791, questions of great interest occurred both amongst Catholics themselves and between Catholics and their parliamentary friends. The history of these questions presents itself in a double aspect to the historian. From one point of view, we see much to regret; from another, much to be proud of. The great and laudable desire on the part of some amongst us to share with our fellow-subjects the liberties of Englishmen, led to imprudent and indiscreet actions, and even in a few instances to what I am afraid must be called schismatical conduct. But the policy and the plans of this party were completely foiled by the vigilance and determination of others amongst us, at the head of whom stands the illustrious Milner. It is to the sorrow and regret of their grandchildren that the ancestors of some of us behaved as they did; but it is, and ever will be, the glory of the Church of England that their action raised up the doughty champion to whom we owe our unfettered liberties, and who will share in history, along with O'Connell and the Irish, the praise of having ensured our complete emancipation. In the proceedings of the Catholic Committee, and subsequently of the Catholic Board, we have most signal instances of the way in which good is brought out of evil. The evil done was transient; and though it kept up dissensions amongst Catholics for many years, it never attained its chief object, and completely died away several years before the great Act of Emancipation passed. But the good done was far greater in proportion than the evil. It was substantial and it was triumphant; it lived on with increasing strength, and, as we shall see in the course of this history, it lasts to this day, and is the solid foundation on which the liberties of the Church stand in the United Kingdom. I will begin by giving, in the words of Mr. Charles Butler, an account of the formation and object of the English Catholic Committee in 1782.

"In the year 1782, Lord Stourton, Lord Petre, Mr. Throckmorton (afterwards Sir John Throckmorton), Mr. Thomas Stapleton, and Mr. Henry Hornyold, were appointed, at a general meeting of the English Catholics, 'to be a committee for five years, to promote and attend to the affairs of the Roman Catholic body in England.'"[1] Husenbeth, in his "Life of Milner," calls the meeting at which the committee was appointed "a meeting of certain Catholics."[2] Husenbeth no doubt changed the word "general," in "Butler's Memoirs," into the word "certain," in order to throw suspicion on the representative character of the meeting. How far Mr. Butler was justified in calling it a general meeting, can only be determined by

---

[1] "Historical Memoirs," vol. iv. p. 2.
[2] "Life of Milner," p. 21.

looking at a list of the names of those gentlemen who attended it; this list I have never seen. In the manner in which the committee was formed there was probably nothing objectionable. As the committee was to deal with Catholic affairs, the bishops should have been consulted beforehand, or at least made aware of the intentions of those who called the meeting, in order that their lordships might give their opinion on the prudence of the action proposed. There exists no published document which proves that the bishops were consulted as to the holding of the meeting, or the formation of the committee; at the same time, there is no published document which proves that the bishops were not so consulted. Many committees of English Catholics since that time, and some of them which have had most important work on hand, and have received the highest ecclesiastical sanction in England, have been originated and formed by laymen, and then submitted to ecclesiastical authority. These committees have often not assumed a representative character, until after several weeks or months the adhesion of individual Catholics throughout England, has at length given that character to them.[1] Dr. Milner, indeed, seems to insinuate that the committee had no representative character whatever. Alluding to the fact that in Butler's first edition of his "Memoirs," there is no reference to the committee of 1782 and their proceedings, Milner says, "Was it because this pretended committee of the Catholics had no commission whatever from any one except themselves?"[2] It can hardly, however, be supposed that what Butler calls "a general meeting of the English Catholics," and Husenbeth "a meeting of certain Catholics,"

---

[1] The committee formed in the year 1850, which drew up the address to Cardinal Wiseman, called a public meeting, and composed the "declaration," which was sent to every member of Parliament, is a case in point.

[2] "Supplementary Memoirs of the English Catholics," p. 47.

had no existence; and if it existed, the committee would have represented at least those Catholics who were present at it, and voted for the formation of the Committee. It is, perhaps, probable that Milner, being under a deep sense of the very objectionable proceedings of the committee, was anxious to throw a doubt on its representative character. The object of this committee as expressed in its appointment was not open to objection. It was "to promote and attend to the affairs of the Roman Catholic body in England." If it had done this in the proper sphere of laymen, as I have endeavoured to explain that sphere in a former chapter, it might have been a most useful body of men. But, unfortunately, they forgot their own duties and invaded those of others. Hence a soiled page in the history of English Catholics; for, to quote the words of Milner, writing in the year 1820, "Here properly begins that system of lay interference and domination in the ecclesiastical affairs of English Catholics which ... has perpetuated disorder, divisions, and irreligion among too many of them for nearly the last forty years."[1]

I will now proceed to what this Committee of Five actually did, and will give, in the first place, Mr. Butler's account. "A variety of circumstances," he says, "prevented them making any particular exertions in the cause entrusted to them; the only measure of this description which engaged their attention was a plan for procuring the Catholic ecclesiastics in this country to be formed into a regular hierarchy, by the appointment of bishops in ordinary instead of vicars apostolic.... The first step of the committee was to ascertain the expediency and practicability of the measure. So far as it was a spiritual concern, it belonged to the cognisance of the Vicars Apostolic. The committee therefore addressed a letter

[1] "Supplementary Memoirs," p. 47.

to each of the four Vicars Apostolic, most respectfully stating their own views, and requesting his opinion upon the subject. It appeared from the answers that their opinions differed ; the committee upon this account dropped the measure."[1] This letter was dated May 24, 1783, and was signed by all the five members of the committee.

We will now see how Dr. Milner describes this letter. He says, "The paper in question contains a series of assertions highly derogatory to the spiritual government of the vicars apostolic, which rest entirely on the authority of those few laymen, and on the theological learning of their juridical secretary.[2] These assertions are accompanied with an offer of theirs (the laymen), 'to aid and support in taking such measures as may be effectual to constitute them (the VV.A.) with full power of ordinaries, in order that the frequent recurrence to Rome for dispensations and other ecclesiastical matters might cease.' There is no doubt that the recurrence to Rome each time a new bishop was to be made, constituted the first head of our five laymen's projected retrenchment. They may be excused from the intention of schism, by their ignorance of theological matters; but how daringly presumptuous must their scribes and advisers have been!"[3] Milner wrote these words in the year 1820, thirty-seven years after the matter occurred upon which they are a comment. It is impossible, therefore, to suppose that they were not written with a deep conviction of their truth. It was his deliberate opinion that the committee wished to bring about a state of things in England in which bishops in ordinary would be appointed without

---

[1] " Historical Memoirs," vol. iv. pp. 3, 4.
[2] The secretary to the committee was Mr. Charles Butler.
[3] " Supplementary Memoirs," p. 48.

any recurrence to Rome. It must be to this that he alluded when he says in effect, that the intentions of the committee were at least materially schismatical. The words of the committee in the short extract quoted above from Dr. Milner, however presumptuous they may have been, do not, in the absence of external proof, contain anything schismatical. The words, "and other ecclesiastical matters," might be taken to mean matters in which the ordinary powers of a bishop would exceed the powers of a Vicar Apostolic, unless there was a reason to suppose that something else was meant.[1] Had Milner any reason to believe that more was meant? He wrote, of course, with the knowledge which subsequent events afforded. One member of the committee, as we shall see hereafter, did, in the year 1790, write several pamphlets, "the object of which," to use the words of Husenbeth, in his Life of Milner, "was to persuade the clergy and laity that they had a right to choose their own bishops, and procure their consecration by any bishop, without reference to the Pope." This was clearly schismatical, though, as Husenbeth says, "it is probable that the layman was not aware at first of the real character and tendency of his system, and he little expected the burst of indignation with which it would be received."[2] This layman was John, afterwards Sir John, Throckmorton. There was also a priest who had been writing some most objectionable works; they contained schismatical doctrine, and in one case were heretical.

---

[1] I am not aware that the letter of the committee to the Vicars Apostolic, of May 24, 1783, was ever published, nor even that it was ever in print. It is not in the "Blue-books." Milner, writing in 1820, says of this letter, it "now lies before the present writer." Milner was then Vicar Apostolic of the Midland District, and no doubt the letter lying before him, and which indeed he calls "an original paper," was the copy of the manuscript letter which was sent by the committee to Bishop Thomas Talbot, Milner's predecessor in the Midland District.

[2] "Life of Milner," p. 28.

This man was the Rev. Joseph Berington, at one time chaplain to Sir John Throckmorton, and under whose influence in this matter Sir John may be supposed to have been. There were also one or two other members of the committee whose opinions on the question of the appointment of bishops were open to grave suspicion. It was, no doubt, from the full knowledge of this that Milner has left to posterity his deliberate judgment that the words "and other ecclesiastical matters" included, in the minds of the lay committee, the election of bishops.

Besides the letter to the Vicars Apostolic, the committee addressed a printed letter to the Catholics of England, dated London, April 10, 1787. Mr. Butler, in his "Memoirs," makes no allusion to this letter. Dr. Milner, however, speaks of it in his "Supplementary Memoirs," and after the words we have quoted above respecting the daring presumption of "the scribes and advisers" of the committee, he says, "The same thing may be said of a printed letter of the same committee dated April 10, 1787." And after giving an extract from the letter, Milner writes as follows:—" This letter (though it bears intrinsic evidence of the pen that wrote it) might certainly pass for a speech of Mirabeau, in the French National Assembly, particularly where it insinuates that the people have an equal authority with their pastors *in regulating every part of the Church discipline*, and that they are competent to make whatever changes they please, in conformity with the laws of the State, without either Pope or Council; yet it is seen by its date to have preceded that schismatical and impious assembly by the space of two years." This is strong language. It was, however, written by Milner thirty-three years after the printed letter was addressed by the committee to the Catholics of England, and may be supposed to express his deliberate opinion. On the other hand, we may suppose that the indignation of the great champion was excited at the time he penned the above lines; for his "Supplementary Memoirs" were written in answer to Butler's "Memoirs," which had just appeared, and which, as we have seen, omitted in the first edition all notice of "the Committee of Five," and throughout the volumes gave but a defective and one-sided account of the questions which had so long agitated the English Catholics. It is perhaps a pity that Milner compared the Catholic Committee and the "scribe" who wrote the letter of 1787, to Mirabeau and the National Assembly. For though the letter was in the highest degree objectionable, though it was a most unwarrantable interference of laymen in the affairs of the Church, and strongly savouring of schism, if not actually schismatical, yet surely there was sufficient difference between Mr. Butler and Mirabeau, and between the Catholic Committee and the National Assembly, to induce Dr. Milner to hesitate before pointing to what was done by English Catholics, as a forerunner of the terrible events of the French Revolution. But in criticizing Milner's words, we must ever remember that they are the words of a victorious soldier of the Church. He began, as we shall see later on, single-handed, to attack the evil spirit of dictation to the clergy by the laity, and of unwise interference in ecclesiastical concerns, which some men in England perseveringly continued; and when he was joined in the fight by others, he was their leader, *facile primus*, at the head of those who combated for the liberty of the Church, and who, in their devoted loyalty to the Spouse of Christ, would have remained for ever under the penal laws, rather than purchase their repeal by surrendering her rights. We rejoice now in the liberty which the Church enjoys in England, in the matter of Catholic discipline. This liberty we owe to the happy result of the differences which existed for so many years amongst ourselves, as much as to the action of the Legislature and of our civil governors. For that result we are indebted in great measure to the clear perception, the strong will, and the persevering energy of Milner. This illustrious man must for ever share, with O'Connell and the Irish, the glory of one of the greatest moral victories ever won, of true Church principles over Erastianism, of the rights of religion over the tyranny of its enemies. Still, Milner was a man like ourselves, and he had his faults, as all men have. What was great in his character was so brilliant that it would have cast into the shade his defects, were it not for this circumstance—that they were defects which had an irritating influence on others. He was plainspoken, sometimes to a degree of rudeness; there was a want of tact, and sometimes of prudence, in things that he said; and his writings on Catholic affairs are continually interspersed with personal observations, which must have been very annoying to several of his opponents, especially to Mr. Charles Butler. In a case of the highest importance, Milner had unquestionably right on his side; and though he was obliged frequently to comment very severely on the actions of individuals, he might perhaps have spared a little of that kind of attack which in a court of law would be called "damaging the character of a witness."

The men with whom Milner had to contend were almost all men of more or less influence among their Catholic brethren; they had each their own followers, although they may not have had that representative character, as members of the committee, which Mr. Butler's "Memoirs" would lead us to suppose. "The Committee of Five" were the first men called upon to act in Catholic affairs after the Act of 1778. The passing of this Act, besides giving substantial relief, raised the hopes of the Catholics that the time was approaching when they would be put on something like an equality with their fellow-subjects. The members of the committee had all received a first-rate education in our colleges abroad; they loved their country, and were at least as thoroughly English as any man in the land. Conscious that there was nothing in the doctrines and discipline of the Catholic Church which was opposed to British liberties, they wished to destroy that prejudice amongst Protestants which leads them to suppose that there is. Some of them were ambitious of entering into public life. An Emancipation Act was all that was required to restore to Lords Petre and Stourton their rights as peers of the realm, to give the descendant of the ancient family of Throckmorton a seat in the House of Commons for his native county,[1] and to enable the first real-property lawyer of the day to be called to the Bar. We can hardly wonder that these men should be inclined to strain a point, in order to accomplish their wishes. I do not for a moment say that the position and aspirations of these men can excuse some of their acts, which were in fact schismatical; but surely they may, to use another legal phrase, be pleaded in mitigation of punishment? These reflections on the members of the committee and Dr. Milner have been written in order to give the reader, at the commencement of this portion of the history, some idea of the men who were chiefly engaged in the lamentable disputes to which I shall have to allude.

Another reflection is forced upon us. It does not seem, from anything which has appeared in print, that the committee received soon enough that decided check from ecclesiastical authority which they should have

[1] Very soon after the passing of the Emancipation Act, Sir Robert Throckmorton, the nephew of Sir John, was returned for Berkshire.

encountered. The old maxim, *principiis obsta*, was not acted upon, or not with that vigour with which it should have been; and we may add, not with the promptness and vigour with which it would be, if any undue interference of the laity in ecclesiastical matters were to be attempted now. Mr. Butler, as we have seen, says that it appeared, from the answers of the Vicars Apostolic to the letter of May 24, 1783, that their opinions differed, and that the committee, upon that account, dropped the measure. Dr. Milner tells us that "it is not to be supposed the Vicars Apostolic of that period looked with indifference on these projected invasions of their own and the chief pastor's just authority, and on the fatal precipice, to the brink of which a precious portion of their flock had been led blindfolded by blind guides. This appears," he says, "by their letters to each other, while the attempts were making, many of which letters are still remaining."[1] It would have been better, we may respectfully say, if the disapprobation of the Vicars Apostolic had been expressed in a letter to the committee and to the Catholics of England. If the proceedings of the committee had been exposed and disavowed by authority at their commencement, it is probable that the next "Committee of Ten," which followed the Committee of Five, would never have existed—at least, constituted as it was; and an immense amount of evil would have been prevented. We have it on the authority of Milner that that glorious confessor of the faith, Bishop James Talbot, did not wish the committee to be dissolved, however much he may have disapproved of their conduct. Milner was a priest at Winchester in the year 1787. When the letter of the 10th of April appeared, he was stung to the quick, and, longing *to be at them*, he wrote an answer showing the schismatical tendency of the letter.

[1] "Supplementary Memoirs," p. 50, and in note to p. 53.

It appears that he showed this answer to his Vicar Apostolic, Bishop James Talbot. Milner himself tells us that "the bishop made him suppress it, because he admitted the utility of having a committee." Bishop James Talbot therefore considered that the co-operation of the laity with their ecclesiastical superiors in Catholic affairs, was a desirable thing. It may seem to us a pity that he did not write to the committee, and tell them his idea of the utility of such a body; where the laymen might be useful and do good, and where they were making themselves officious and doing mischief. It appears also, from Dr. Milner's account of the committee, that besides writing the two letters I have mentioned, they were harassing the Vicars Apostolic with other matters, particularly in trying to force them to adopt for a general signature a *doctrinal test* chosen by the lay committee, and not approved of by the bishops. The interference of the committee was, in fact, such that Bishop James, writing to his brother, Bishop Thomas Talbot, Vicar Apostolic of the Midland District, says, amongst other things, "some there are who want to put us (bishops) in leading strings, and themselves to hold them." During the time of "the Committee of Ten," Bishop James Talbot prepared a formal protest against them—and well he might, as we shall presently see—but it does not appear that he ever published it. And "when he was on his death-bed, he told his spiritual friend, the Rev. Mr. Lindow, that if he recovered he would write against the committee."[1] It might have been well if he had done so at the commencement of their proceedings.

But all honour to Bishop James! The penal laws had dragged him more than once into the dock; and he had been tried for his life at the Old Bailey for saying Mass.

[1] "Supplementary Memoirs," note to p. 53.

We must not be too ready to find fault with him for having omitted to do what we now (perhaps in our foolishness) think that he ought to have done.

The Committee of Five was, as we have seen, elected for five years; its power, therefore, having expired in the year 1787, a new committee was formed. This took place at what Mr. Butler calls a general meeting of the English Catholics, on the 3rd of May, 1787. The object of the formation of the committee was, as expressed at the meeting, "to watch over and promote the public interest of the English Roman Catholics;" it was to be under the same rules and regulations as the late committee; it was to consist of ten members, of whom five were to be elected at the meeting, one from each of the four districts to be elected by the gentlemen of those districts, and the remaining one to be chosen by the gentlemen of Lancashire and Cheshire.

The meeting elected Lords Petre and Stourton, Mr. Throckmorton, Sir Henry Englefield, and Mr. Fermor. Lord Clifford was elected by the Western District, Sir John Lawson by the Northern, Sir William Jerningham by the Midland, and Mr. Hornyold by the London District. Mr. Towneley was elected for Lancashire and Cheshire. At a meeting which Mr. Butler again calls "a general meeting of the English Catholics," held on the 15th of May, 1788, the three following clergymen were added to the committee, namely, Dr. James Talbot, the Vicar Apostolic of the London District; Dr. Charles Berington, the coadjutor Bishop of the Midland District; and the Rev. Joseph Wilks, a Benedictine.[1]

According to Milner, the election of the three last-named clergymen was brought about in the following manner. The committee wished to exclude all clergymen

[1] Butler's "Historical Memoirs," vol. iv. pp. 4, seq.

from their body, and, indeed, from the management of Catholic affairs. A leading member of the committee publicly declared that if any clergymen were admitted into it, he would withdraw himself from it.[1] It was now the intention of the committee to submit to their fellow-Catholics for general signature an instrument declaratory of our opinions on certain points.[2] The members of the committee then suddenly bethought themselves that they would not be able to get many Catholics to sign it, unless it should have been previously sanctioned by the clergy; hence they elected three clergymen members of the committee. But they would not allow the clergy to nominate their own representatives; the lay members chose for them Dr. Berington and Mr. Wilks, who had gone along with them in all their past measures, and Dr. James Talbot, whom they could not pass by, and whom they hoped to hoodwink.[3]

We must now proceed to the acts of the committee. At what Mr. Butler calls "a general meeting of the English Catholics," on the 10th of February, 1788,[4] a memorial was voted to be presented to Mr. Pitt. It described the state of Catholics under existing laws, abjured certain opinions falsely attributed to them, and asked for relief. The memorial was presented to Pitt, and on the 9th of

---

[1] In a letter, dated March 22, 1788, from Bishop James to Bishop Thomas Talbot, giving an account of a meeting which had just taken place at the Thatched House, in order to address the King, and of the Catholics who attended it, Bishop James says—"But the Church is excluded, and therefore I have never been summoned, though I had some title, as a gentleman, and could have given some useful information relative to an application lately made to us" ("Supplementary Memoirs," p. 52).

[2] This turned out to be the celebrated "Protestation," to which I shall shortly allude.

[3] "Supplementary Memoirs," pp. 52, 53.

[4] This was no doubt the meeting to which Bishop James Talbot alludes in the letter to his brother above quoted, and from which "the Church was excluded."

May, 1788, Lord Petre, Sir Henry Englefield, and Mr. Fermor had a conference with the minister, who assured them that the Government was anxious to grant what relief it in prudence could give ; but that it was desirable, before any bills should be brought into Parliament, that " he should be furnished with authentic evidence of the opinion of the Catholic clergy and Catholic universities, with respect to the existence or extent of the Pope's dispensing power." The deputation communicated to the committee, on the same day, the result of their interview with Mr. Pitt. In consequence of Mr. Pitt's suggestion, three questions relating to the temporal and dispensing power of the Pope, and the accusation commonly made against us, that we hold the doctrine that faith need not be kept with heretics, were sent to the Universities of the Sorbonne, Louvain, Douay, Alcala, and Salamanca. The universities all returned answers which were satisfactory to the Government.

The next act of the committee was to pass a resolution, at a meeting held on the 19th of April, 1788, "that Mr. Butler should prepare the draft of a bill for the repeal of the laws against the English Catholics." Butler accordingly prepared the bill. It was upon the principle of placing Catholics, in respect to all civil rights, on a level with the Protestant Dissenters. "It contained no oath, but in some instances the benefits which it conferred were extended to those only who had taken, or who should take, the oath contained in the Act passed in 1778 for the relief of the Catholics." [1]

The next object to which the committee turned their attention was the too-celebrated "Protestation," and the oath connected with it. The conduct of the committee in this matter is perhaps the darkest page in our English

[1] Butler's " Historical Memoirs," vol iv. p. 16.

Catholic history during the last hundred years. The whole truth of the matter can hardly be said to be known even now, and perhaps it never will be. I will endeavour to explain it as clearly and concisely as I can.

According to Mr. Butler, Lord Stanhope was endeavouring to form a combined effort on the part of members of the Established Church, the Dissenters, and the Roman Catholics, to procure a modification of the statutes of uniformity. In order to strengthen the union, it was thought advisable that Catholics should solemnly disclaim some of the tenets imputed to us. Lord Stanhope then, according to Mr. Butler, "without the slightest communication with any Roman Catholic, framed the Protestation"—that is, the disclaimer above alluded to.[1] Milner says that he "is satisfied that Lord Stanhope *patronized* the Protestation; but that he *composed it*, he can no more believe than that he wrote the *Summa Theologiæ* of S. Thomas of Aquin."[2] Lord Stanhope sent the Protestation to Lord Petre, who forwarded it to Mr. Butler, the secretary to the committee, who in his turn transmitted copies of it to the four Vicars Apostolic.

We have it on the authority of Mr. Butler, that all the Vicars Apostolic at first made some difficulties about signing the Protestation.[3] "They did indeed afterwards sign it, but Bishop Walmesley complained that he was surprised into his signature, and withdrew it." Bishop Matthew Gibson directed that if "his name was absolutely necessary, it should be affixed by Bishop James Talbot, *in sensu Catholico*. The clergy generally felt the same repugnance as their superiors: 'but,' says Milner, 'what

---

[1] "Historical Memoirs," vol. iv. pp. 16, 17.
[2] "Supplementary Memoirs," p. 54.
[3] Husenbeth's "Life of Milner," p. 23, quoting from Butler's "Red Book," fol. 14.

with the explanations, assurances, and promises of the different agents of the committee,' they and their flocks were mostly induced to subscribe it; many from the positive assurance given that the *Protestation* would not be followed by any new oath. The total number of signatures was 1523."[1] Before the Protestation was signed, some alterations had been made in it, at the suggestion of some of the Vicars Apostolic; but even as signed, it contained, according to Milner, several errors and inaccuracies. He instances one inaccuracy which he and some others desired to have corrected; but the "patrons of the Protestation" laughed at them, and refused to make the alteration.

The next proceeding of the committee was, we are sorry to say, disgraceful. Notwithstanding the assurance given that no new oath should be proposed, they did frame a new oath.[2] Mr. Butler excuses this act of the committee on the ground that strong representations were made to them (which they were backward in acceding to) that a new oath was necessary. But the act was inexcusable, and the committee began to prove their loyalty to the Crown by being disloyal to their own friends, and disloyal to their own Church. No Catholic ever attained his object who began in this way.

With regard to the substance of the new oath, it was, in several places, in the highest degree objectionable. Mr. Butler says that the oath "in its original form was an exact transcript of the Protestation, and consequently contained nothing more than what the bishops, with the body of English Catholics, had already signed and approved;" and that after it had received some alterations suggested by the Ministry and approved of by the ecclesi-

---

[1] Husenbeth's "Life of Milner," pp. 23, 24.
[2] This new oath was to be substituted, in the bill prepared by Butler, for the oath in the Act of 1778.

astical members of the committee, it was kept by Bishop James Talbot for two days, and returned by him with a verbal declaration that he saw nothing in it contrary to faith or good morals.[1] But Milner positively asserts that the oath was never once communicated by the committee to the Vicars Apostolic; but that it was shown to the Archbishop of Canterbury, and altered at his suggestion, while the Catholic bishops were left to learn its contents from a newspaper.[2]

At the final settling of the oath, the chief of the many objections to it were, that it condemned the doctrine of the deposing power of the Pope in strained and exaggerated terms, and far stronger than the Parliament required; it condemned the spiritual power of the Pope in this country in words which not only no Catholic could swear to in their plain sense, but which made Dr. Horsley, the Protestant Bishop of St. David's, say, in the House of Lords, that *there were things in the committee's oath which he as a Protestant could not swear.* But another insuperable objection to the oath was, that it surrendered the names "Catholic" and "Roman Catholic," and took, as the designation of each one of us who has inherited or professes the faith of St. Edward, the title of "Protesting Catholic Dissenter." It is difficult for us in these days to believe that such a thing could have been done. We hardly know how to characterize it; whether to call it horrible and monstrous, or ridiculous and absurd. To say the truth, we are now rather inclined to laugh at it. It was one of those atrocious things which has its ridiculous side; when it is first forced upon us, we are affected with horror, but we leave it with derision. These chief objections to the oath arose from new matter inserted into it which was not

---

[1] "Historical Memoirs," vol. iv. pp. 25, 26.
[2] "Supplementary Memoirs," p. 59.

in the Protestation.[1] And we must here remind the reader that it was the object of the committee to impress upon their fellow-Catholics the notion, that the oath contained nothing in it of consequence which was not in the Protestation. The reason of this was that they hoped to get all who had signed the Protestation to agree to the oath.

It was now time for the bishops to interfere with the whole weight of their authority. They accordingly met at Hammersmith on the 19th of October, 1789, and then and there formally condemned the oath, declared it unlawful to be taken, and forbade their subjects to take it. Besides the four Vicars Apostolic, namely, Bishops Walmesley, James and Thomas Talbot, and Matthew Gibson, there were also present Dr. Sharrock, coadjutor to Bishop Walmesley; Dr. Berington, coadjutor to Bishop Thomas Talbot; the Rev. Robert Bannister, Professor of Theology; and the Rev. John Milner. With the knowledge we have of the glorious career of Milner, it is well worthy of notice that he was present at this meeting, when the bishops first made a bold stand against the committee. We can hardly suppose otherwise than that the result of their deliberations was owing, in great measure at least, to his energetic advice. "The above-quoted decision of our VV.A.," says Milner, "which fixed the faith and conduct of their flocks in general, was echoed back to them in accents of applause from the prelates of Scotland and Ireland, as likewise from the Holy See."[2]

"In face of this solemn condemnation by the four

---

[1] Most Catholics, who have some knowledge of these affairs, are under the impression that the words "Protesting Catholic Dissenter" occurred in the Protestation. But such is not the case. They were confined to the oath, which formed part of the Relief Bill proposed by the committee. Those, therefore, who signed the Protestation did not style themselves by the obnoxious title.

[2] The Cardinal Prefect of the Propaganda, writing to the bishops, says of the oath, "Formula juramenti non erat *fidei* ac Patrum regulis *consentanea*."

bishops in England, Mr. Charles Butler wrote a long appeal addressed to the Catholics of England, dated November 25, 1789, in defence of the *protestation* and *oath;* which appeal was signed by two clerical and five lay members of the committee. On the same day was signed by the same members a long letter to the bishops, remonstrating against their censure, and containing words in which, Dr. Milner says, both 'they and the Holy See are grossly insulted and calumniated.'

"Two of the Vicars Apostolic died soon after the condemnation of the oath, Dr. James Talbot on the 26th of January, 1790, and Dr. Matthew Gibson on the 19th of May following. These deaths led to active intrigues on the part of the committee to procure the appointment of two successors who might favour their views, and they were particularly anxious to have Dr. Berington appointed to the London District. He was a member of the committee, and had all along acted with it."[1]

It was at this time that Sir John Throckmorton, one of the committee, wrote several pamphlets, to which allusion has already been made, to prove that the clergy and laity had a right to choose their own bishops and to procure their consecration by any bishop without reference to the Holy See. These pamphlets were immediately answered by Milner, Father Charles Plowden, S. J., and the Revs. Dr. Strickland and William Pilling. Milner, in his last pamphlet, gave the finishing stroke to what he calls "an open attempt to separate the clergy from the faith and communion of the Church." It would appear from Milner's "Supplementary Memoirs" that there was some sort of election on the part of a certain number of the clergy and laity of the London District; for he says that one of the committee wrote to Dr. Berington, and entreated him to

[1] Husenbeth's "Life of Milner," pp. 25-27.

stand firmly by his election to the London District. However, if there was any such election, it was of no more consequence than if it had been a practical joke; for the Holy See proceeded to appoint Dr. Douglas to the London District and Dr. William Gibson to the Northern District as Vicars Apostolic.

The continued action of the committee against the Church obliged the bishops to renew their condemnation of the oath, especially as two of those who originally condemned it were dead, and their successors had been appointed in their place. Drs. Gibson and Douglas had been consecrated at Lulworth; and before they left the castle they and Dr. Walmesley agreed upon and signed an encyclical letter, in which they again condemned the oath, and asserted the exclusive right of the bishops "to determine on oaths or instruments containing doctrinal matters, and rejecting the appellation of 'Protesting Catholic Dissenters.'"

But this fresh condemnation of the oath by the Vicars Apostolic did not produce any good effect upon the committee. Though it gives pain to do so, I must quote Mr. Butler's own words on the subject. He writes as follows:— "The condemnation of the oath by the Vicars Apostolic did not withhold the committee from continuing their exertions to obtain the passing of the bill, or induce them to take any step for obtaining an alteration of the oath."[1] This is a lamentable admission of a gross dereliction of duty. The oath was, in the first instance, condemned by all four of the Vicars Apostolic. The alterations made in it did not satisfy three of the Vicars Apostolic, nor the successors of two of them who died between the two condemnations. Five Vicars Apostolic out of six had therefore condemned the oath in its altered state.

[1] "Historical Memoirs," vol. iv. p. 34.

It was the undoubted right of the bishops to pronounce upon the lawfulness of the oath, and it was their exclusive right. It was a pure case of conscience, and the laity had lawfully no voice in the matter. To proceed, therefore, with their arrangements for ensuring the passing of the bill with the obnoxious oath, was a step on the road to schism. Bishop Thomas Talbot did not sign the second condemnation of the oath. His position seems to have been this: he condemned the original oath as framed by the committee, but he thought the alterations made in it put it into such a shape that it was not absolutely necessary to condemn it as altered. I am inclined to think that Bishop Thomas Talbot thought that in the then state of affairs, it was necessary, to ensure the passing of a bill, that the committee should continue to act, and that they might cease their work if they were irritated by a second condemnation.

The proceedings of the committee now passed the bounds of spiritual obedience and common sense, and began to look like a public entry into schism. They published what has since been known by the name of "the Schismatical Protest." It was dated February 2, 1791.[1] It "occurs," says Husenbeth, "at the end of a letter of eighteen quarto pages, addressed to Bishops Walmesley, Gibson, and Douglas, and written by the Rev. Joseph Wilks, though the protest itself was evidently drawn up by Mr. C. Butler.[2] This protest Milner stigmatizes as a "complication of profaneness, calumny, schism, and blasphemy." It "publicly and schismatically disclaims submission to their bishops acting in the strict discharge

---

[1] This, if it be not the correct date, is within a day or two of it. It can only be verified by reference to the "Blue-books," a copy of which I have not seen for some years.
[2] "Life of Milner," p. 34.

of their pastoral duty;" it "protests and calls upon the awful name of God, again and again, to witness their schismatical protest against every *clause, determination, matter, and thing* contained in the first as well as the second encyclical; it condemns the bishops as being "arbitrary and unjust," and charges them with "inculcating principles hostile to society and Government, derogatory from the allegiance due to the State."[1] It concludes by appealing from the bishops "to all the Catholic Churches in the universe, and especially to the first of Catholic Churches, the Apostolic See, rightly informed."

Such, then, was the state of things amongst the English Catholics at the beginning of February, 1791. The day was rapidly approaching when the second Relief Bill was to be brought into Parliament. The committee was maturing its plans for emancipating those only of the Church who would swear that they were "Protesting Catholic Dissenters." They were confident of success; they smiled incredulously at ecclesiastical authorities who told them that they would not succeed, and made merry when they were told that the venerable Bishop Walmesley used to repeat with confidence, "*I have asked my Master that this bad oath may not pass, and He will grant my prayer;* they ridiculed the idea that the Vicars Apostolic would find any support in Parliament; they had made friends, as they thought, in both Houses—allies who would help them to defeat their bishops, and to establish a lay supremacy in the Church in England; they were ready for the battle, boasted of what they were going to do, and rejoiced in the coming success.

---

[1] "Supplementary Memoirs," pp. 74, 76. It will be remembered that all four of the Vicars Apostolic signed the first condemnation of the oath. As, therefore, the "Protest" condemns this first condemnation, the committee had not the excuse that one of the Vicars Apostolic was not against them.

Of the bishops Milner says, "They had little else to trust to for the success of their cause but its native goodness and the Divine assistance."

But the days of the committee were numbered, and their designs were to come to naught. The decree had gone forth that the rising Church in England should be free at least from internal lay domination; the chains struck off by her enemies were not to be replaced by fetters forged by her own children. The bishops now summoned to their aid a willing champion, a man in the very prime of life, full of energy and zeal, a learned and pious priest, able and willing to be God's instrument to free His English Church. I have, therefore, now to recount

HOW MILNER FOUGHT AND BEAT THE COMMITTEE.

Milner was the *Cœur de Lion* of controversy. What we read both in history and fiction of Richard Plantagenet, and his mode of carrying on war, seems to apply to Milner, in the method in which he conducted his bloodless but hardly less fierce contests. In both there was the same apparent inaction, the same quiet watchfulness for the right moment, the same sudden onslaughts, rushing into the very thickest of the fight, following up blow after blow, right and left, in the midst of a multitude of foes, loving rather a crowd of adversaries than a single antagonist.

He is quietly seated at Winchester, writing his classical work on the history and antiquities of that ancient city. February in the year 1791 arrived; the recess was over, and Parliament again met. It appeared certain that within a few months a Relief Bill would pass. The committee entrusted their bill containing the condemned oath to Mr. Mitford, afterwards Lord Redesdale. Now had come the time for action. The voices of the Vicars Apostolic calling on their champion were heard in the study at Winchester. Milner started from his chair, for now the battle-axe was to be seized. He set off for London, leaving, as he says, his friends at home to pray for him. He wrote a pamphlet in the coach on the way.[1] When he arrived in London he put this pamphlet into the hands of the printer, and then called on Edmund Burke. Burke introduced him to Fox and Windham. He had a conference with Dundas in presence of Pitt, also with three of the Protestant bishops and with Wilberforce and William Smith, and several other members of Parliament. They all listened to him with the greatest kindness, and interpreted the oath in the plain sense of its words, and not in the lax unnatural manner they were said to do in the Blue-books.[2] He convinced them that the great body of Catholics looked up to their bishops for guidance, and not to the committee. They were all sincerely desirous of passing a bill which, as far as it should go, should embrace and satisfy all Catholics, and Milner prepared them for the reception of a bill from the committee which would exclude the greater number of their Catholic fellow-subjects. The bill, as drawn up by the committee, was introduced into the House of Commons on the 1st of March.[3] Milner was present in the midst, as he says, of "a crowd of exulting adversaries." Mr. Mitford, in his opening speech, distinguished between the "Protesting Catholic Dissenters," for whose benefit the bill had been brought in, and the "Papists," who were to be excluded from relief. "The illustrious Fox," says Milner, "spoke with his accustomed enlargement of sentiment, and Burke

[1] This pamphlet was entitled "Facts relating to the contest among the Roman Catholics."
[2] The "Blue-books" were the books in which the committee published their objectionable "Letters," "Protests," etc.
[3] The bill was drawn by Charles Butler, and settled by his friend and fellow-labourer on Coke-upon-Littleton, Mr. Hargraves.

dissipated the gathering mists of bigotry with the bright rays of his glowing imagination and benevolent heart. Mr. Pitt spoke at great length, but in such obscure and ambiguous terms that Fox was obliged twice or thrice to call upon him for an explanation of his meaning. The fact is, he had not then made up his mind whether there should be one Act, to comprehend both parties, or two Acts, one in favour of the Protestant Catholic Dissenters, whom, in a former speech, he had praised as good subjects, the other barely to save from the gallows the traitorous, perfidious, and bloody-minded Papists, as he then considered them.[1] At length the Attorney-General, afterwards Lord Chief Baron, Sir Archibald Macdonald, rose and said that, *As he was entering the house a paper had been put into his hand which proved that one of the Catholic parties was as good subjects and as much entitled to favour as the other.*"[2] This was the pamphlet written in the stage-coach on the way from Winchester, and copies of which an officer of the House, who was a friend of Milner, distributed to the members as they went in. This announcement instantly produced an extraordinary effect. Pitt was undeceived as soon as he heard it, and indeed said, soon after, "We have been deceived in the great outlines of the bill; either the other party must be relieved, or the bill not pass." From this moment the fate of the obnoxious parts of the bill was decided. One member proposed that the word *Dissenters* should be omitted from the eccentric appellation given to us by the committee. Another member then said that the title would be *Protesting* or *Protestant Catholics*, which

---

[1] From this it would appear that either Milner did not enter so fully into the matter in his talk with Dundas as he did with the others, or Pitt did not pay attention to what he said. We can hardly suppose that so great a man would have allowed his mind again to receive the poison which had been extracted by Milner.

[2] "Supplementary Memoirs," p. 79.

would be ridiculous. The word *Protestant* was then struck out, and *Catholic* alone remained, to which was added the word *Roman;* that word, of which every Catholic is most proud, and which in our days in England is peculiarly the test which tries whether one who calls himself a Catholic is really a Catholic or only an impostor. The Ministry required the committee to drop the absurd name of *Protesting Catholic Dissenter*, and adopt the title of "Roman Catholic." The committee obeyed, and, to use Milner's phrase, resumed *the family name*. The oath, too, underwent many alterations in the House of Commons, but still remained unsatisfactory to the bishops. The committee in the mean time was not completely beaten. It formally called upon Milner to prove that he was authorized to act for any other Catholics than himself. It denied his right to act. He asked for an hour to write his answer, and then produced a document ready if necessary to be printed, in which " he proved that the great body of Catholics throughout England looked up to their bishops to procure for them in the existing juncture an unobjectionable and proper form of oath ; that two parts in three of the London clergy had signified this to them in a formal manner but a few days before ; that fifty-three in Lancashire had called upon them in a printed paper, which he had with him, to this effect, testifying at the same time that very few of their laity would take the committee's oath." Lastly, he produced a formal deputation to him from the bishops to act as their agent in the present business. "Never," says Milner, "was an attorney more fully authorized to transact another person's business than he proved he was to circulate the unanswerable hand bill, which had produced so great an effect in the House of Commons." Notwithstanding this complete justification the committee drew up a "Statement of Facts," counter to the one written on the way from Winchester to London, which they printed and circulated among members of Parliament, in which they denied that the supporters of the oath were a minor part of the Catholic body, or that real scruples existed among Catholics as to its lawfulness, adding that "one John Milner" could only produce the names of *three persons* as his authority for his assertions, and that the committee and those for whom they were acting were ready to repeat the Protestation (that is to say, says Milner, the oath) as often as called upon."[1]

"One John Milner!" Yes—Butler could not have given Milner greater praise, nor have put him in a higher position than he did by these very words with which he meant to damage him. Milner was well supported by three out of the four Vicars Apostolic; and we can hardly suppose that the fourth, Dr. Thomas Talbot, did not secretly wish him success. There were some others also who were active in opposing the committee, amongst whom Milner mentions Mr. Weld of Lulworth, and Father Charles Plowden of the Society of Jesus. But Milner was the avowed champion of the good cause: he was put forward by the Vicars Apostolic as, to use a vulgar phrase, the fighting man; he worked night and day, during his stay in London, to defeat the enemy and win the battle for the Church. He was, therefore, the special mark singled out by the committee, but he was proof against them.

The bill came before the House of Lords in the first week of June. Lord Rawdon began the debate, and asserted that *the bill would not extend to relieve a considerable*

---

[1] As well might a Saracen have called out that it was only "one Richard Plantagenet" who was charging against their ranks. The "three persons" were three Vicars Apostolic, so that the committee might be likened to the man who represented his adversary, in some question of right of way, as having only ten men in his favour, suppressing the fact that the ten men were ten out of the twelve judges.

number, *perhaps a majority of the Catholics*. This was, of course, because it was known that the majority would not take the oath as framed by the committee. Lord Rawdon was followed by the Archbishop of Canterbury, and by the Bishops of St. David's and Salisbury, all in favour of the bill, but all thinking it imperfect. Mr. Butler himself, as quoted by Milner, has given us a sketch of the Bishop of St. David's speech. " He called God to witness his wishes to serve the Catholics; but the present bill was very imperfect: so imperfect that he doubted whether it could be mended. He then repeated, with little variation, the whole of Mr. Milner's last publication at the door of the House of Commons. If the bill passed, with the oath in its present form, *one set of Catholics were at the mercy of the other*. He saw the streets full of informers, the prisons crowded," etc.[1] The Duke of Leeds and Earl Fauconbergh were friendly to the bill, but thought it should go over to the next session. The debate was adjourned until Thursday, when it was stated that Dr. Douglas, on the part of the Catholics, had sent in his ultimatum, consisting of four alterations; but stating that the oath prescribed by the Irish Relief Act of 1778 would be agreeable to every one. The debate was again adjourned until the next day, when the Bishop of St. David's proposed the Irish oath. Lords Guildford and Grenville insisted on a clause being inserted, by which we swear allegiance to the succession in the Protestant line. With these alterations, the bill was carried without a division: and it was sent down to the Commons, who agreed to the Lords' amendments. And thus the bill passed unanimously through both Houses. It received the Royal Assent; the Committee of Ten was dissolved; and Milner went back to Winchester. He laid aside, but did not throw away, the battle-axe. He resumed the his-

[1] " Supplementary Memoirs," p. 85.

tory of the ancient city, and remained quietly on the watch.

Having given a short history of the passing of the Relief Act of 1791,[1] it remains to tell the reader to what extent that relief actually went. This will best be done by giving a short analysis of the Act.

In the preamble Catholics were still called "Papists, or persons professing the Popish religion;" and it was recited that it was expedient that those who should take the oath thereinafter mentioned, should be relieved from certain penalties and disabilities. The reader will bear in mind that the word "expedient" in this act was meant in its sense of, *proper under the circumstances*, and in opposition to *just*. No claim of right was admitted. In the then state of affairs in Europe it was desirable that all the inhabitants of the British Isles should be as united as possible, and therefore an act which would help to conciliate was passed.

Though the Act in its preamble called us by the vulgar nickname "Papists," we were not required to call ourselves Papists. The oath which the Act prescribed begins with the words: "I, A. B., do hereby declare that I do profess the Roman Catholic Religion." After thirty-eight years we were treated more civilly, and in the great Act of 1829 we could not only call ourselves, but King, Lords, and Commons condescended to call us "the Roman Catholic subjects of his Majesty." This was Protestant progress. The oath itself was, as we have seen, the same as the Irish oath of 1778. The common sense of Parliament had substituted this oath in the English Act for the eccentric and, as Dr. Walmesley called it, "the bad oath," which the Committee of Ten wished to force upon their Catholic brethren. The oath was much the same in substance as

---

[1] 31st Geo. III. cap. xxxii.

the English oath of 1778; but it contained no special reference to the claims of the Stuart family. No person could take advantage of the relief given by the Act who had not previously taken the oath. Those who had taken the oath could not be prosecuted for not resorting to some parish church, nor for being a "Papist," nor for hearing or saying Mass, nor for being a priest or deacon, nor for entering or belonging to any ecclesiastical order or community of the Church of Rome, nor for being present at or performing any rite, ceremony, practice, or observance of the "Popish religion, or maintaining or assisting others therein." It was, however, enacted that no assembly for religious worship should be allowed under the Act, till it should have been certified to the Quarter Sessions; and no person could perform any ecclesiastical functions therein, until his name and description had been recorded by the clerk of the peace. This provision was, we believe, generally obeyed, and some of the old missions still preserve the certificates, obtained from the clerk of the peace, of the record of the chapels and of the priest who was then serving the mission. One curious provision of the Act was that the doors of no Roman Catholic chapel should be "locked, barred, or bolted" during the time of service. The framers of the Act seem to have had some strange suspicion that Catholics would make use of their chapels for treasonable or some other unlawful purpose, for they showed themselves especially anxious to secure this clause by enacting that no person attending a service, or a "meeting," as the Act expresses it, with closed doors, should take any benefit from the Act, although he might have taken the oath of allegiance. Another provision of the Act, which, at least in these days, is rather amusing, is that a Catholic might thenceforth be a constable by deputy, and also a churchwarden and overseer of the poor, but still only by deputy.

A priest who had taken the oath was exempted from serving on a jury; any person disturbing a congregation or "misusing a priest" is by this act liable on conviction to a penalty of twenty pounds. A clause which shows into what inconsistencies false doctrines will lead intelligent people, is one which enacts that the law which compels every one to go to church on a Sunday shall still be in force, but that going to a Catholic chapel will count for the same. So that England, which was then essentially Protestant, and whose people universally believed Catholics to be idolaters, made a law under which if a man was determined not to go to church, he must attend an idolatrous worship. The following restrictions were also put upon priests. No priest could claim the benefit of this Act if he officiated in any place with a steeple and bell;[1] if he should officiate at any funeral in any church or churchyard, also if he should wear the habit of his Order, or exercise any rite or ceremony of his religion save within a certified chapel, or in a private house, where there should not be more than five persons assembled beside those of the household.

The Act extended to schoolmasters, who thenceforth could not be prosecuted, provided they had taken the oath; but it was provided that "no person professing the Roman Catholic religion should obtain or hold the mastership of any college or school of royal foundation, or of any other endowed college or school for the education of youth, or should keep a school in either of the Universities of Oxford and Cambridge. The seventeenth section of the Act provided "that nothing in this Act contained should make it lawful to found, endow, or establish any religious order or society of persons bound by monastic or religious

---

[1] It will be observed that steeples and bells are not forbidden by the Act; it only punished the priest who should presume to officiate beneath them.

vows, or to found, endow, or establish any school, academy, or college by persons professing the Roman Catholic religion within these realms, or the dominions thereunto belonging; and that all uses, trusts, and dispositions, whether of real or personal property, which immediately before June 24, 1791, shall be deemed to be superstitious or unlawful, shall continue to be so deemed and taken, anything in this Act contained notwithstanding."

In the year 1791 there was, as far as I know, no religious house of men in England. The French Revolution had not at that time driven across the Channel the English houses established on the Continent. But there were many men in England belonging to religious orders. They were scattered about on various missions. There were Benedictines and Franciscans and Dominicans. There were also others who had taken the vows of religion, who in their hearts remained true and faithful to their vocation, and who were only waiting until God in His mercy, by the mouth of His Vicar upon earth, should allow them to meet together again in the Society of Jesus.

Although by section xvii. of the Act no Order could be established,[1] the members of Religious Orders then in England were included and *nominatim* included, in the full benefit of the Act. For section iii., which protects from prosecution persons who had taken the oath, extends, as we have seen, not only to priests and deacons, but to any one "entering or belonging to any ecclesiastical order or community of the Church of Rome." So that the Act of 1791 made no distinction whatever in the benefit which

---

[1] It must at the same time be said that clause xvii., inasmuch as it is directed against Religious Orders, seems open to very considerable argument, in which "a good deal might be said on both sides," whether, for instance, founding a ,'house" is founding an "Order"; and if several men belonging to a Religious Order were to choose to live together, which of them could be prosecuted for "establishing a Religious Order or Society."

it gave, between the secular and regular clergy who were then in England; and further, though by section xvii. it forbade an order to be established, by section iii. it expressly allowed a man to "enter an order" and remain in England. The Act of 1829 contains, as is well known, clauses for providing for the gradual suppression of Religious Orders; but the Act of 1829 goes further than the Act of 1791 and makes a most invidious distinction between the secular and regular clergy then in England: for "Jesuits," who had the distinguished honour of being specially named, "and members of other religious orders, communities, or societies of the Church of Rome, bound by monastic or religious vows," are obliged by the Act of 1829 to register themselves as such. And moreover, whereas the Act of 1791 allowed a man to "enter an order," that is, to take the vows of Religion in an Order, the Act of 1829, made any man who should do so liable to banishment, and if he evaded that sentence, to transportation for life. In short, whereas by the Act of 1791, though no one could found or establish an order, any one might enter an order; by the Act of 1829, any one entering an order is punished as a felon. So that the Act of 1829 virtually repealed a portion of the relief which had been granted by the Act of 1791.[1]

Are the Catholics of the United Kingdom generally aware that the great Emancipation Act deprived us of benefits which were granted when the repeal of the old penal laws began; that religious orders, before the law, have been since the Emancipation Act, and still are in a worse position than they were in between the years 1791 and 1829?

The attention of the legislature has several times been

[1] In one or two other points regarding Religious the Act of 1829 contrasts unfavourably with the Act of 1791.

directed to the clauses of the Emancipation Act against Religious Orders. Some attempts have been made to obtain the repeal of those clauses, though the Catholics of England have never backed up the attempt as they ought to have done. A few years ago the subject was spoken of in the House of Commons, and Lord Beaconsfield, then in the Lower House, opposed the repeal of the clauses against Religious Orders, on the ground that though Jesuits and others were now perfectly harmless, yet they might become dangerous, and it might be as well to hold the clauses over them *in terrorem*. Passing by the expression of unjust suspicion in which we may hope Lord Beaconsfield had too much sense to be sincere, it may fairly be said that whatever may be the opinions of "the great Liberal party," the Conservatives of England, at least, might be well content to allow a man to enter a Religious Order in the year 1880, when William Pitt, the whole bench of Bishops, the Houses of Lords and Commons unanimously, and King George III. himself, were content to allow a man to do so in the year 1791.[1]

The remaining portion of the Act, we may give in the words of Mr. Butler. It "enacts that in future no one shall be summoned to take the oath of supremacy prescribed by 1 William and Mary, s. 1, cap. viii., and George I. s. 2, cap. viii., or the declaration against Transubstantiation, required by 25 Charles II.; that 1 William and Mary, s. 1, cap. ix., for removing Papists or reputed Papists from the cities of London and Westminster, shall not extend to Roman Catholics taking the appointed oath; and that no Peer of Great Britain or Ireland,

---

[1] In the last days of Lord Beaconsfield's Government notice was given of a bill to be introduced into the House of Commons to repeal the obnoxious clauses of the Emancipation Act. Why did we hear nothing more of this bill in the days of a Government which professed to conciliate Catholics?

taking the oath, shall be liable to be prosecuted for coming into his Majesty's presence, or into the court or house where his Majesty resides, under 30 Charles II. s. 2, cap. i.; the Act also repeals the laws requiring the deeds and wills of Roman Catholics to be registered and enrolled; and dispenses persons acting as a councillor at law, barrister, attorney, clerk, or notary, from taking the oath of supremacy, or the declaration against Transubstantiation, for acting in those capacities.[1]

Thus we see that no Catholic could be called to the bar, or practise as an attorney, before the passing of this Act. The statute 7th and 8th William and Mary interdicted the bar to Catholics. The last Catholic called to the bar before the statute of William and Mary was Mr. Nathaniel Piggott, who was called in the year 1688.[2] The first Catholic called to the Bar after the passing of the Act of 1791, was Mr. Charles Butler himself, who had drawn up the Act. Much as we differ from Mr. Butler in his action on the Committee, it must be admitted that from his learning and position, he was well entitled to be the first to take advantage of the clause which enabled Catholics to be called to the Bar. Previous to the year 1791, several Catholics had attained great eminence as conveyancers. Lord Campbell, in his "Life of Lord Eldon," relates that Mr. Duane, "an eminent Catholic conveyancer," gave John Scott (afterwards Lord Eldon) "the run of his chambers," in consequence of the young student not having sufficient money to pay the regular fee. And in a note to this passage Lord Campbell adds: "At this time (1775) conveyancing was chiefly in the hands of Roman Catholics. Being long disqualified by their religion from being called to the Bar, they practised

---

[1] "Historical Memoirs," vol. iv. pp. 47, 48. 1st Edition of 1822.
[2] Ibid., vol. ii. p. 337. Edition of 1819.

successfully in Chambers; and being employed at first by their co-religionists, their industry and learning forced them into general business. Charles Butler, whom I well knew, may be considered the last of this race."[1]

This act did not extend to Scotland: the Scotch Catholics had to wait two years more for their first relief Act.

Up to this time Catholics had been subject to a double land-tax. Mr. Butler, at the end of his description of the Act of 1791, says: "The double land-tax being imposed on Catholics by the annual land-tax Act, a repeal of it could not be effected by any prospective Act, but it was repealed by omitting from the annual land-tax Act the clause imposing it."[2]

Still, however, Catholics continued to pay double land-tax. This seems to have arisen partly from the plan indicated by Mr. Butler, not having been sufficient to relieve us from the unjust burden; for in the year 1831 an Act was passed to relieve Catholics from the payment of double land-tax. And it arose also in great measure from the difficulty in discovering what lands were actually paying double tax. Immediately after the passing of the Act of 1831, a professional man made it his business to find out the lands which were subject to double tax, in consequence of their owners being then or having been Catholics. He then proposed to the owners to prove the fact and obtain relief under the Act. His conditions were, that if he failed in obtaining the exemption, he was to receive no fee whatever; if he succeeded, he was to receive the annual amount which he had recovered, for three years. In this way many Catholics were relieved of the tax.

Such, then, was the Relief Act of 1791. It was a great boon to Catholics. It legalized the public worship of the

---

[1] "Life of Lord Eldon," p. 40.
[2] "Historical Memoirs," vol. iii. p. 48.

Catholic Church. Schools could be opened, a priest could offer the Holy Sacrifice, and the faithful could assist at it without molestation, and under the protection of the law. Several disabilities under which Catholics lived were removed. It was essentially a new beginning—a much more fair, if not altogether a fair start for truth in its contest with error. So great was the relief, that Mr. Pitt called it emancipation, and said that "the term emancipation was not in the smallest degree applicable to the repeal of the few remaining penal statutes to which Catholics were still liable."[1]

If Mr. Pitt was justified in calling the Act of 1791 "emancipation," he could only have been so by confining his meaning of the word to what he found by tracing it back to its classical origin. It was not emancipation, as an Englishman would understand the term. A free man in England, without some of the most important rights of a free man, would hardly consider himself emancipated. Until the year 1829, no English Catholic could even vote at the election of a Member of Parliament. Gerards and Towneleys would scarcely look upon themselves as emancipated, when, solely because they were Catholics, their broad acres were not represented. And the voice of the public seems to have proclaimed that Pitt, standing in the British House of Commons, put too narrow a construction upon the word emancipation. For the Act of 1791 was never called more than a Relief Act, whereas the Act of 1829, from the first introduction of the Bill, was universally called Emancipation. Nevertheless, the Act of 1791 was a very great step in advance; and as these are days in which centenaries are celebrated, those amongst us who shall be spared to see the year 1891 should not let that year pass without renewing our thanks to God for His good providence over His English Church.

[1] "Pitt's Speeches," vol. iii. p. 421.

CHAPTER VII.

THE ACT OF 1791, AND SUBSEQUENT EVENTS.

Why the Committee failed—Meeting at the Crown and Anchor—The Cisalpine Club—The Mediation—The "Buff Book"—Father Charles Plowden —The "Roman Catholic Meeting."

IN giving an account of the Relief Act of 1791 in the last chapter, I omitted to mention, that in the clause which permitted a Catholic to keep a school, it was provided that "no schoolmaster professing the Roman Catholic religion should receive into his school for education the child of any Protestant father." This unjust and penal proviso, introduced into a Relief Bill, was repealed by 9 and 10 Vict. cap. 59. And with regard to this proviso, it may be noticed that it was not merely a penal law against Catholics; it was an infringement of the liberty of British subjects, inasmuch as it crippled the freedom of Protestants in the choice of school for the education of their children. The Act 9 and 10 of the Queen cap. 59, also repealed two other portions of the Act of 1791. It may be interesting and perhaps also useful to mention these. It repealed so much of the Act of 1791 as enacted "that nothing therein contained should be construed to give any ease, benefit, or advantage to any person who should by preaching, teaching, or writing, deny or gainsay the oath of allegiance, abjuration, and declaration thereinbefore mentioned and appointed to be taken as aforesaid, or the declarations or doctrines therein contained, or any of them." This clause was certainly an infringement of the liberty of speech. Under it no Catholic could speak in public, or write against any part of the oath, even for the purpose of obtaining its repeal, without depriving himself of the benefit of the Act. If a Catholic had preached or written against, for instance, the insulting declaration against "evasion, equivocation, and mental reservation" in the taking of the oath, or against the vile insinuation that he had a "dispensation already granted by the Pope," to perjure himself, he would have made himself liable to prosecution. The Act 9 and 10 Vict. cap. 59, also repealed that part of the Act of 1791 which provided that "no person professing the Roman Catholic religion should be permitted to keep a school for the education of youth until his or her name and description as a Roman Catholic schoolmaster or schoolmistress should have been recorded at the Quarter Sessions." Any restrictions upon Catholic primary education existing now are not the result of what we call the penal laws; these have in this respect been swept away: they are the result of modern laws, professedly enacted for the benefit of all her Majesty's subjects, but in which the venom of hatred of all religion, especially of the Church, is as clearly to be seen as in any of the old penal laws themselves. About forty years ago, it used to be the fashion amongst some of the older members of the Catholic communion in England, to say to their younger and more ardent brethren: What have you to complain of? What is the necessity of Catholic associations, and meetings, etc.? or, "What are you pretending to watch?" But the history of the last forty years, and the tendency of legislation in our own days, must convince (to use one of Lord Brougham's phrases) "the most foolish of our foolish kind" that they were right who took it for granted that the evil spirits would not, as far as their power extended, allow the ways of the renascent Church in England to be the ways of pleasantness and peace. But we must proceed with our history, reserving further remarks suggested by this subject for a future page.

It will be worth while, however, before any further mention of the facts, to consider for a moment what it was that caused the Catholic committee to fail so signally in their work, and to expose themselves to the ignominious defeat I have narrated. We are bound in common gratitude to attribute the failure chiefly to that special Providence which has so clearly watched over us. But of secondary, or instrumental causes, to what can we assign the complete collapse of all the elaborate arrangements of the "Committee of Ten?" They made two practical, and what we may call diplomatic, mistakes. The first mistake was in framing a new oath to be taken by Catholics, instead of the old one which they had taken since the year 1778, when the first Relief Act was passed. In their eagerness to convince Protestants of the falsehood of certain doctrines attributed to us, they wished us to swear to everything that was in the Protestation. And this eagerness induced the committee, as we have seen, to break faith with their fellow-Catholics; for they had given an assurance that no new oath should be proposed. They introduced the new oath, and, thank God! it was the first step to their ruin. The second mistake of the committee was the assurance they felt that the new oath being introduced, every one would sign it who had signed the Protestation. In this they found themselves most completely deceived. So that it might have been said truly of the committee, *Lacum aperuit, et effodit eum: et incidit in foveam, quam fecit.*[1] In speaking of the differences

[1] "He hath opened a pit and dug it: and he is fallen into the hole he made" (Ps. vii. 16).

between the Oath and the Protestation, and which I have specified in a former chapter, Dr. Milner says: "It may be added, with respect to the errors, in general, of the instrument, that conscientious Catholics made a great difference between a declaration made to their fellow-creatures and an oath made to God. Being deluded to believe that all the first characters in the nation understood certain expressions, as the secretary explained them, they thought at first that it was lawful to *subscribe them;* but when the question was *about swearing to the truth of them 'in the plain sense of the words,'* their consciences revolted at the proposal." [1]

To those who interest themselves in matters of this kind, it must always be a matter of great surprise that Charles Butler, whose acquaintance with Catholics of all classes, must have been at least equal to that of any other man in England, should have fallen into these, to him and the committee, fatal mistakes. For it was these two mistakes that enabled Dr. Milner to take up a position which was impregnable, and from which he was able to attack his enemy and put him to the rout. Of some of the other members of the committee we are not so well able to judge; but of Mr. Butler it may be said that he was a man of strong intellectual power, and a logical mind, and though he held strong opinions, and could prosecute them earnestly, yet he was singularly free from prejudice, and was remarkably tolerant of opinions opposed to his own. A man who had the habit of jumping to a conclusion because he desired the conclusion, and one whose prejudices governed his actions, might easily have made the blunders which Butler made on the Catholic Committee; but that he himself should have acted as he did is, at first sight, unaccountable. The only solution

[1] "Supplemental Memoirs," p. 60.

which appears to be at all satisfactory is that which seems to be suggested by the result of his mistake, and by the happy state of freedom in which the Church now is in England. He was in this matter opposed to Providence; and *he had eyes that saw not, and ears that heard not.* And here it may be well to caution any one who may be interested in the matters alluded to in this history, not to judge too hastily of the whole character of Mr. Butler from his action as we have seen it on the committee, and from his subsequent action on the Catholic Board. Though his conduct both on the committee and at the Board must be condemned, yet for other reasons he is entitled to the gratitude of Catholics, and as I hope hereafter to show, he possessed and exercised some qualities in whch he might be taken with advantage as an example.

Two days after the passing of the Relief Bill, that is, on June 9, 1791, a meeting of Catholics took place at the Crown and Anchor Tavern, in the Strand. There were about two hundred gentlemen present. The first business of the meeting was a resolution proposed and seconded, conveying the thanks of the meeting to the committee for their conduct in the affair of the bill. It had been previously arranged at a meeting of the clergy summoned by Dr. Douglas, that an amendment should be proposed to the above resolution. This amendment was for the purpose of including the bishops in the vote of thanks. And it is well worthy of being told, as an example of the fair-mindedness of Milner, that whereas at this meeting of the clergy Dr. Douglas declared his opinion that thanks "could not conscientiously be given to persons who had so long and so violently endeavoured to impose a condemned oath of heterodoxy and schism on the Catholics of England;" Dr. Milner contended "that the committee might properly be thanked for their exertions *in procuring the civil benefits of the Act*, provided the bishops were thanked *for their vigilant zeal in obtaining an orthodox oath.*" Milner's proposal was adopted, and accordingly as soon as the resolution of thanks to the committee had been proposed and seconded at the Crown and Anchor meeting, the Rev. J. Barnard, Dr. Douglas' vicar-general, proposed the amendment agreed upon. Milner seconded the amendment. The chairman, however, refused to put the amendment to the meeting, and persisted in his refusal, though he was continually reminded by Milner "of the established rule of deliberative assemblies, which requires that a proposed amendment of a motion must be disposed of before the original motion itself." According to Dr. Milner, pressure seems to have been used upon the chairman, to force him to act as he did. "Certain gentlemen," writes Milner, "who surrounded the chair insisted upon it that the amendment should not be put to the vote, and accordingly it was not put to them."[1]

The principal object, however, which, according to Milner, the committee had in calling the meeting at the Crown and Anchor, and the only object which Butler mentions in his "Memoirs," was to pass the following resolution :—

[1] The account of this meeting at the Crown and Anchor is taken chiefly from Milner's "Supplementary Memoirs." It is extraordinary that Husenbeth in his "Life of Milner" makes no allusion to the meeting of the clergy summoned by Dr. Douglas, as mentioned in the text. It was, as we have seen, in consequence of Milner's advice that the clergy consented to join in any vote of thanks to the committee. Though Husenbeth mentions that Milner seconded the amendment at the Crown and Anchor meeting, his account of the whole proceeding is so meagre, that he lets pass a grand opportunity of putting into striking contrast the great fairness of his hero, in proposing a vote of thanks to the committee, and the great unfairness of the committee in refusing to thank the bishops. This is only one instance out of many in Husenbeth's "Life of Milner," which have caused it to be so often observed, that the life of Milner has yet to be written.

"That as the oath contained in the Bill for the Relief of English Catholics is not expressed in the words of the Protestation, the English Catholics take this occasion to repeat their adherence to the Protestation, as an explicit declaration of their civil and social principles, and direct the committee to use their endeavours to have it deposited in the Museum, or some other proper place of public institution, that it may be preserved there, as a lasting memorial of their political and moral integrity."

The meeting divided on this resolution, and it was carried by a majority of 32; the numbers being 104 for the resolution, and 72 against it.[1] Mr. Butler accordingly deposited the Protestation in the Museum. He looked upon this as a great triumph, and used frequently for many years after to speak of it as such to his friends. But it was not such a great triumph after all. In the first place, it was and is a matter of great doubt, whether the Protestation deposited in the Museum was the original and identical document which was signed. Butler declared that it was; Milner maintained that it was not, and certainly brought strong proofs to support his assertion. In the second place, the Protestation was, according to those best able to judge, a loosely and inaccurately worded document. The doubt as to its authenticity with the proofs, and the fact of its inaccuracy in several statements, are also recorded in papers which Milner deposited at the Museum. The importance of the document is therefore considerably lessened; in fact, it is not of much value. Its existence in the British Museum need not be a matter of any anxiety to English Catholics.

With regard to the number of Catholics who took the oath prescribed by the Act of 1791, I am not aware that

[1] The majority consisted of twenty-one priests and eighty-three laymen, and the minority of thirty priests and forty-two laymen. The priests in the minority included Bishop Douglas and Bishop Walmesley's deputy, the Rev. Mr. Coombes.

any account has been collected and published. The only allusion to it I have met with, occurs in the debate on Sir J. C. Hippesley's motion in the House of Commons, in March, 1813. Mr. Canning, in his speech on the 11th of March, said, "The hon. baronet" (Sir J. C. Hippesley) "has, with infinite assiduity and industry, collected information that not more than five thousand Catholics had taken the oath prescribed by the last Act passed for the relief of the Roman Catholic body."[1]

I must now put before the reader a short account of the establishment of what was for so many years known amongst Catholics as "the Cisalpine Club." We saw in a former chapter that the Committee of Ten was formed on May 3, 1787, and was to last for five years. The five years terminated on May 2, 1792. But as the services of the committee were no longer required after the passing of the Act of 1791, the committee transacted no further business, and considered themselves virtually dissolved. They determined, however, to preserve in another association the principles and spirit of the old committee, which might still be said to have some existence, as its term had not run out. The leading members of the committee and a few of their friends, to the number of thirteen in all, met on April 12, 1792, at the Freemasons' Tavern, and formed themselves into the Cisalpine Club. The principles of the late committee were to be the principles of the club. Milner says that the professed object of the club was to oppose the alleged usurpation of the Pope, and the tyranny of the Vicars Apostolic.[2] The members themselves expressed one object of the club in these words—"We are determined in all similar situations to resist any ecclesiastical interference, which may militate against the freedom

---

[1] Canning's Speeches, edited by Therry, vol. iii. p. 405.
[2] "Supplementary Memoirs," p. 99.

of English Catholics."[1] The name Cisalpine sufficiently indicates to Catholics the spirit and objects of the club; the title " Cisalpine" being of course chosen as opposed to Ultramontane. A special object of those who formed the club was to educate the young men of the Catholic body in the principles which had guided the committee. This appears in a letter written by one of the "principal founders and patrons of the committee," as quoted by Milner. "The merits of it" (the Protestation), says the writer of the letter, "would soon be frittered away, if the spirit of that Protestation were not preserved by such a meeting, where the young men may continue to support their fathers' principles, who signed the Protestation before they came into the public world."[2] Cardinal Newman, in the second of his most admirable lectures on "The Present Position of Catholics in England," represents "tradition as the sustaining power of the Protestant view," of that view of which fable is the basis, prejudice the life, assumed principles the intellectual ground, and ignorance the protection. The Cisalpine Club was founded in order to begin within the Catholic Church in England an evil tradition of Cisalpine principles, based upon assumed principles, some false, others dangerous, some the offspring of English natural prejudices, others borrowed from unruly foreign Catholics; all protected by ignorance of the Church's rights. And if this tradition could have been preserved, it would have been the cause of great mischief; and would have made the position of English Catholics as unenviable as it is now honourable and respected throughout the world-wide Church.

But the flow of the tradition was soon to be stopped.

[1] Buff Book, p. 23, cited by Milner. The word "similar," means, of course, situations similar to that in which the Committee of Ten had placed themselves.

[2] "Supplementary Memoirs," p. 101.

The Cisalpine Club did indeed continue to exist for many years. During the first few years of its existence it did some mischief, but none which had permanent consequence. And its influence will continually lessen as years flow on. Indeed, it would seem that in proportion as it increased its members, it diminished in Cisalpine principles. It soon ceased to act at all as a body having any influence in Catholic affairs. Catholics who have celebrated their jubilee of life can well remember all the later members of the Cisalpine Club. And it would not be too much to say, that in remembering them, they call to mind men who were remarkable for their respect for Church authority, and who carefully instilled that respect into the hearts and minds of their sons. During the term of office of the last secretary of the Cisalpine Club (who was also the first secretary of the Emancipation Club [1]) no Cisalpine business whatever was transacted.[2] The club soon became a mere dining club, which used to meet three times a year, during the London season, at the Thatched House Tavern.

The Cisalpine Club in its origin never had, nor pretended to have, any representative character. If in the course of years it possessed that character, it was representative only of the laudable desire of English Catholic gentlemen to assemble together occasionally at a friendly and convivial meeting.

Soon after the meeting at the Crown and Anchor Tavern, an attempt was made to bring about a reconcilia-

---

[1] When the Emancipation Bill passed, the Cisalpine Club, chiefly, I believe, at the instance of Mr. Edward Blount, of Bellamore, changed its name to "Emancipation Club."

[2] This secretary was Mr. Charles Turvile, of Gray's Inn, who continued secretary to the Emancipation Club until his untimely death in 1839, he having been an early victim to the dangers of railway travelling. All who can remember him know him to have been a man not only of distinguished honour and virtue, but also one who was remarkable for his respect for authority and submission to ecclesiastical superiors.

tion between the members of the committee and the Vicars Apostolic. This attempt at reconciliation was called at the time "the Mediation." In order that the reader may understand the proceedings connected with the mediation, it will be necessary to make some introductory remarks.

It has been already noticed that one of the clerical members of the Committee of Ten was the Rev. Joseph Wilks. Mr. Wilks signed the *schismatical protest*, and in doing that he put himself in direct opposition to his own bishop, Dr. Walmesley, the venerable Vicar Apostolic of the Western District. Dr. Walmesley was bound in duty to maintain his authority, schismatically attacked by one of his own priests. His lordship accordingly suspended Mr. Wilks "from the exercise of all missionary faculties, and all ecclesiastical functions," in the Western District.

We have already noticed that Milner was assisted in his attack upon the committee by the Rev. Charles Plowden. Mr. Plowden was one of those who at that time were commonly called ex-Jesuits. He had entered the Society before its suppression in the year 1773. He was a powerful writer, and wrote a trenchant "Answer to the Second Blue Book"; that is, the book which contained, amongst other things, the schismatical protest. In this answer, Father Plowden asserted that he wrote at the request of the three Vicars Apostolic, Drs. Walmesley, Douglas, and Gibson. It appears that Father Plowden had consented to write the answer on condition that he alone should be answerable for its contents.

The mediation originated with three Catholic laymen, whom Butler calls, "gentlemen of the highest respectability," and whom Milner calls, "respectable and religious Catholic gentlemen." They were John Webbe Weston, of Sutton Place; Francis Eyre, of Warkworth Castle; and William

Sheldon, of Brailes. These three gentlemen requested the committee to state the grievances of which they complained, and which were obstacles to a reconciliation between themselves and the Vicars Apostolic. The committee mentioned three grievances: (1) "The depriving Mr. Wilks (one of their ecclesiastical colleagues) of his faculties;" (2) "The publishing of the 'Answer to the Second Blue Book,' by the Rev. Charles Plowden, in which the author asserts that he wrote at the request of three Vicars Apostolic," (3) "That the ecclesiastical government of the Catholic bishops in this country is not conformable to the known rules and canons of the Church, by which the clergy of the mission ought to possess the rights of parochial clergy."[1] The mediators then laid this statement of grievances before the bishops. Their lordships answered, in the case of Mr. Wilks that, "if the reverend gentleman under an interdict would express his submission to their decision, they would respectively concur to the removal of it."[2] To the second point—that is, the grievances arising from Father Plowden's pamphlet—"the bishops answered agreeably to the wishes of their advocate, that they had requested the Rev. Charles Plowden to answer the Blue Book, but that if he had written anything amiss, he himself was to answer for it." As to the third grievance—that is, that the missionary clergy were not parish priests—"the bishops contented themselves with saying that they would consider of it."[3] To this last answer, Milner, in his "Supplementary Memoirs," in the page already cited, adds as follows:—"In fact, these lay gentlemen did not understand the ecclesiastical business they had embarked in. They wished our scattered missionaries to be changed into parish priests, before there were any parishes founded for them to govern.

[1] Milner's "Supplementary Memoirs," pp. 97, 98.
[2] Ibid., p. 98.   [3] Ibid., p. 98.

They were *all* of them to be alike *rectors*, without any vicars; like an army of officers without any soldiers! And this to restrain the bishops from deciding doctrinal questions, or at least from censuring those of their clergy who might refuse obedience to their decisions."[1]

When the answer of the bishops in the case of Mr. Wilks, was sent to the committee, and they saw that their lordships required that reverend gentleman's submission to their decision in the matter of the oath before the suspension could be removed, they "unanimously and decidedly rejected" the condition. With regard to the answer of the bishops in Father Plowden's case, Milner makes the following characteristic remark:—"The secretary of the committee had no stomach to come to close quarters, and in such a cause, with the Rev. Charles Plowden."

The three mediators published their proceedings in a book, which, from having a buff covering, was known by the name of the "Buff Book." In justice to the committee, I insert a passage from this book, as quoted by Butler.[2]

"In the course of this negotiation," say the mediators, "we had an opportunity of seeing and laying before three of the Vicars Apostolic, the *original bill* prepared by order of the late committee, and also the *second bill*, with the several alterations, and particularly the variations in the oath, which had been the unfortunate cause of so much difference of opinion. *These were produced, with such incontrovertible evidence that those alterations, and particularly the variations in the oath, were not formed or proposed*

---

[1] The reader interested in this matter would do well to compare Milner's remarks on this subject with an article on "Ecclesiastical Organization," by Cardinal Wiseman, in the *Dublin Review* for August, 1842.

[2] "Historical Memoirs," etc., vol. iv. p. 58. Edition of 1822.

by the gentlemen of the late committee, that we feel ourselves called on, both by candour and impartiality, to declare that we were perfectly convinced that the Vicars Apostolic appeared to us satisfied; and that we really hope no doubts will any longer be entertained on that subject."[1]

The mediators no doubt wished to deal as mercifully as they could with the members of the committee. It was probably proved to them that Lord Stanhope and his friends had framed and proposed the alteration in the oath, and therefore they excused the committee from having originated them. If the Vicars Apostolic appeared satisfied, it must have been only on the question of the origin of the new oath. The report of the mediators does not take anything material from the blame which the committee deserved. The committee had no right to accept the proposal of a new oath. It was their duty to keep faith with their fellow-Catholics, who had been assured that no change should be made in the oath. And when the committee determined upon a change, they should have inserted nothing without the knowledge and consent of the Vicars Apostolic. When the Vicars Apostolic condemned the oath, the committee should have instantly withdrawn it. It is a very small excuse for them to say that they did not originate the oath. In fact, the old saying seems to apply to them—*the receiver is as bad as the thief.*

With the aid only of the published documents connected with this mediation, it is not possible to form a positive judgment as to its precise results. From the extracts I have cited from Milner, it would appear that things remained in a very unsettled state, and that the bones of contention still lay between the two parties. Butler,

[1] The italics are Mr. Butler's; but he does not say whether they were his own, or those of the mediators.

however, leaves a very different impression in the following passage from his account of the mediation. "Thus," he writes, "by the interference of these respectable mediators, and the gentlemanly and Christian disposition of the parties principally engaged in the discussion, the contention was happily terminated; on each side the word of peace was spoken, and silence promised. The peace thus spoken, and the silence thus promised, have been observed inviolate, both by the committee and their adherents, and by the three objecting prelates."[1]

It is clear from Milner's account that the answers of the bishops did not satisfy the committee, and one of their answers the committee absolutely rejected. Still, we cannot but accept what Butler says, writing after thirty years had passed, "The peace was spoken, and observed inviolate." Comparing the two accounts by Milner and Butler, and judging by the light of subsequent history, it would appear that on neither side was any actual concession made; but that the parties to the difference shook hands, and by a sort of tacit agreement said nothing more about the matter.

I cannot conclude this portion of the history without making some reflections on the noble conduct of Father Charles Plowden. Father Plowden, as I have said, was one of those who were commonly called ex-Jesuits. He was born in the year 1743, entered the Society of Jesus, and was thirty years of age at the suppression of the Society in the year 1773. He lived to see the restoration of the Society over the whole world in 1814, and he died in the year 1821, in the seventy-ninth year of his age. He held the highest offices in the Society. On what Dr. Oliver calls "the partial revival of the Society" in the year 1803, he was appointed Novice Master at Hodder

[1] "Historical Memoirs," vol. iv. p. 59.

Place, and later on he was appointed Rector of Stonyhurst College, and Provincial of the English Province. He was a finished scholar and a highly accomplished man; he had great knowledge and experience of the world and of the characters and manners of men. In judging of what Father Plowden did in 1791, he must be judged as a Jesuit, and not as what he, strictly speaking, was at that time, a secular priest. He had been brought up and ordained priest in the Society; and from the time of its suppression he, like so many other faithful men, never allowed his affections to turn away from his first love. He longed and sighed for the restoration of the Society of Jesus. His heart was where his treasure was, in the poverty and obedience of a Religious Order. He thought and spoke and wrote as a Jesuit. When in 1803 he took charge of the novices at Hodder, so far from having lost anything of the spirit of his Order, his high appreciation of it, his love and affection for it, were as great as when he took his first vows at Watten. It may be said of him that the thirty years of his nominally secular life, had deepened in his heart the roots of every virtue and quality which fitted him to be a true son of St. Ignatius. From 1773 to 1803 he preserved unimpaired the traditions of the Society, both in its internal government, and in its relations to the Holy See, to bishops and vicars apostolic, and to all who were not members of the Society. From 1803 these traditions, preserved intact, were the rule of his conduct as Rector, Master of Novices, and Provincial. What Father Plowden did during the days of the Committee of Ten was done by one who must to all intents and purposes be called a Jesuit. I may venture to repeat the words: he thought, he spoke, he wrote as a Jesuit. How, then, did he act? When the Vicars Apostolic were in their utmost need; when their authority was attacked by priests and laymen; when a formidable combination of Catholics rose up to assist a clique of Protestants in forcing schismatical declarations upon the clergy and laity of England, Father Plowden came to the rescue, proved his loyalty to the Church and to the Episcopal Order, and aided nobly in the combat which ended in victory. It derogates nothing from Father Plowden to say that he was second to Milner in the fight. Milner, it appears abundantly clear, was especially raised up by God to be the great leader in the contest. It was a great honour to any man to be what Father Plowden was—the gallant lieutenant of a chosen chief. The honour which Father Plowden won at the end of the last century, the members of the Society of Jesus claim now to share; and they may claim it on the double title, that Father Plowden was a member of the Society, and that he was emphatically a representative man. It is sometimes said that when one individual Jesuit expresses an opinion, it is attributed by the public to the whole body. But if this be a rule which has its exceptions, Father Plowden is not one of those exceptions. In his attack upon the schismatical productions of the second Blue Book, he spoke the opinions of all who, like himself, were waiting to return to their old home. In particular, he spoke and wrote with the full and entire consent of the venerable Father Stone, who, though he could not then be called Provincial, was looked up to by all in Father Plowden's position as a father, and who was in fact the first Provincial of the restored Society in England. To such an extent was Father Plowden what I have called a representative man, that I believe it would not be too much to say that, if the English Fathers of the Society were called upon to name *one* man since the restoration, by whose principles and conduct they would be content to be judged, Father Plowden would be the one named. His action was the action of his brethren at the time he lived, and he has transmitted his spirit to our own days. His support of lawful authority was the support which the English Jesuits gave to the Vicars Apostolic when they wanted the help of any one who could give it.

Father Plowden in after years, as Novice Master and Provincial, was not the man to impart to his successors principles different from his own. He gave and he left a great lesson which he taught both by word and example, and that lesson has never been lost in the English Province of the Society. One sentence of that lesson was, loyalty to every lawfully constituted authority upon earth. It was the lesson handed down to him, and which he faithfully passed on to others: it is a lesson as well understood and acted upon in these days, as when Father Plowden lived. The tradition has its source in the sainted founder, and it is passing through our days full and pure.

As for more than three hundred years the Society of Jesus has, in moral theology, held the balance between the rigorous and the lax, so, in the relations of a Religious Order to the Episcopate, it has always held the balance between an unbending adherence under all circumstances to its privileges, and that weak compliance which would surrender a right to secure a temporary advantage, or win the evanescent smile of patronage. A true Jesuit, like every other true and faithful religious man, would always be ready to *stand by his Order*, and by those privileges which the Holy See, for the general good of the Church, has conferred upon it, in order that its special work may be protected. On the other hand, as it is well known to be the boast of the Society that obedience is the chief virtue inculcated, we may add that no Jesuit has yet been found so far to play the hypocrite, as to flatter himself on his obedience, and exclude from its object any authority which over him has lawful power. As it was at the end of the last century, so it would be now. Though no body of men can be more anxious than members of the Society of Jesus that young Catholic laymen should, in their proper sphere, interest themselves in those affairs which affect the Catholics of England; so no men could be found who would be more ready to warn those young men if they should meddle with matters not within their province. At present it would appear that a spirit of inactivity pervades the mass of those who are almost of age to take their fathers' places. But should there be a reaction from this state of inactivity, and should the reaction take a line—which God forbid—opposed to ecclesiastical authority, the bishops of England would see in these days what they saw in days gone by, the Society of Jesus in the front rank of those who would stand up to support them.

Before passing on from this portion of the history of English Catholics during the last hundred years, I must mention the establishment of another Catholic club, the existence of which is not even alluded to in Butler's " Historical Memoirs," but about which we find a few words in the " Supplementary Memoirs " of Dr. Milner. Milner's account is headed THE ROMAN CATHOLIC MEETING; and what he writes about it is verbatim as follows :—

"The notorious anti-Catholic spirit of the Cisalpine Club caused another club to be formed under the above-mentioned title, in effecting which the respectable mediators named above were mainly instrumental. The first meeting was held and the eighteen rules of it settled at the Crown and Anchor Tavern, on May 1, 1794, when the following members of it were present: Bishop Douglas, the Lords Newburgh, Stourton, Arundell, and Clifford; the Baronets Fleetwood, Jerningham, Blount, and Haggerston, with about forty other respectable gentlemen. The greatest hopes of general benefit to the Catholic religion and the Catholic cause were conceived from the continuance of this Society; but owing to some mismanagement or jealousy which the writer has not fully discovered, it fell to pieces in the course of a very few years."[1]

This is the only published account, as far as I know, which has ever appeared of the Club, which Milner calls the Roman Catholic Meeting. It is interesting in several respects. As according to Milner the mediators were mainly instrumental in forming the club, it would seem that they were so dissatisfied with the spirit of the Cisalpine Club, and consequently of the Committee of Ten, that they considered it advisable to form another club to counteract the evil. The words "forty other respectable gentlemen," written by Milner, most probably mean forty men of well-known Catholic families. These forty, along with four peers and four baronets, make up a considerable party—indeed, a very large party of Catholics in those days. This shows that the Cisalpine Club was very far from representing the Catholics of England. It is also a matter of interest to know the names of some, at least, of those families who were opposed to the ideas and proceedings of those who formed the Cisalpine Club. We have also to notice with regret, in Milner's short account of the new club, the cause of its failure after a few years. Mismanagement and jealousy ruined it, and in ruining it destroyed the hopes of those who looked to it for general benefit to the Catholic religion and the Catholic cause. Mismanagement and jealousy have destroyed many a good work amongst the Catholics of the British Isles since the time of which I am writing. The fault of mismanagement and the passion of jealousy are perhaps the two evils which most commonly prevent a combination of men from learning wisdom by experience.

[1] "Supplementary Memoirs,' p. 101.

CHAPTER VIII.

THE RECEPTION OF THE FRENCH CLERGY AND OF THE ENGLISH COMMUNITIES IN ENGLAND.

The French clergy—Letter of the Bishop of St. Pol de Léon—English Communities abroad—Douay and St.Omer's—The Benedictine dames of Brussels —The providence of God over the Church in England—Mean action of some Cisalpines—Kindness of the royal family to the religious—George III. and the Taunton nuns—The Prince Regent and the Princethorpe nuns.

WE now come to that time in which I have to recount one of the grandest acts of national charity which the world has ever witnessed. And it was national in the fullest and best sense of the word. An act may be called national if it be done by the Parliament or by the governing power in a country, whatever that power may be. But still a Parliament might pass a measure which would be national inasmuch as the Parliament is representative, but which would not be national inasmuch as the great body of the people might sympathize little or not at all in the act. In the matter I am going to speak of, the people of England individually, and collectively in Parliament, threw themselves heart and soul into the good deed.

The reader will readily understand that I allude to the reception in England of the French clergy and the twice-exiled British communities who were expelled from France during the great Revolution, and who found a home in the British Isles. It was a grand act of charity;

grand in the number relieved, and in the amount of the relief, grand in the motive by which it was prompted, and, let us add, grand in the reward which it received. In giving credit to our countrymen for their magnificent act, we must not forget that its value was enhanced by the promptness with which, in time of necessity, all religious rancour and hatred were sunk in the desire to succour the oppressed.

The expulsion of the clergy and religious seems to have been timed most providentially for England. They began to arrive on our shores in the year 1792, the year after the passing of the Relief Act of 1791. This Act had legalized the Catholic religion in England, and there had been no reaction from the liberal spirit in which the measure had been conceived. If in the minds of some, a protest against the French revolutionists constituted along with charity a mixed motive for benevolence, the desire of making a protest was certainly not the dominant motive in what was done. France did not declare war against England until February, 1793, and therefore the favour shown by England to the French Catholics was not the result of feelings of animosity engendered by war. The relief given by England to the exiled French was a work of almost pure benevolence. England never regretted the good work of those days; and glories in it to the present time. Amongst Catholics there seems to have been from the beginning, and there is now, a universal impression that the reception of the French clergy by our Protestant fellow-countrymen has brought, as its reward, many blessings upon the country.[1]

On August 19, 1792, the decree for the transportation

---

[1] Often as I have heard this subject mentioned, I never remember to have heard it spoken of without the accompanying expressed conviction that it must have brought a great blessing from Heaven.

of all priests who would not take the revolutionary oath passed the French Legislative Assembly. On the 2nd of September began the atrocious massacres of priests in the prisons of Paris. Then followed another decree of transportation, and the flight to England began. Well may the writer in the *Catholic Directory* for the year 1794 say: "1792 and 1793 will be ever remarkable in the annals of time. Amidst the various nations which have afforded an asylum and succour to the French clergy whom a strict adherence to their religion has exiled from their native soil, England, beyond a doubt, must have the pre-eminence for generosity and compassion. During the course of September and October, 1792," says the writer, " more than six thousand clergymen were received in either England, Jersey, or Guernsey; nor was it long before the number was augmented to eight thousand. Great Britain has proportioned her munificence to the number of the suffering objects. By the benevolence of Government, the Royal Palace at Winchester has been fitted up in order to accommodate some of them with lodging and other necessaries, without expense. Already more than six hundred and sixty are provided for there. The nation at large has opened a subscription, and every parish has contributed its part; the amount of which in August, 1793, was £67,000, and at the same epoch four thousand eight hundred of these suffering exiles were supported by it. We might also mention," continues the same writer, "£10,000, the donations of some charitable but nameless individuals, without even taking notice of the succours several of them have received in private families, where they have been caressed almost like children of their own."

Dr. Milner says that there were one thousand of the clergy in the King's House at Winchester; and as he was living in that city at the time, his number is probably correct.

The private collections for the exiled priests and laymen were set on foot, and earnestly prosecuted, by the great Edmund Burke. Burke also established a school for the education of the sons of the French noblemen who shared the fate of the non-juring priests.[1] The University of Oxford printed a fine edition of the Vulgate New Testament and presented a copy to each one of the French priests who desired to have one. The acts of kindness to the *émigrés*, as they were called at the time, were universal over the whole kingdom. But the crowning act of charity was the grant by the House of Commons, on the proposal of William Pitt, of an annuity of £20 a year to each one of the exiles. This gift they continued to receive so long as they remained in England and had need of the bounty. In order to make the money they received go further, many of the priests used to live together in a kind of community life.[2]

A considerable number of these were employed by the Vicars Apostolic to work in missions where the number of English priests was not sufficient. Some of them were sent to be chaplains in private houses where the inmates from having been educated abroad were well acquainted with the French language. And as the *émigrés* themselves became able to speak English, they began new missions in various parts of the country.[3] A large number of the

---

[1] One of the French noblemen educated in this school was the Marquis de Lys, the father of the late Marquis Francis de Lys, whom many remember with affection.

[2] A considerable number of the priests and also of the laymen congregated in the suburb of London called Somerstown. A Catholic who was living at the time told the author that the development of this suburb was chiefly owing to the number of priests who resided there.

[3] If any one would undertake to make a list of the missions in England which were begun by the French *émigrés*, it would be an interesting contribution to the history of the Church in England during the last hundred years.

priests helped to support themselves by teaching the French language, some in schools, others in private families. They were often engaged for this purpose by both Catholics and Protestants.[1]

Catholics who well remembered those times used to say that the dispersion of the French clergy amongst the aristocracy of England helped in a very great degree to soften the bitterness against the Church which at that time prevailed. This effect was produced by the high principles, the blameless conduct, and the polished manners of the guests. The reader will no doubt be pleased to read an account of the French clergy which was written many years ago by an English Catholic, who was born in the middle of the last and who lived until very near the middle of the present century.[2]

Mr. Browne Mostyn says: " Having myself inhabited France full thirty years with but short absences, and having seen and frequented clergy society during that time both in the north and south of France, and mixed in society with all ranks, I believe no Englishman can more fairly than myself assume to give an opinion, which at your request, I will give with pleasure and as strict adherence to truth as conviction will allow me to do. . . . I will begin with the bishops ; . . . they were almost all men of high rank in society, all having had the best education, and mostly men of great information. Their opulence, high connections, and distinguished rank in society, induced most of them to repair a great deal to Paris and about court, unfortunately and improperly, but their dioceses were not for that neglected, but governed during their absence by able *grand-*

---

[1] The late Sir Robert Peel, amongst many others, received his earliest lessons in French from an *émigré* priest.

[2] This was the late Charles Browne Mostyn, of Kiddington. The extract which appears in the text is from a manuscript which was never printed, and which was written at the request of Miss Turvile, of Bosworth Hall.

vicaires as administrators for them. That some of them led worldly lives cannot be denied, but, with *very few exceptions indeed*, I did not hear of anything like vice or dissolute conduct laid to their charge. In the great day of trial at the Revolution, when called upon by the Assemblée Nationale to take the obnoxious civil oath, or to forfeit their rich benefices, on the day appointed they appeared at the bar, and when called nominally to take the oath, out of one hundred and twenty-four Bishops, only three conformed; Talleyrand was one, the Bishop of Orleans another, and one whose name I forget, but who was notoriously deranged. All the others forfeited voluntarily their livings and exposed themselves to finish their lives by the guillotine or in exile, ending their days in beggary and want. So fine an example is not to be found in all ecclesiastical history. How very different was the conduct of our English bishops on a similar trying occasion, when *one only*, Fisher of Rochester, remained steady to his duty! The conduct of the French bishops was so magnanimous as to force from their most powerful enemy, Mirabeau, then present, that honourable testimony: "La force et les bayonettes sont pour nous; mais ma foi, l'honneur est pour eux!" The *curés* and *vicaires* and parochial clergy throughout France were a most respectable and, generally speaking, respected body, always at their posts, constantly and daily employed in their duties and those duties very hard, as in the constant exercise at their churches, morning and evening, their confessionals, visiting the sick, administering the sacraments, catechising, etc. They were poorly provided for ... To say that among such an immensely numerous body of clergy there were not some solitary examples of misconduct of some kind or other cannot be expected. But, indeed, such examples were unaccountably rare. Whenever they occurred the bishops took cognizance of it and the usual punishment was confinement in the seminary for months or years, according to the gravity of the case."

Such, then, according to the testimony of one who knew them well, were the French secular clergy. Such were the men, eight thousand of whom found a home in the British Isles, and were hospitably entertained for several years. The great body of them remained the honoured guests of the English, uutil the ratification of the Concordat by Pope Pius VII., August 15, 1801, and the solemn re-establishment of the public exercise of Catholic worship in France on Easter Sunday of the following year, enabled them to return to France. Many of them, however, remained in England, and died on the missions they had founded. The gratitude of the French clergy was equal to the generosity of the English nation. Two expressions of heartfelt thanks, I will put before the reader. The first was that of Louis XVI. on the scaffold. We read in the *Laity's Directory* for the year 1796, the following short but touching account:

"In 1793, Louis XVI. of France, having been perfidiously condemned to an ignominious death by a portion of his own subjects, and having chosen for his confessor, to assist him in his last moments, the Rev. Mr. Edgeworth, an Irish priest, who performed this heroical duty in the prison of the Temple and upon the scaffold at the imminent risk of his life, His Majesty inquired of him what was become of his faithful clergy: when upon learning that a considerable portion of them had found an asylum in England, he expressed his most lively emotions of gratitude towards His Majesty and the English people."

The other expression of gratitude is so grand and consoling that though the extract is somewhat long, the reader will easily forgive its length. It is contained in a letter of the Right Rev. John Francis de la Marche, Bishop of St. Pol de Léon, addressed to the French clergymen refugees in England, and translated into English from the original French.

"Let us admire the all-wise ways of Divine Providence, which, to prepare us an asylum in this place, disposed the British legislation to adopt a system of toleration very different from that which prevails in our unhappy country, a toleration which on our arrival opened chapels for the public practice of religious worship, and altars prepared to receive our devotion and the Victim we are permitted to present to the Eternal Father in thanksgiving for His favours, while we call down His mercies on those through whose hands we receive them. Let us, then, take advantage of this liberty; let us hasten to these altars, these sanctuaries; let us pour forth the effusions of our gratitude; let us join in prayer with the pious natives who edify us by their fervour and the constancy of their faith; let us conjure our Lord to bestow His blessings on the nation at large, according to the measure of our obligations; let us beseech Him to turn away the fatal principles which are inconsistent with the tranquillity of government, and that He would send His guardian angels to secure the throne of its kings; let us beg of Him that He will be graciously pleased to preside over that august senate, the representatives of the people, the interpreters of its wishes and wants, the defenders of its rights, the oracle of its duties, in their important deliberations, where the interests of nations are discussed, the weighty concerns of peace, war, commerce, finance, and everything which concerns the public welfare, is debated with wisdom and eloquence; let us entreat our God to direct their councils in framing laws to be sanctioned by the King, and in adopting measures that may bring prosperity to the kingdom. May union ever prevail among the different parts which compose the British Empire, and continually give additional strength and energy to its power and greatness. May England be a stranger to civil discord and anarchy, which must be fatal to the commerce, the prosperity, and liberty of her subjects.

"May Heaven, attentive to our prayers, grant peace and plenty to a country where we are so hospitably entertained. May every revolving year give an increase to the harvest of a people so ready to share it with the unfortunate. May the Ruler of the winds and seas guide their vessels, and enrich them with the treasures of the East and of the West. May England exhibit to all other nations the picture of perfect happiness, as she has held up to them the model of Christian benevolence."[1]

When we consider that this prayer for our country was drawn from grateful hearts by a really grand act of national charity, it is difficult not to believe that the great temporal and spiritual blessings which England has received since the prayer was uttered, are its fruit. It is now ninety-three years since the French clergy found an asylum in England. France cannot be said to have been in a settled state ever since that time. In the turmoil of contending factions a party is now in the ascendant which has in that country renewed against the Church the violent measures of the early days of the Revolution. The bishops and secular clergy have been hitherto let alone; but almost all the religious orders of men have been proscribed, and the members of one order, numbering several thousands, have been expelled from their country. Many of them have again found refuge in England. In 1792 the French clergy were received in this country with open arms; in 1880 they were received with a respectful silence. The expulsion of the Jesuits is not a new sign of new times—it is the old sign that things are in a bad state on the other side of the Straits of Dover. But the kind of reception they have met with here is a new sign. Let those study it and learn a lesson from it who love their country and their religion.

The decrees of the legislative assembly promulgated in the year 1792, affected only French subjects. The houses

[1] The letter from which the above is an extract is dated "London, December 30, 1792," and was published by Coghlan in the following year.

of the religious, both men and women, who were British subjects remained for a few months unmolested. These houses had been established abroad in consequence of the penal laws which forbade their existence in Great Britain and Ireland. The two principal houses belonging at the time of the French Revolution to the English secular clergy, were the celebrated colleges of Douay and St. Omer's. Douay had always belonged to the seculars. It was commenced by Cardinal Allen in the year 1568, and during the course of its existence, which lasted for two hundred and twenty-five years, it "produced one cardinal, two archbishops, thirty-one bishops and bishops elect, three arch-priests, about one hundred doctors of divinity, one hundred and sixty-nine writers, many eminent men of religious orders," and what was its greatest glory, "one hundred and sixty martyrs, besides innumerable others, who either died in prison or suffered confinement or banishment for their faith."[1] The College of St. Omer's was a college of the Jesuit Fathers. It was founded by the illustrious Father Persons in the year 1594, exactly two hundred years before the commencement of the now famous College of Stonyhurst. It remained in the hands of those to whom it belonged for a hundred and sixty-eight years, that is, until the year 1762, when the power of hell, which cannot prevail against the whole Church, was permitted to prevail against that portion of the Church, and no mean portion of the Church, formed by the Society of Jesus in the kingdom of France. The dissolution of the society in France was, in the usual order of such things, followed by robbery, and the College of St. Omer's was handed over by the Parliament of Paris, which had seized it, to the secular clergy of England. They kept it until

---

[1] "Notices of English Colleges and Convents," by the Hon. Edward Petre.

the Revolution, when they in turn were robbed of it by the infidel.[1]

Of the houses of the English regular clergy in France in the year 1793, perhaps the most celebrated was the Benedictine priory at Douay, the origin of which dates (according to Mr. Petre) from the year 1605. In this college was continued, in unbroken succession, the old English presidency of the Benedictine order, the oldest presidency, I believe, in the world. There was also a Benedictine priory at Paris, and a convent of Franciscan Recollects at Douay.

Of religious houses of women there were in France, at the time I am writing about, the Canonesses of St. Augustin at Paris, a Benedictine abbey at Paris, a Benedictine abbey at Dunkirk, a convent of the Poor Clares at Gravelines, a convent of the same order at Dunkirk, a convent of the same order at Aire, a convent of the same order at Rouen, and the nuns of the Conception, or Blue Nuns, at Paris.

Having thus mentioned our English establishments in France, I must now proceed to the march of events in that country. On the 1st of February, 1793, the National Convention declared war against England. On the 10th of October in the same year, the National Convention issued a decree by which the subjects of his Britannic Majesty in France were stripped of their property and imprisoned. The alleged reason for this atrocious measure I will give in the words of Dr. Coombes, in his narrative

---

[1] Alban Butler was the second secular president of St. Omer's. Charles Butler, in his life of his uncle says, "On his being named to the presidency of the English college at St. Omer's, doubts were suggested to him, on the justice or propriety of his accepting the presidency of a college, which, in fact, belonged to others. He advised with the Bishop of Amiens and the Bishop of Boulogne upon this point, and they both agreed in opinion that he might safely accept it."

of his own escape from Douay.[1] "The pretext which served to cloak this inhuman proceeding was the supposed indignity shown to the French nation in the person of Beauvais, one of the representatives of the people. This man was said to have been put to death by the English at Toulon, and, as Barrère stated in his report to the Convention, not to have suffered like a freeman, but to have been hanged like a slave. After the recapture of Toulon, Beauvais was 'found alive and in good health.' It then appeared that his conduct had exposed him to the resentment of his countrymen, and that he had been indebted for his safety to the generous protection of the British officers. Impressed with the noble behaviour of the enemies of his country, he set off for Paris, with a full determination to make known the humanity of the English towards him, but he was despatched on the road by the secret orders of the Committee of Public Safety." Men who could commit so cowardly a murder were fit instruments to carry out the decree of the 10th of October. Two days after the promulgation of the decree, namely, "on the 12th of October, the College of Douay (writes Mr. Petre) was seized by the French, and its inmates were conveyed prisoners to the citadel of Dourlens. There they remained until the 24th of November, 1794, when they obtained permission to return to Douay, being twenty-six in number. They were still prisoners in the Irish College, but under less restraint. In the following February they were set at liberty, and arrived in England on the 2nd of March, 1795.

"The College of St. Omer's was also seized in consequence of the decree of the 10th of October, and its members were imprisoned at Arras. In May, 1794, they were sent as prisoners to Dourlens. From Dourlens they

[1] *Laity's Directory* for the year 1800.

were sent back to St. Omer's and confined in the French College. In 1795 they were set at liberty, and returned to England."[1]

It would occupy too much of the history to follow the fortunes of those Religious Houses of English subjects which I have mentioned above. Suffice it to say that, after enduring imprisonment, privations, insults, and threats of death, these communities, some of them with numbers diminished by persecution, found their way to England during the years 1794 and 1795.

We have seen that the forced emigration of the French clergy and many of the laity from France to England was caused by the decree of the Legislative Assembly on the 19th of August, 1792; and that the seizure of the persons and property of the English secular and regular establishments in France, and their arrival at last in England, were brought about by the decree of the National Convention of the 10th of October, 1793. In the following year, 1794, the success of the French revolutionary forces in Belgium caused the flight to England of the English religious houses which had been established in that country. These religious houses were many and famous. Of the religious houses of men there were the barefooted Carmelites at Tongres— who lived in a house which had belonged to the Jesuit Fathers up to the time of the suppression of their Order— the Dominican Convent and College at Bornheim, near Antwerp, the Dominican College at Louvain, and the College of the Jesuit Fathers of Liege. The reader may ask how it was that the Jesuit Fathers could possess a house in the year 1794, when their Order was suppressed in the year 1773, and not restored until the year 1814. It happened in this way; and as the story cannot be told better than it has already been by Dr. Oliver, I will quote

[1] "Notices of English Colleges," by the Hon. Edward Petre.

his words. Father John Howard was the last rector of the Liege College before the suppression. He "saw the suppression of his house on the 9th of September, 1773. After the dissolution of the Society the Prince of Liege restored the house to this Father John Howard, and under the name of "The Academy," it served as a place of education for the English Catholic gentry, as well as a seminary for ecclesiastics. Father Howard presided over the new establishment until his death, 16th of October, 1783. He was succeeded by Father William Strickland, a man of superior merit, who, after introducing some considerable improvements, delivered up the government to Father Marmaduke Stone. This last respected and conciliating Superior continued in office until the final emigration to Stonyhurst."[1]

After the bull of Pope Clement XIV., the Academy at Liege could not strictly be called a Jesuit establishment, but, if the expression may be allowed, it was as much like one as it could well be. The Dominicans of Bornheim, after their arrival in England, settled first at Carshalton in Surrey, and established a school there in 1795. In the year 1810 they removed from Carshalton to Hinckley, in Leicestershire. In the year 1852, when the Passionist Fathers left Woodchester, Mr. Leigh, the founder of the church and adjoining convent, presented both to the Dominican Fathers. The first prior of Woodchester was Father Proctor, so well known for many years in the midland counties as the superior at Hinckley.

The convents of religious women in Belgium which were compelled to break up when the country was invaded by the French, were the Canonesses of S. Augustine at

[1] "Historical Catechism," chiefly relating to the English Province of the Society, p. xi. Mr. George Clifford, the father of the present Sir Charles Clifford, was the last student at Liege; accompanying the Fathers in their emigration, he became the first student at Stonyhurst.

Louvain; a convent of the same Order at Bruges; the Canonesses of the Holy Sepulchre at Liege; the Benedictine Abbeys of Brussels, Cambray, and Ghent; the nuns of the Third Order of St. Francis at Bruges; a convent of Dominicanesses at Brussels; and convents of Teresian or Carmelite nuns at Antwerp, Lierre, and Hoogstraet. There were other English communities on the Continent at the time of the French Revolution; but as they did not return to England I have not mentioned them.

There is a circumstance connected with the arrival in England of one of the communities, which will no doubt interest the reader. The Benedictine dames of Brussels dated their beginning from the year 1587, when they were founded by Mary Piercy, daughter of the Earl of Northumberland, Dorothy and Gertrude Arundell, Jane Berkley, daughter of Sir John Berkley, of Baverstone, and several other English ladies. There was "a constant prevailing opinion in this community, said to be founded on ancient predictions, that as this was the first entire religious establishment of our nation, that was founded on the Continent, so they should be the first of this kind that should return to their native country. Certain it is," says the account from which I take this, "that this event, contrary to all expectations and appearances, has taken place. They did not leave their house at Brussels until June 22," 1794, "when passing on to Antwerp, they arrived at Rotterdam the 26th; embarking from thence July 2nd, they landed at St. Catherine's Stairs early on the 6th of the same month, where they met with the utmost humanity and respect even from the lowest ranks of Englishmen."[1] The community to which the above refers was that whose successors are now established at East Bergholt in Suffolk.

[1] *Laity's Directory* for the year 1795, from an article continued in the *Directory* for the years 1796 and 1797, and signed J. M. (John Milner).

And so, the English colleges and religious communities which had been founded in France and Belgium, came at last to their own country. There is something so wonderfully providential in this event that it cannot be dismissed with a mere mention. But it is only one link in a chain of events, which seem evidently to prove that the Almighty has a special care for this land of ours, and that we have every reason to hope that the Church in England is advancing in a triumphant march. Our history during the last hundred years shows in a remarkable manner how the Providence of God makes use of the political necessities of nations and the changes in Empires, to bring about the glory of the Son of God and the victory of His Spouse upon earth. This appears very clearly in the events which happened in consequence of the revolt of our American Colonies, and of the breaking out of the French Revolution. We have seen that political motives chiefly induced the British Legislature to relax the penal laws. The want of troops to send to America, and subsequently to defend our own shores, led naturally to a desire to unite as much as possible all the subjects of George III. A less active hatred of the Church in the hearts of the majority of the people, a strong sense of the injustice of the penal laws in the minds of many influential statesmen, also contributed to make the time favourable for acts of relief. It is a most remarkable coincidence that the first Act of practical relief should have been passed the year before the French clergy were driven to our shores, and only two years before our own exiles began to return. Had there been no expulsion of our communities from France, and had they simply taken advantage of the Act of 1791 to come over to England in a body, it is very doubtful how they would have been received. The liberality which caused the bill to be introduced might have been exhausted when the

Act had been passed. Before the Jews were admitted into Parliament, many people used to say they would vote that a Jew might be elected, but would certainly never vote for a Jew themselves. And so, many Englishmen might have voted that Catholics might open schools, and religious orders exist in England; and yet would not have been prepared to see St. Omer's, Douay, and Liege come immediately to England, and scores of religious in various convents forthwith recommence the work which had been destroyed at the Reformation.

It is very improbable indeed that the liberality of the time would have been enough to make our countrymen take an invasion of Catholic religious communities much more calmly than an invasion of soldiers from the Continent. Providence came to our aid, or rather so governed events, that the actual arrival of the colleges and the religious orders was celebrated with a more popular reception than the passing of the Act of 1791 itself. As the minds of the English had been prepared to pass the Act by political motives; so the kind reception which the communities received here was mainly due to the base and tyrannical motives which caused their expulsion from France and Belgium.

There is in the English people a strong tendency to sympathize with those who suffer unjustly, and to run to the succour of the oppressed. The conduct of the French Government roused and put in active motion this natural characteristic of our countrymen. Hence this great natural virtue of compassion supplied whatever might have been wanting of religious toleration, and Protestants vied with Catholics in welcoming communities, which made England far more Catholic than it was before. Political motives, national vices and national virtues, were all instruments in the hands of God. What had been flung away from England by the Reformation was thrown back again from France by the Revolution. The virtue of the English, under the command of God, was more than a match for the vice of the French, and a victory was won for the Church. Just at the moment when Englishmen were best prepared to sanction it, the Church resumed its normal condition in England. This was a great blessing in store from all eternity for a country in which God had once been well served.

In the first chapter of this history I classed under three heads the active agencies which have brought about so wonderful a change in the Church in England during the last hundred years. Under the first head was comprised all that has been done by English Catholics themselves. And here must be included all that has resulted from the return of the English communities: for the preservation of these communities abroad until the appointed time, was essentially the work of English Catholics. The good that has resulted from the presence of our institutions is enormous. Before the Act of 1791 and the French Revolution, the Church was in a decaying state. It had just been in its worst days, with no prospect of better things. It was a Church without schools and without religious orders.[1] It is impossible to deny that the existence in England of Oscott, Stonyhurst, Old Hall, Ushaw, Downside, and Ampleforth, have in many respects been of the greatest advantage to religion. If none of them have yet attained the reputation of old Douay and St. Omer's, they have at any rate, in their steady advance towards being schools of the first order, shown what the vitality of the Church is, when she sets to work under almost every conceivable obstacle.

[1] Two or three schools of a secondary order existed, and one religious community, namely that at York.

Then as to the return of the religious orders, their presence has made a great change in the state of the Church in England. If a religious order be curtailed of its privileges, or be thwarted in its own proper work, the effect is that of maiming one of the limbs of the Church. But the Church in a country where there are no religious orders, is in a state which may be compared to paralysis; it would be difficult to preserve in the body even a *scintilla* of life; and life would gradually become extinct. It may be said that the Church in Ireland is a proof to the contrary. But Ireland is an exceptional case. Religion in Ireland was, under God, preserved as it was in the first three centuries of the Church by the strength of faith undergoing a continual persecution. In England faith gave way before persecution, and at the time I am writing about, there were probably not a hundred thousand Catholics, including the Irish, in the country. There has always been in England a tendency to nationality in Church government. Religious orders, besides constituting the *state* of perfection, and besides the special good which each order does by prayer and good works, bind a church more closely to the successor of St. Peter; they do this in the very origin of their constitution, by their position in the Church, and by their well known loyal devotion to the Holy See. If the religious houses had not returned to England when they did, there is some reason to think that Church government in England would either have fallen under lay domination, or assumed a national character which would have dimmed the glory of its resurrection. The grand spirit of Milner was strong in the land no doubt, but it had formidable adversaries, and it might not have remained always in the ascendant.

And what I have said above of our colleges, I may say of our convents. New Hall, Taunton, Stanbrook,

East Bergholt, and Oulton, better known as Caverswall, represent well-nigh three hundred years of education of Catholic girls, an education which did so much to preserve the faith in England during the dark days of persecution, and which many a man has blessed in its fruits up to the present day. Long may our old convents live; and long may they hand down the memories of bygone days, and the spirit which inspired their first foundation.[1]

Let us thank God that He so disposed of events as to restore our colleges and convents to us, and let us hope and pray that they may all long flourish, the pride and the boast of English Catholics.

The general welcome which was accorded to the religious houses which were driven to England by the French Revolution had a few exceptions, but these exceptions only tended to mark the generous spirit of the great bulk of the English people. Milner, after stating that none contributed more cheerfully to the relief of the communities than the Established clergy, says, "The only persons who did not partake of this benevolent spirit were the Jacobins of England, a few bigots among the Dissenters, and certain Catholic Cisalpines."[2] Following Milner's account of this portion of our history, he says that

[1] The reader who is not sufficiently acquainted with the history of our convents may perhaps be surprised not to see the name of Princethorpe mentioned with the rest. The reason is that this account refers only to the return of those convents which were of English origin. Princethorpe was of French origin. The community was expelled from France at the time the French clergy were expelled. From the time of its arrival in this country in 1792, up to the present day, this community has educated a large number of girls of the best families of Great Britain and Ireland, and so from companionship in exile, and the thoroughly English as well as Catholic education it has given, has earned the same gratitude from us as the other convents have, and in honourable mention can never be separated from them.

[2] The reader must always distinguish, especially in the writings of Dr. Milner, between the acts of the Cisalpine Club and the acts of members of that club in their individual capacity. The club did not act in the matter of the Religious mentioned in the text.

"a great leader of the club wrote to a venerable character (who could not but disapprove of his sentiments), under date of September 8, 1794, 'What a quantity of nuns, monks, and friars are arrived! What is to be done with them? It is well worthy of the consideration of the Vicars Apostolic how far it is advisable, safe, and prudent to encourage their establishment; how far we are bound by our oath, by our honour, not to connive at a wilful transgression of our Act of Parliament.'" So that while the whole nation, with hardly an exception, was forgetting any penal law that might still exist against religious orders, and was anxious only to gratify the yearnings of a noble British spirit, these few Catholics of the Cisalpine Club were meanly raking up the old and bad laws, and parading a hypocritical spirit of loyalty, to cover their dislike to religious orders. This bad leaven amongst the English Catholics, which, thank God, was not destined to corrupt the whole mass, had however some effect amongst the Protestants. As this disagreeable subject has come naturally in its turn, I may as well follow it to the end and have done with it. This cannot better be done than in the words of Milner. After quoting the words of the letter from the Cisalpine, he continues as follows: "When it is known that Catholics of power were thus disposed in regard of the most inoffensive, the most pure and pious, and the most *useful*[1] description of English Catholics, next to the officiating clergy, it is easy to account for a circumstance which took place respecting them in 1800. A religious controversy had taken place in one of the cathedral cities between a prebendary and the Catholic pastor of that city, in which the latter, owing to the advantage of his cause, was allowed to have had greatly

---

[1] "Allusion is here made to the virtuous and religious education given by the ladies to the youth of their own sex."

the advantage.[1] In this posture of affairs, it was resolved on by the worsted party to have recourse to Parliament for an Act to annoy the Catholics, though it was not settled on which side to attack them. At one time it was intended to lay restraints on the French clergy, some of whom had been actually sent out of the kingdom for making converts, but at length it was resolved on to torment the poor nuns, by putting them under a species of *Alien Act.* Accordingly a bill was brought into the House of Commons for this purpose, and, as it was at first countenanced by the minister, it seemed sure of succeeding.[2] At length, however, being opposed by Messrs. Sheridan, Hobhouse, Windham, etc., it became weaker and more relaxed in every stage of its progress, and was likely to be totally lost, when the first-mentioned member proclaimed to the Commons that, 'a compromise had taken place.' Accordingly the bill met with no further opposition among them, though, after all its changes, it was still in such a state that, as O'Leary said in his excellent pamphlet on the subject,[3] 'The ladies would say of it, "Send us back to the French guillotines rather than subject us to the conditions proposed in the bill."' The fact is, Mr. Sheridan, who was extremely intimate with the Cisalpines in question, never doubted of their being authorized to make terms for the poor recluses; and, to give a colour to such a pretence, they had actually written to them for their certificates and other documents, with a promise of protecting them. The upshot of the business was, a real friend of theirs informed them that they were betrayed, and advised them to throw themselves on the humanity of the House of Lords, without any Cisalpine

---

[1] The Catholic pastor was, of course, Milner himself.
[2] This bill was brought into the House by Sir Henry Mildmay.
[3] "Remarks on Sir Henry Mildmay's Bill."

interference whatever.[1] This they did, and the bill was 'quashed at once.'"[2]

Religious orders will always have enemies—they will have them both inside and outside the fold. No sooner did they take their place again in England, after nearly three centuries of proscription and exclusion, than they found enemies, few in number indeed, but active in their evil work, and amongst Catholics as well as Protestants. Whenever these enemies appear, and wheresoever they appear, may they be always crushed, as they were crushed in the year 1800, by the resistance of the great majority of Catholics, backed by the fairness and chivalrous sentiment of the English people. But if ever any English Catholics, in their dislike of religious orders, should so far lose the true spirit of their religion, and should be so tainted with Erastianism as to congratulate themselves that some religious orders are still under the ban of the law, let them also congratulate themselves that they must trace back their descent up to the shabby half-dozen Cisalpines, who, at the beginning of this century, brought discomfiture and disgrace upon themselves by the mean conduct which has just been put before the reader.

It is pleasing to turn from this unworthy conduct of a few Catholics to the conduct of the English royal family in regard of the communities expelled from France and Belgium. It is a remarkable thing that George III. and his sons, though some of them were most bitter opponents of the Catholic claims, always showed, not merely civility and politeness, but extreme kindness, in their personal relations with Catholics.

[1] Who this real friend was Milner does not say, but there can be little doubt that it was himself. He loved religious orders, he hated Cisalpinism, and could spot a traitor quicker than any other Catholic in England.

[2] The friends of the nuns might have exclaimed, as Cobbett once exclaimed, and as we may exclaim now, "Thank God, we have a House of Lords."

The determination of the old King himself not to consent to our complete emancipation is well known. George IV. was in 1829 inclined to be quite as obstinate as his father, and but for the influence of the Duke of Wellington and Sir Robert Peel, might have refused his consent to the great Act. The Duke of York, as is well known, also took a solemn oath in the House of Lords that he would never, under any circumstances, give his consent to admit us into Parliament. The Duke of. Cumberland amongst his other supposed enormities, was the grand master of the Orangemen, and therefore our most bitter enemy. I am not quite clear as to the disposition towards us of the Duke of Cambridge. The Duke of Kent, the father of the Queen, was friendly to us. But the Duke of Sussex was the only active friend we had amongst the King's sons, in the advocacy of our political rights. It so happens that the most remarkable acts of kindness which Catholics received from the royal family were precisely from those members of it who were most actively opposed to the Relief Bill. These were George III., George IV., and the Duke of York. Some examples of this kindness on the part of the King and his sons cannot fail to interest the reader. We take the first example from a letter written by Dr. Coombes to Coghlan, and published in the *Laity's Directory* for 1800. Dr. Coombes was one of those who escaped from Douay, and in this letter he describes the adventures of some of the Douay students who had been captured and imprisoned at Doulens. The conclusion of the letter is in the following words:—

"After crossing the country with infinite hazard and danger, and performing the journey of nearly forty miles in the space of one night, they arrived safe on the frontier of France, and reached the head-quarters of the British army under the command of the Duke of York. His Royal Highness beheld with the deepest concern the situation to which young men of a liberal education had been reduced; he sincerely pitied their misfortunes, and was visibly hurt at the wretched appearance which they made both as to their persons and dress; he kindly inquired about their friends whom they had left in prison, requested a list of their names undoubtedly for the same benevolent purpose, and with a generosity peculiar to himself, gave to each one present an ample pecuniary supply for the prosecution of his journey. This, sir, is an instance of humanity which should never be forgotten. It is an action worthy of a prince and a hero; and ought to be reserved for the instruction and example of those who have yet to learn that the exercise of humanity, compassion, and generosity adds the brightest ornaments to the splendour of rank and the fame of military exploits. I cannot dismiss this subject without expressing my earnest wish and prayer, that this generous and gallant Prince may long be the boast of the illustrious family which fills the throne, and the pride and glory of the country which gave him birth."

The annals of the Franciscan nuns of Taunton also relate of the Duke of York as follows:—

"During his stay in Bruges, his Royal Highness honoured our community with a visit, and considerately brought in with him only one English officer as an attendant. The Bishop of Bruges met him in our refectory, for he had come unexpectedly while we were at dinner. The abbess and sister F. Sales Weld, who was a novice, went round the house with him. On taking leave of the abbess, he recommended to our prayers the success of his arms, and after his departure he sent back one of his suite, with a present to the community of twenty-five guineas. His Royal Highness did the same to the Austins;[1] and we were told, visited every English establishment in the places through which he passed." The account also adds that "his Royal Highness Prince Ernest Augustus [the Duke of Cumberland] likewise honoured us with a visit at a later period of the year."

The next instance which I shall give is of the kindness of the King himself; and it is taken from the same manu-

[1] What is now called the English Convent at Bruges.

script account from which I have just quoted.[1] It is as follows :—

"Our afflicted abbess was all anxiety to have a letter from Mr. Weld, whose two daughters were with us. She had immediately informed him of our emigration and where we were, and was hurt at not having a speedy reply, and his advice in her distress. At last she received a most kind and consoling letter. It informed her that it providentially happened that when he received the account of her having left Prinsenhof, the King was at Weymouth. Mr. Weld went there to pay his respects, and the good King asked him with great interest what had become of the English communities in the Low Countries, and especially after that in which his daughter was novice. Mr. Weld described the situation all were in, and that they knew not whither to take refuge. The King immediately desired he would tell us to come to England, and that he would take care we should not be molested, and added of his own accord, 'Tell them to bring their Church vestments, breviaries, and such like; I will give orders that they shall pass the Custom House.' His majesty recollected that by law these things were condemned to the flames. He made Mr. Weld give him down the names of the superiors of the different communities."

The community having arrived at London, the account continues :

"The next morning, the 8th of August, Mr. Grafton, Sister Frances Chantal Howse, and Sister Mary Austin Hutton went to the Custom House (at London) to see to the landing and examining of our goods; and discovered how cleverly and secretly the King had managed for all the religious communities. Only the chief or head officer knew his Majesty's orders; a sort of examination therefore took place; and when he sent the men out of the room into another with bales or trunks he had done with, he asked which contained Church vestments, breviaries, etc.,

---

[1] This manuscript is an account of the adventures of the community of Franciscan nuns who were established at the Prinsenhof at Bruges, in their flight to England ; and I am permitted to publish it through the kindness of the reverend mother abbess of Taunton.

and when the officers returned, he pretended he had examined those trunks, and ordered them to be carried away."

One of the most interesting accounts showing the kindness of the royal family to the exiled communities, is that which is preserved at St. Mary's Priory, Princethorpe; and a translation from which I can give the reader through the kind permission of the Reverend Mother Prioress. The community was at that time purely French, and they had been established for many years at Montargis. In the year 1792 they were expelled from their convent with the rudeness and insolence which characterized the French revolutionists. They determined to make for England with the intention of passing immediately from England to Belgium, where they hoped to find a home. But they unexpectedly found a welcome home in England. They arrived at the port in France from which they were to embark for our shores. I now continue the narrative in their own words.

"The captain of the ship in which we had taken our passage, having learned that we had obtained passports, had given out on leaving Brighton that no doubt he should take us on board on his return journey. This accounts for our having found the beach at Shoreham crowded with a large number of carriages and a mass of people, some of whom had been attracted by the sight of an entire community disembarking on this island, where for two hundred years the religious state was proscribed; others of whom, and these in greater number, had come in their eagerness to succour it. Scarcely had we stepped out of the small boats which landed us, when we were conducted by the crowd to a neighbouring house, in the midst of great cheering and the most touching marks of kindness. Some of them said to us, 'Come, come and forget amongst us all that those villains have made you suffer: we will take away the least trace of your misfortunes.' Others said to us, 'You will find here none but feeling and compassionate hearts, who will esteem themselves happy in repairing the injustice and the cruelty of your fellow-countrymen.' Others again said, 'We will make every effort to procure you that happiness and peace which you could no longer enjoy in France; take courage, therefore, you have nothing more to fear.' The truth of these assurances was soon made evident to us. Persons of quality, who had come in their carriages, hastened to make us get in with them; while the rest of the community were conducted to hired carriages which had been sent from Brighton. In a few moments we all found ourselves carried off, without any one of us knowing where she was going or with whom she was, and all of us in the greatest surprise at a reception which we had no idea we should receive. We arrived at Brighton, a town situated at a distance of six miles from Shoreham, where we had disembarked; and we were set down at the hotel, where apartments had been engaged for us by our generous benefactors. Those who had brought us, all united in renewing their assurances of the most sincere compassion. It was there we learned the protection accorded to us by the Prince of Wales through the intervention of Mrs. Fitzherbert, who came herself to see us on our arrival. We did not, however, as yet know that this protection extended so far as to defray all our expenses in this town, and that all the nobility who were there had subscribed for this act of benevolence. We were only informed of this the next morning, when the Prince of Wales sent his physician to inquire if we were treated at the hotel according to the orders which had been given. During the course of this day we were visited by a multitude of our benevolent hosts. The Prince of Wales himself came to see Reverend Mother. He entered into the minutest details of everything which concerned us. Having learned that we intended to leave immediately for Brussels, he persuaded Reverend Mother to remain in England; 'for,' said he, 'the Low Countries being threatened with a French invasion before long, a residence there will only expose you to danger, and the same bad treatment you have just met with in France. Remain in England,' he continued; 'you will find here a great number of your countrymen and countrywomen, and the English will consider it a duty to make you happy. At least, go to London, and pass some time there; you will see what turn affairs will take, and then you can leave for Brussels, if you can do so without fear of the consequences; but believe me, a hasty voyage there may place you in the greatest possible embarrassment.' This advice, coming from the mouth of the heir apparent of the Crown of England, was as much as a manifest order of the will of our Lord in our regard; and although we did not then see all the consequences of it, it was at least an earnest of the favourable reception which awaited us, to whatever part of the kingdom we might go. After the Prince had left, the physician whom we have already spoken of supported his advice more in detail, adding that the passage from Brighton to Ostend being very little frequented, we might run great danger: whereas it would be much safer to take the ordinary way by Dover, in case we should be able to go to Belgium. The opinions of all directing us to London, Reverend Mother determined to go there, and thought only about the means of transit. The Prince again came to see us, and this time he asked to see the community. Reverend Mother having assembled us all, he received us with a kindness truly royal. He conjured Reverend Mother (these were his words) to make the community sit down while he remained standing. He repeated the advice which he had given the evening before about our journey to Brussels, and he invited us in the most obliging terms to go to London, where we should find all the inhabitants disposed to recompense us for our losses. The want of chairs prevented many of us from being able to sit down. The Prince perceived this, and, turning to Mrs. Fitzherbert, he said in that kind manner which is his characteristic, 'See, we are keeping them standing; let us be off; I cannot suffer this any longer.'

"Whilst Reverend Mother was turning over in her own mind, as we have already said, our departure for London, a lady obligingly offered her two places in her carriage, for Friday. The hour for starting was just settled, when the landlord came to tell us that the Prince of Wales had taken upon himself the expenses of our journey and the transport of all our baggage, and that ten of us could start the next morning. So, Reverend Mother changing the plans she had already made, named those who were to start on the next and the following days."

When George IV. died in 1830, a miniature of Mrs. Fitzherbert was found tied round his neck. This lasting attachment to a virtuous wife has often been cited as one, if not the only one, redeeming quality in the character the King. His conduct to the exiled community of Montargis may certainly also be mentioned in his favour. For it was not only in consequence of his civility and kindness, but in consequence of his urgent and repeated advice, that the sisters settled in England, and that we are indebted for one of the largest and most flourishing communities we possess. It is at least interesting, that both these traits of goodness should have been taken from the conduct of George IV. towards Catholics.

If, as we cannot doubt, Almighty God has blessed our land for the hearty welcome which our religious orders received, we may hope that the royal family of England has earned a special blessing for itself, in consequence of the special kindness which its members showed in our regard.

CHAPTER IX.

REV. MR. WILKS AND THE "STAFFORDSHIRE CLERGY."

BEFORE giving an account of the progress of emancipation in Ireland and Scotland, it will be necessary to mention an episode in the history of English Catholics. This episode was something very like a small schism amongst the Catholic clergy; and was for many years afterwards well known under the name of "the Staffordshire Clergy." This unfortunate affair lasted only for a short time. Its temporary character showed that anything like schism could not take any hold on English Catholic ground. From the end of its brief existence until the present day, no clergy have shown more zeal, more devotion to the Church, and more submission to authority than the whole body of priests in the county of Stafford.

The origin of this schism was as follows. It has been already stated that the Rev. Joseph Wilks was a member of the "Committee of Ten;" that he signed, and in fact wrote, conjointly with Mr. Butler, the "schismatical protest". against the condemnation by the Vicars Apostolic of the oath proposed by the committee in 1791. Dr. Milner says of Wilks that he went all the unlawful lengths of the committee, continued to promote its oath after it had been censured by his bishop, signed the two "Blue-books, and obstinately refused to retract these scandalous measures."[1]

[1] "Supplementary Memoirs," p. 92.

In consequence of this rebellious conduct, Dr. Walmesley, the Vicar Apostolic of the Western District, suspended Mr. Wilks. The letter of suspension was as follows:—

"Bath, Saturday, February 19, 1791.
"As you have evidently refused submission to the ordinances of the Vicars Apostolic; if, before, or on Sunday next, the 26th instant, you do not make to me satisfactory submission, I declare you suspended from the exercises of all missionary faculties, and all ecclesiastical functions in my district. Let this one admonition suffice for all.
"CHARLES RAMATEN, Vicar Apostolic.

Mr. Wilks did not immediately submit. He had not submitted at the time of the meeting at the Crown and Anchor Tavern on the 9th of June. We have seen that the suspension of Mr. Wilks was one of the grievances brought forward by the committee at that meeting. On that occasion "the agent of Bishop Walmesley," says Husenbeth, "being called upon to declare for what criminal fault Mr. Wilks had been suspended, read the following from a letter of the bishop, dated June 1, 1791:—"Because Mr. Wilks has rebelled and protested against the divine established government of the Church by bishops and their authority—a crime not less than schism."[1] In the mean time, and before the Crown and Anchor meeting, "different laymen and women," says Milner, "had used their efforts in vain to oblige the prelate to reverse a sentence which he had conscientiously pronounced."[2] The case being clearly an ecclesiastical one, we have it on the authority of Milner that the committee, or at any rate those ladies and gentlemen who were most anxious to have the suspension reversed, solicited priests to interfere in the matter. "The principal clergyman applied to for this purpose," says

---

[1] Husenbeth's "Life of Milner," pp. 40, 41.
[2] "Supplementary Memoirs," p. 92.

Milner, "was one who had always shown his obsequiousness to the secretary and leaders of the committee."[1] Milner, who is always cautious in mentioning proper names, does not name this "principal clergyman." It was the Rev. Joseph Berington, who had published some very objectionable books; who took the worst possible view of the state of the Catholic Church in England; who had publicly suggested that Catholics owed their unemancipated state to themselves, for not taking the oath of supremacy; and who was one of those men, one or two of whom may be generally found amongst us, who live in a chronic state of dissatisfaction with superiors and opposition to ecclesiastical authority.[2] Joseph Berington was well acquainted with the clergy of the Midland District, and especially with those of Staffordshire. He had been on the mission at Oscott before the mission house there was enlarged to commence the college.[3] Berington applied to some of his acquaintance amongst the Staffordshire clergy to join him in taking the part of Mr. Wilks against his bishop. Thirteen of them consented to do so: and these thirteen, along with Berington, joined in signing a letter, "most probably," as Husenbeth says, "composed by Berington," and addressed to the Committee of Ten, in which they "pledge themselves to make the cause of Mr. Wilks their own, and doubt not but they shall receive such co-operation from all the clergy of England as shall secure success to their endeavours in restoring to their delegate the good-will of

---

[1] "Supplementary Memoirs," p. 92.

[2] Joseph Berington had published a book entitled, "The decline and fall of the Roman Catholic Church in Great Britain." Poor man! He wrote this only just before the Catholic Church in Great Britain rose up again, and, with a new life, began a new fight, in which she has never had a fall, but with God's blessing has obtained many a victory.

[3] This house is now called Maryvale, that name having been given to it, at the suggestion of one of his companions, by Cardinal Newman when he went to reside there.

his bishop and the exercise of his ecclesiastical functions." "Never," says Milner, "was there an ecclesiastical proceeding more irregular and disedifying."[1] "The names of these priests were subsequently signed to other reprehensible documents, and one more joined them, making the whole number fifteen; and they were known as the "Staffordshire clergy."[2]

In justice to the memory of these men, we must add another sentence from Milner's "Supplementary Memoirs." "These last signatures, which were made by some of the thirteen without any knowledge, and by the rest with only an imperfect knowledge, of the cause which they had *made their own*, were the source of disquietude and misery to them for several years, till by the grace of God they successively, either in health or on their death-beds, fully retracted them."[3]

The bad spirit which caused the unpleasant proceedings above mentioned continued to work for a few years. But when Milner was consecrated bishop, and appointed Vicar Apostolic of the Midland District in the year 1803, it had entirely died out. The late Dr. Husenbeth, in an unpublished manuscript, corrects an error relating to this matter which occurs in Canon Flanagan's "History of the Church in England."[4] As this error represents the evil of the "Staffordshire clergy" to have lasted longer than it did, it is well that the reader should be aware of the correction. Dr. Husenbeth writes as follows:—"It is stated,

[1] Husenbeth's "Life of Milner," p. 41.
[2] "Supplementary Memoirs," p. 93.
[3] Milner says that one of the publications of the "Staffordshire clergy" contained *implied heresy*. This publication was "an appeal to the Catholics of England," and the proposition which Milner condemns was as follows:—"Of this (Catholic) Church we believe the Bishop of Rome to be the head, *supreme in spirituals by Divine appointment, supreme in discipline by ecclesiastical institution.*"
[4] Vol. ii. p. 443.

in Canon Flanagan's History, that these priests" (that is, those known as the "Staffordshire clergy") "often assembled at Sedgley Park, and that Dr. Milner frequently appeared among them, to call their attention to reasons and facts, and bring them to a better sense. But this is a sad mistake. Their opposition had been entirely given up under his predecessor, Bishop Stapleton, and when Dr. Milner became Bishop in 1803, eight of the fifteen were dead; another, Rev. Joseph Berington, had left the district; and one, Rev. John Perry, had so far gained Dr. Milner's confidence that he made him his vicar-general and his confessor. All indeed fully retracted, ... and 'as to Mr. Southworth' (the President of Sedgley Park when Milner was made bishop), 'he, with the remaining five, had retracted two years before. He was on the best of terms with Bishop Stapleton, who confirmed in his new chapel at Sedgley Park, soon after it had been opened in 1801. It is certain, therefore, that these priests never assembled at Sedgley Park in Dr. Milner's time, nor is it likely that they all met there together at any time.'"[1]

Amongst some other manuscripts left by Dr. Husenbeth, he gives, under the heading "Staffordshire clergy," a list of thirteen priests, with the residence of most of them and the date of their deaths. As this list may prove of interest to some readers, I give it as follows:—

> Rev. Thomas Flynn, died August 18, 1797.
> Rev. George Beeston, Tixall, died August 15, 1797.
> Rev. William Hartley, died July 8, 1794.
> Rev. Joseph Berington, Oscott, died Dec. 1, 1827.
> Rev. Thomas Stone, Moseley, died March 7, 1797.
> Rev. John Carter, Wolverhampton, died March 24, 1803.
> Rev. John Coone, Stafford, died August 4, 1816.
> Rev. Thomas Southworth, Sedgley Park, died June 9, 1816.
> Rev. James Tasker, Cresswell, died July 15, 1815.

[1] "MS. Memoirs of Parkers:" Rev Thomas Southworth.

Rev. Edward Eyre, Longbirch, died Nov. 15, 1834.
Rev. John Roe, Blackladies, died June 28, 1838.
Rev. John Wright, died July 23, 1797.
Rev. John Kirk, Pipe Hall, died Dec. 20, 1851.

These, with the Rev. Thomas Perry, make up fourteen; who the fifteenth was, I am not aware. Mr. Wilks retracted his error, and died an edifying death at Douay.

A few years later than the time I have been writing about, some of the French priests in England were engaged in the schism which followed the Concordat between Pope Pius VII. and Napoleon, and which I shall have occasion to allude to. But from the time of the "Staffordshire clergy" down to the present day, the word "schism" has never been seriously pronounced in relation to the English Catholic clergy. If ever through thoughtlessness or ignorance the word has been rashly uttered, there never has in fact been any foundation for its use.

In this history we have now come, so far as the Church of England is concerned, down to the end of the last century. At the opening of the present century, twenty-two years had passed since the repeal of the penal laws had begun, and nine years since what is called freedom of worship had been granted to us by Act of Parliament. The remnant of the Catholics of England had been reinforced by the return of our colleges and convents from abroad, and we had derived great help in several ways from the residence of the clergy who had been exiled from France. The large emigration of the Irish to England had not begun, and the "Oxford movement" was three and thirty years in the future. The new growth of the Church sprang from the old roots. The sapling took a firm hold of the ground, and, though exposed in its early life, as we have seen, to some rude shocks, it showed proofs of a strength well able to bear them. It shot up and became a stately tree; and when shelter had to be provided for thousands, its branches were spread out to cover them all.

If the parable of the mustard-seed may be applied to the Church of any one country, it certainly illustrates the state of the Church in England at the close of the last century and its growth in succeeding years. The arrival of the Irish added enormously to our numbers, and the Oxford movement, besides numbers not inconsiderable, brought the Church into, or into close connection with, almost every family of the upper classes in the country. These two providential events infused elements into the Church of England which now form essential parts of our state and condition. But still they were joined on to the old stock and amalgamated with it. And whatever may be the progress which the Church may make in our country, even if it should own the English people for its children once again, the Church preserved in the old Catholic families, the Church of the garrets and cellars, will have been the seed from which the tree grew which produced such abundant fruit, though some of its branches may have been grafted on the stem.

It is not unlikely, indeed, that had there been no emigration from Ireland and no "Oxford movement," the Church in England would have been in a state so lowly that we do not like to think of what might have been. But truly, in thinking over these things, our thoughts are lost in the mysterious designs of God. The seed *had* fallen to the ground, and *had died*, beaten down and trodden underfoot. But because it had fallen to the ground and had died, it was not *left alone*. It received two companions (if the expression may be allowed), bringing new life and strength—two as great blessings as God ever gave to a Church; and we see it now, bearing *much fruit*, only one of the myriad proofs that God's Word does not pass away.

CHAPTER X.

PROGRESS OF EMANCIPATION IN IRELAND.

The influence of Ireland—Duty of English Catholics towards Ireland—Catholic associations in Ireland—John Keogh—Keogh and O'Connell—O'Connell—Union is strength.

WE have now to follow the progress of emancipation in Ireland. This is a great and instructive subject. Though the history of the emancipation of English Catholics be a matter of more interest, as relating to our immediate home affairs, still what was done in Ireland by her own people towards gaining the freedom of British subjects is of greater importance, because it brought into action a great political power—the only great political power which the Catholics of the British Isles possess. I repeat here what has been written in a former chapter, that the political power of Ireland is the political power of Catholics in the United Kingdom. An English Catholic has many things to be proud of. There is a great deal in our past history of which we may justly boast. England, as well as Ireland, was at one time entitled to be called, as she was called, an Island of Saints. The history of England, when England was Catholic, though there are many blots upon its leaves, presents many centuries of wisdom and strength in government, of steady progress and persevering energy in its people, and of bravery and glory in war. Though an English Catholic has to lament that brute force drove the Church out of the land, leaving only a handful of members who were to form the stock out of which, in after years, true religion was again to grow, yet he has to rejoice in the fidelity of that handful, and to thank God for the increase He has given in our days. An English Catholic may also point to that sense of religion, that reverence for God, which undoubtedly exist in many of our countrymen and women, and passing over for the moment the wrong direction which that sense of religion and that reverence for God have taken, through the wiles and deceits of the enemy of human nature, he may stretch his view back to those days when all that is good in religion, was brought over to our forefathers with the first coming of the Roman Catholic Church.

We may, indeed, now look upon the realization of almost the fondest hopes of English Catholics who were young and eager forty years ago. We see a great increase in numbers; we see freedom before the law, and the law administered with greater fairness; we see churches, schools, and institutions of all kinds rapidly on the increase, and the number of priests yearly augmenting; we see religious orders multiplying, and a hierarchy gradually developing into settled organization. We have much to be proud of in the past; we have much to be proud of in the present. But there is one thing that we cannot boast of: we cannot boast of political power. If we want to use political power we must go to Ireland to get it. Have English Catholics ever got anything from Parliament or the Government which the Irish Catholics have not got first, or which has not been got for us by Irishmen? By Irishmen I here mean the power of Catholic Ireland. Could English Catholics force a bill; should we ever dream of forcing a bill through Parliament? The Irish have forced bills through Parliament; they forced bills before 1829, they forced one in 1829, and they have forced several since that time. Look at Canning's speeches, and see the emancipation of English Catholics brought in as an afterthought, as a sort of corollary or note, at the tail end of one of his grand orations for the emancipation of the Irish. And when to-day a Catholic priest is stung by the refusal of some local authorities, or by the Home Office, to give some direction which justice and common fairness would dictate to an administrator of the law, what is it that he is told to do; what do people say to him? They say to him, "Get an Irish member to bring it before the House of Commons."[1] Why an Irish member? Because an Irish member has power at his back to support his demands. For some years past only one constituency in England has returned a Catholic member. It is, indeed, thought by some that it is our own fault that we have not some Catholics representing English constituencies. It is said that there are a few Catholic gentlemen who, if they took their proper position in public affairs, would succeed in occasionally winning a seat in Parliament. This is a subject that I may have occasion to refer to in some subsequent page. But this question does not affect what I am now insisting upon. For whether it is in consequence of the neglect of their duty by Catholic gentlemen, or in consequence of the bigotry of the majority in every English constituency, the fact remains that, with one exception, the only representation of Catholics by Catholics in the House of Commons is by members sent from Ireland. So that if the Home Rule party should gain its end, there might not be a single Catholic in the Lower House of Parliament.

[1] This was perfectly true at the time it was first written. It is not true now, because folly has taken the place of wisdom in our counsels.

Nothing is more dangerous in practical politics than for a politician to mistake the ground on which he stands. Nothing is more useful to a man who has some political question in charge than to tell him the truth. There are amongst us some who, judging from what they say and write, greatly overrate the power of English Catholics. That we have more power in one respect now than we had some years ago is true. There are more constituencies in which the number of Catholic votes adds considerable weight when put into the scale at an election.[1] In another respect we have not so much power as we had. To have Catholics in Parliament is a power, especially when we have a man there like the late Mr. Langdale. At one time we had several English Catholics in the House, representing English constituencies. Now we have only one. The injury we do ourselves by exaggerating our power is this: it tends to make us undervalue the importance of preserving as close a connection as we can with the Catholics of Ireland and their representatives in Parliament. If we think that power is where power is not, we shall underrate and perhaps neglect and even ignore power where power really is. We must understand our position as it is, not as it was, nor as it may be in the future. Parliamentary power is the supreme political power in the British Empire; and the parliamentary power of Catholics comes wholly and solely from Ireland. But we need not despair; things will get better. We shall some day, and perhaps before long, have a few representatives in Parliament. We may be as sanguine as we please, but until we have about fifty English Catholics in the House of Commons, and until about a quarter of the tradesmen

---

[1] This is in consequence of the increase of Catholics in England; but is it in consequence of the increase in the number of English Catholics?

in Oxford Street are Catholics, we must not consider that our power has attained any degree to boast of. We know, our countrymen know well, the whole world knows, that the power of the Catholics of Ireland is great in the British Parliament. The power of English Catholics, unaided by the Irish, is nothing. If we think it to be something, whereas it is nothing, besides mistaking our own interests, we shall run the danger of putting ourselves into the ridiculous position represented in the old fable, of the frog which tried to swell itself to the size of the ox, and was ruined in the attempt.

The Catholics of Ireland have much more to boast of than we have. They have preserved the faith as a nation; they possess great political power; they have, by emigrating in large numbers to England, increased the Catholic population, and contributed a large share of whatever importance we may have in this country. In the highest interests which we have in this world, we and the Catholics of Ireland stand on the same ground; we have the same rights to demand, and the same rights to defend when gained. It is our interest to keep up as close a connection as we can in every respect with Irish Catholics. Our relations with Irish Catholics, whether they be in England or in Ireland, ought to be so friendly that, if any English Catholic should disapprove of anything done by Irish Catholics, his inclination should be to let his disapprobation be dissolved in those more potent motives, which would urge him to allow nothing to diminish the friendship between him and them. When a man hears the actions of his true friend condemned, his generous impulse is to defend his friend: if he should think that he cannot defend him, he at least shows a disinclination to hear his friend abused. Such a man is honoured for his fidelity. It should be the ambition of every English Catholic to be thus honoured. And it appears to me that there is something even dishonourable as well as impolitic in the conduct of those amongst us who, in order that they may please their Protestant fellow-countrymen, separate themselves from Irish interests, and make it appear that they have as little sympathy with the Irish people as they have with Basutos and Boers. And when we consider the enormous importance which the Irish people are to the welfare of the Church in the British Empire, it seems treason against the Church to say or do anything which would weaken the power of Ireland. I would venture to say that an English Catholic who has little sympathy with the Irish has little sympathy with the Church. And one who would diminish the power and influence of the Irish, would diminish the power and influence of the Church in the British dominions. To be a Catholic before everything is the boast of many in England, and loudly do some sound the cry, in order that it may be heard in Rome. But little would "the Christ on earth"[1] rely upon the sincerity of those who, while they assert so loudly the words "Catholic before everything," show, by the manner in which they speak of Ireland, that they are English first and Catholic after.

It must not be supposed that I in the least undervalue the influence which English Catholics really possess. There are so many Catholics who in these days hold positions in which influence is exercised, that, though the number is small in comparison with that of the Protestants in such positions, yet the amount of influence arising from such sources does not stand at just one degree above zero, as it does in the House of Commons. Good and staunch Catholics, scattered however sparsely over Great Britain, produce some effect in social life. The various offices

---

[1] St. Catherine of Siena's name for the Holy Father.

which they hold in boroughs, counties, and cities bring them into relation with those who can only learn by actual experience that Catholics can be as truly English as they are truly Catholic. Every now and then a Catholic is put into a position of high trust and dignity. Though it may not be very perceptible at the moment, such appointments as those of Serjeant Shee[1] to the Queen's Bench, and Lord Ripon to the Governor-Generalship of India, break down, subsequently to the appointment, even more prejudice than has been broken through in order to effect it. That Catholics have fairer play than we had been accustomed to is well shown by this, that when a man has made such a position for himself that he cannot be overlooked or thrust aside, his claims are admitted, as would be the claims of a Protestant. In proportion as Catholic young men choose to employ usefully the undoubted talents which many of them possess, they will arrive at a position in which the value of their services will be recognized. There is reason to hope that influence acquired in this way will continue to increase; and the time may come again when English constituencies will return Catholic members. But at present it must be acknowledged that we have none of that first-rate political influence which is given by seats in the House of Commons. This influence is a matter of necessity when any section of the community has separate interests. We have it not amongst ourselves. Ireland does possess it; and therefore in all matters relating to Catholic interests a first axiom for our guidance should be, what I again repeat, and what should be instilled into the mind of every Catholic young man in Great Britain, and urged until it become a practical conviction—THE POWER OF IRELAND IS THE POWER OF THE CATHOLIC

---

[1] Mr. Serjeant Shee was the first Catholic raised to the bench in England since the Revolution.

CHURCH IN THE UNITED KINGDOM. To keep that power strong ought to be an object in the conduct of every English Catholic: it is difficult to see how it is not a positive duty. The authority which is exercised under the Constitution of England by Queen, Lords, and Commons is as lawful an authority as that exercised by any absolute monarch who ever reigned. The loyalty of a subject to a sovereign is not greater than the loyalty of an Englishman to the authority of Queen, Lords, and Commons. If an absolute monarch were a pillar of the Church as well as a pillar of the State, it would be double disloyalty in a Catholic to be unfaithful to such a man. How, then, can an English Catholic, owing fealty in the British Constitution to Queen, Lords, and Commons, escape a charge of disloyalty if he is not loyal to that special element in the authority which he obeys, which is the only representative in Parliament of the interests of his Church?

Loyalty ought to be above suspicion; and I venture to say that never a word should escape the mouth of an English Catholic which should lead any one to suppose that he does not value at a great price the power of Ireland. Our object should be to keep as closely connected as possible with the Irish power; and we should deem it a disgrace to say or do anything which would show a tendency to patronize English Protestant ideas at the expense of those which are Irish and Catholic. An English Catholic appreciating the true value of the power of Ireland would rather incur the censure of meaner natures finding fault with him for not being sufficiently English, than merit the stigma of cowardice by siding, through human respect, with those who would weaken, because it is Irish and Catholic, that power which it is his interest to protect. If it were known generally throughout the Empire that

English Catholics were faithful to the only power which they possess in Parliament, and that they looked upon the power of Ireland as a man in the midst of a shower of arrows would look upon his shield, English Catholics would be regarded as men of sense and as men of moral courage, and as such they would be respected. The power of Ireland, too, would be more thought of and brought into account. For no considerable body of Englishmen, though they may be even a small minority, can worthily attach themselves to a good cause without raising the importance of that cause itself, and without, I dare to say, forming a conviction in the minds of the majority that, though the time may not have come, it is not far distant, when the cause will have gained its end.

I have thought that these introductory remarks may help to show the reader that the history of emancipation in Ireland is for them an interesting and a useful study.

The great Catholic Association of 1828 was one of the most powerful engines of political action that was ever organized. It proved for all time what the moral force of a united people is capable of doing. The Catholic Association and the Clare election carried the emancipation of the Irish and British Catholics. The obstinate prejudice, the deep-seated bigotry, and the jealous selfishness of the English Protestants were struck, beaten down, and for the time rendered powerless by a union of the Catholics of Ireland, brought about and governed by the genius, the energy, and the determined will of one man. This great Association, of which I shall have to speak more at length in future chapters, had its precursors. According to Mr. Sheil, "the confederates of 1642 were the precursors of the Association of 1828."[1]

The object of the confederates of 1642 is thus stated

[1] "Legal and Political Sketches," vol. ii. p. 157.

by Lingard: "To procure freedom of conscience, to maintain the just prerogative of the Crown, and to obtain for the people of Ireland the same privileges which were enjoyed by the people of England." ... "A national Association," writes the same author, "for the purpose of effecting them" (that is, the objects above mentioned), "was formed, and the members, in imitation of the Scottish Covenanters, bound themselves by a common oath to maintain the free and public exercise of the Catholic worship, to bear true faith and allegiance to King Charles, and to defend him against all who should endeavour to subvert the royal prerogative, the power of Parliament, or the just rights of the subject."[1] I do not enter into the history, civil and military, of this association. It ceased to exist when Cromwell, to use the words of Sheil, "crushed the Catholics to the earth."

From this time until the year 1727, there seems to have been no common action on the part of the Irish Catholics. In that year George I. died, and was succeeded by George II. The Catholics of Ireland had been told that some of the most ferocious of what Edmund Burke called "the ferocious Acts" of Anne and George I., had been passed to punish them for not having presented a loyal address to Queen Anne on her accession to the throne. The Catholics, therefore, bethought themselves that they might prudently, and perhaps with some little profit to themselves, present a loyal address to George II. An address was therefore prepared. Mitchell says it was "an humble congratulatory address;"[2] Sheil says it was "servile."[3] It testified "unalterable loyalty and attachment to the King and his royal house." Some kind of temporary

---

[1] "History of England," Charles I., A.D. 1642.
[2] Mitchell's "History of Ireland," vol. i. p. 88.
[3] Sheil's "Sketches," vol. ii. p. 159.

organization had no doubt taken place amongst the Irish Catholics, in order that this address might be representative. It was presented to the lords justices at Dublin Castle by Lord Delvin at the head of a deputation, in which the principal Catholic families were represented. The only consolation which the Catholics had on this occasion was, that they were not scolded for daring to present the address, and for venturing so near to the shadow of royalty as they did when they entered the Castle of Dublin. They got no answer to the address, neither from the King nor from the lords justices. It was received in solemn silence, and when Mitchell wrote his history, only a few years back, it was not known whether the address was ever sent from Dublin to be laid before the King, nor whether the lords justices ever engaged to send it. Sheil attributes this neglect to what he calls the "utterly despicable and degraded condition" in which Catholics then were. What was supposed to be a practical answer to the daring of the Catholics in presenting a loyal address, immediately followed. An act was passed depriving Catholics of a right which they had hitherto possessed, to vote at elections for members of Parliament.[1] The following year a bill was introduced to take away from Catholics the right to practise as solicitors. This bill was the occasion of the next combination of Catholics, though it was only a partial and incomplete organization. I give the account of it in the words of Mr. Sheil. "Here," he writes, "we find, perhaps, the origin of the Catholic rent. Several Catholics in Cork and in Dublin raised a subscription to defray the expense of opposing the bill, and an apostate priest gave information of this conspiracy (for so it was called) to bring in the Pope and the Pretender. The transaction was referred to a committee of the House

---

[1] 1 Geo. II. ch. 9, sec. 7.

of Commons, who actually reported that five pounds had been collected, and resolved 'that it appeared to them, that under pretence of opposing heads of bills, sums of money had been collected and a fund established by the Popish inhabitants of this kingdom, highly detrimental to to the Protestant interest.' These were the first efforts of the Roman Catholics to obtain relief, or rather to prevent the imposition of additional burthens. They did not, however, act through the medium of a committee or association."[1]

A most important step in advance towards organization was made in the year 1757. This step was in consequence of a gross and insulting act of injustice and of a threatened new penal law. The act of injustice which contributed to the important consequences we shall presently see is thus stated by Mr. Mitchell. "A young Catholic girl named O'Toole was importuned by some of her friends to conform to the Established Church; to avoid this persecution, she took refuge in the house of another friend and relative, a Catholic merchant in Dublin, named Saul. Legal proceedings were at once taken against Mr. Saul, in the name of a Protestant connection of the young lady. Of course the trial went against Saul, and on this occasion he was assured from the bench that papists had no rights, inasmuch as 'the law did not presume a papist to exist in the kingdom; *nor could they so much as breathe there without the connivance of Government.*'[2] And the court was right, for such was actually the 'law,' or what passed for law, in Ireland at that time." The threatened penal law, which had actually been framed into the "heads of a bill," aimed at the destruction of the Catholic hierarchy.

[1] "Political Sketches," vol. ii. pp. 159, 160.
[2] "History of Ireland," vol. i. pp. 125, 126. Mr. Mitchell, as all the world knows, was an ultra-Nationalist. In his history he makes no secret of his advanced opinions. But in his statements of historical facts he is remarkably accurate.

To oppose this bill, and to protect Catholics as far as possible from oppression similar to that which they had suffered in the Saul case, the first "Catholic Committee" was formed. According to Mr. Sheil, this committee was formed in the year 1757. But it would appear from Mr. Mitchell's history that it must have been in 1758. The formation of this committee was, as I have already said, a great step in advance. No organization like it had been hitherto attempted; and from that time forward the Catholics of Ireland have almost continually possessed some association for the management of their affairs. Mr. Sheil calls the committee of 1757 "the parent of the great Convention which has since brought its enormous seven millions into action."[1]

In the year 1759 this committee, as was noticed in an early chapter of this history, was recognized by the Government as representing the Catholics of Ireland. The gentlemen especially active in forming this committee were Mr. Wyse, of Waterford; Charles O'Connor, of Belanagare; Dr. Curry, who wrote the "Historical Review of the Civil Wars;" and Lords Fingall, Taaffe, and Delvin. The committee continued to act, and to act with vigour. Taking advantage of the difficulties of the Government in consequence of the revolt of the American colonies, it obtained one concession after another, until in 1782 the Act was passed which enabled Catholics to purchase and dispose of landed property. "Thus," says Mr. Sheil, "they were rashly placed beyond the state, but were furnished with that point from which the engine of their power has been since wielded against it."[2] Theobald Wolfe Tone, as quoted by Sheil, describes the Catholic Committee in 1792 as composed of "the bishops, the county gentlemen, and of a certain number of merchants and tradesmen, all

[1] "Political Sketches," vol. ii. p. 160.   [2] Ibid., p. 162.

resident in Dublin, but named by the Catholics in the different towns corporate to represent them."

We now come to another phase in the management of their affairs by the Catholics of Ireland—that in which one man controlled proceedings and became the acknowledged leader. The state of things in the committee was not altogether satisfactory. The spirit of the Irish Catholics had been roused, and they had begun to see the power which they possessed. The members of the committee were over-cautious, and frequently timid in action; they were sometimes even time-serving. They wished also to keep the management of affairs so entirely in their own hands, and directed by their own ideas, that they would not listen to the voice of the millions who were their real support. The Catholic aristocracy, along with the clergy, were in fact the controllers of the action of the Committee. The members of the committee who did not belong to the aristocracy at length resisted the dictation of the others; they were backed by the people, and their resistance was successful. The aristocracy, instead of yielding to the pressure of the times in a patriotic spirit, and instead of continuing to act with the others, and so preserving the union of all, adopted an unfortunate course. They resigned in a body. Their successful opponents were not discouraged by this foolish and impolitic act. At their head was John Keogh, who, Mr. Sheil says, "was, in the years 1792 and 1793, the unrivalled leader of the Catholic body." As he was the first leader of the Irish Catholics in these latter times, the reader will no doubt be interested in having Mr. Sheil's description of him. "He belonged to the middle class of life, and kept a silk-mercer's shop in Parliament Street, where he had accumulated considerable wealth. His education had corresponded with his original rank, and he was without the graces and refinement of literature; but he had a vigorous and energetic mind, a great command of pure diction, a striking and simple earnestness of manner, great powers of elucidation, singular dexterity, and an ardent, intrepid, and untameable energy of character. His figure was rather upon a small scale, but he had great force of countenance, an eye of peculiar brilliancy, and an expression in which vehement feelings and the deliberative faculties were combined. He was without a competitor in the arts of debate. Occasionally more eloquent speeches were delivered in Catholic Convention, but John Keogh was sure to carry the measure which he proposed, however encountered with apparently superior powers of declamation." [1]

In a much improved form of representation the committee continued to act under the guidance of Keogh. In the year 1793 the Irish Catholics acquired the elective franchise. We English Catholics did not obtain it until 1829. The rebellion of 1798, and the Act of the Union which followed it, completely set aside all agitation for the right of sitting in Parliament. In the restoration of the right to vote for Members of Parliament, the Catholics of Ireland had an enormous power placed in their hands, which it may be fairly said they won by their own union and consequent strength. Keogh continued for some time to be the leader of the Catholics, but, being advanced in years, he gradually retired from public business, or rather from continued attendance at the meetings of the committee. His place was to a great extent filled by Mr. Dennis Scully, of Tipperary, whose wisdom in council, power in writing, and general services to the Catholic cause have hardly received in history and the memory of his countrymen that distinguished notice to which they are entitled.

As I have traced the organization of the Irish Catho-

[1] "Political Sketches," vol. ii. p. 166.

lics up to the beginning of this century, I may as well continue it until the great Act of Emancipation. In the year 1808 a change in leadership took place. Keogh, though in comparative retirement, was still considered up to this time, more than any other man, the leader. But he had had his day. As he had deposed the oligarchy of aristocrats, he was now to be deposed himself. He was to be deposed by a stronger and a greater man than he had ever been, by one of the greatest men that not only Ireland but any other country ever produced, the illustrious O'Connell, the Liberator of the Catholics of the United Kingdom. The occasion on which O'Connell defeated the policy of John Keogh is thus described by John O'Connell in his edition of his father's speeches. "In January, 1808, the Catholic Committee, as the agitators of the day styled themselves, assembled to debate the advisability of an immediate petition to Parliament for the total abrogation of the penal laws. The negative was strongly urged by some of their number, supported, as was rumoured, by the opinion of the celebrated John Keogh, the Catholic leader of that day, who was, however, prevented by illness from attending in person. His object was said to be founded on the idea that it was beneath the dignity of the Catholic body to petition so repeatedly, and that it would be more advisable for them to remain quiet, watching in 'dignified silence' the course of events and the conduct of their parliamentary friends." O'Connell was the principal speaker in opposition to any delay in presenting the petition. The original motion was proposed by Count Dalton, and it "went to express the anxiety of the Catholic body to petition Parliament for the repeal of the remaining penal laws."[1] Mr. O'Connor, of Belanagare, proposed an amendment, the effect of which would have been to postpone the petition.

[1] Plowden's post-union "History of Ireland," vol. iii. p. 614.

Mr. John O'Connell, and with him Francis Plowden and Mitchell agree, says that "the result of the debate was a withdrawal of the amendment, and the unanimous carrying of the resolution to petition."[1] The Rev. John O'Rourke, in his "Centenary Life of O'Connell,"[2] gives either a different version of the same meeting, or an account of another meeting about the same time in which some of the same incidents occurred. He says, "At the meeting of the Catholics in the Assembly Rooms in William Street, where this question" (that is, the question of presenting the petition) "was debated, O'Connell's advice prevailed over Mr. Keogh's by a majority of 134 to 110. Mr. Keogh was not present until the meeting was in the act of dividing; had he been present earlier the result might have been different—he was only in to witness the defeat of his own views. At this meeting the policy of delay, well meant, no doubt, may be said to have come to an end, and O'Connell's immortal flag, bearing the words, 'Agitate! Agitate! Agitate!' was hoisted, and the nation rallied round it and fought under it, until it won complete unqualified emancipation. O'Connell was now the undisputed leader of the Irish people." It will be observed that this account differs from the others, inasmuch as it gives a division on the question, and only a small majority against Keogh's views, whereas the other accounts say that the question was carried against Keogh unanimously.[3]

O'Connell seems to have played a subordinate part at this meeting, having only spoken in support of a resolution proposed by another gentleman. But it is clear, from the different accounts, that the influence of O'Connell dominated the meeting. Mr. Mitchell, in his account of this meeting,

[1] "Select Speeches of Daniel O'Connell," vol. i. p. 15.
[2] Page 26.
[3] Perhaps there were two meetings on the same question, one preliminary to the other.

says, "O'Connell's influence was, even thus early, very powerful in softening down irritation, soothing jealousies, and inspiring self-abnegation, for the sake of the common cause. It was this great quality, not less than his commanding ability, which made him soon afterwards, the acknowledged head of the Catholic cause." Mr. Plowden says, "The meeting was preserved in unanimity by the power of Mr. O'Connell's eloquence." And Mr. Sheil, in concluding his notice of Keogh, writes as follows :—"He had been previously defeated in a public assembly by a young barrister, who had begun to make a figure at the Bar, to which he was called in the year 1798, and who, the moment he took part in politics, made a commanding impression. This barrister was Daniel O'Connell, who, in overthrowing the previous leader of the body upon a question connected with the propriety of persevering to petition the Legislature, gave proof of the extraordinary abilities which have been since so successfully developed.[1] Mr. Keogh was mortified; but his infirmities, without reference to any pain he may have suffered, were a sufficient inducement to retire from the stage where he had long performed the principal character with such just applause."[2] It is quite evident from these accounts that O'Connell was the dominating spirit of the meeting; and the secondary part he seemed to play was perhaps owing to the fact that being comparatively a young man, he yielded the place of honour to his seniors, Count Dalton and Mr. John Byrne, who proposed and seconded the resolution to present the petition. I have dwelt the longer upon this meeting, because as it was the occasion on which our great liberator and master in political conduct, began

---

[1] This account was written between the Clare election and the passing of the Emancipation Act.

[2] "Political Sketches," vol. ii. pp. 169, 170.

to take the lead, it cannot fail to be of extreme interest to the reader.

In 1810, there was a new organization of the Irish Catholics, under the immediate direction of O'Connell, who was now, by all, the acknowledged leader. The organization consisted of permanent boards holding communication with the general committee in Dublin. In the following year, 1811, the Government put down the committee by prosecuting some of the members for a breach of the Convention Act. Shortly after this a "Catholic board" was established; but that again was suppressed in 1814 by proclamation. But O'Connell was not to be foiled, and under his direction "the agitation," says Mitchell, "took the form of aggregate meetings, thus avoiding all possibility of incurring the penalties of the Convention Act; while the meetings were even more useful than the board in arousing the people, diffusing sound information as to their rights and their wrongs, and keeping up a continual public commentary upon current events."[1] "Thus," says Mr. Sheil, "matters stood till the year 1821, when the King intimated his intention to visit Ireland."[2] Agitation ceased for a time, but the Irish people soon found that they were disappointed in the hopes of better things which had been raised at the time of the King's visit. In the year 1823, O'Connell and Sheil established the great and famous Catholic Association, whose efforts, crowned by the election of O'Connell for Clare, at last forced the British Government to yield.

I have rapidly sketched the history of Catholic organization in Ireland from the year 1642 to the year 1829. From the subjection of Ireland by Cromwell until the year 1727 nothing was done. Beginning with the year 1727, we

---

[1] "Mitchell's History," vol. ii. p. 266.
[2] "Political Sketches," vol. ii. p. 183.

have traced the continued development of Catholic power during a period of one hundred and two years, from the time when Lord Delvin and his deputation humbly approached the lords justices with an address of loyalty which never received an answer (unless a new penal law was the answer) up to the day when O'Connell at the head of seven millions of people demanded and obtained their rights. The subject naturally suggests some reflections which I cannot omit. Some years ago people used often to speculate on the true answer to the question: How was it that O'Connell, who forced the British Legislature to yield in the matter of the Catholic claims, so completely failed in his agitation for repeal? Some used to say that repeal was an impossibility. The more intelligent of those who said so, adopted Canning's formula—"Repeal the Union!—restore the Heptarchy!" The others were content to express the same idea in a more homely way, which was embodied in one of Punch's cartoons, where the great agitator was represented as a gigantic baby crying for the moon. It was added by many, that England would fight to the last man before yielding to the cry for repeal. There were other people again who said that O'Connell was not himself earnest in desiring a repeal of the Union, and that the more influential of his countrymen were perfectly aware of this. Ill-natured Englishmen and malicious Irish Protestants used to say that O'Connell continued the agitation in order to keep up his own popularity; and some used basely to add that his views were mercenary. But O'Connell was undoubtedly in earnest; and in the year 1843 he thought he was about to wrest an Act of Repeal from the Legislature. If his views had been mercenary, he would have pursued a lucrative practice at the Bar, or retired from the Bar with the salary and afterwards with the pension of a judge. There were others, again, who said that O'Connell's object was to be King or President of an independent Ireland, and that this could never be: the number of these, however, was not perhaps very large; the idea was too absurd for sensible men, except those men whose common sense was, when O'Connell was concerned, obscured by bigotry and hate. Another reason given for the success of O'Connell in his first agitation and for his failure in the second, was that whereas there was a large party in the Protestant House of Commons in favour of emancipation, there was no party in the House amongst the English, who were in favour of repeal. This circumstance, no doubt, made the attempt to gain repeal much more difficult; but it did not make it impossible: it was an obstacle, but not an absolute bar. The real reason why O'Connell failed in 1843, seems to be this: that whereas in 1829 he brought sufficient moral force to bear down all opposition, in 1843 he did not.

There is an old story, which some years ago used to be a very hackneyed one, that once upon a time a French cook, being very desirous to produce an English plum-pudding to set before a distinguished English guest, applied to an English friend for a receipt. The receipt was immediately supplied, and the French cook, scrupulously adhering to it, turned out, not that beautifully formed ball so well known to us all, but a confused mass which resembled less a pudding than a thick *potâge*. In his despair he sent for his friend, and on his arrival explained, with violent gesticulation, how he had made the pudding with the greatest exactitude after the receipt given. The Englishman smiled, and said, "There is just one thing wanting." "One thing wanting, sir! What is wanting, sir?" "A pudding-cloth, sir." I venture to think that in the agitation for repeal a *pudding-cloth* was wanting. There was nothing to unite together all those whose interests were affected by a repeal of the Union. In 1829 O'Connell spoke for the Catholics of Ireland, and the Catholics of Ireland were all with him; in 1843 he spoke for all Ireland, but all Ireland was not with him. The Catholic Association included all Catholics; the Repeal Association did not include all Irishmen. In the first place, comparatively speaking, very few Protestants were repealers. Amongst the Catholics, a large number of the upper classes were decidedly not repealers, and many were strong in favour of the English connection. Then, again, amongst those Catholics who called themselves repealers, and who, when in Ireland, considered themselves obliged to say they were such, were not really heart and soul in the cause. What gave O'Connell such extraordinary power in 1829 was that he spoke for all who were concerned in the question of emancipation. The moral power consisted in this, that all Catholics demanded emancipation; seven millions did in reality act and speak as one man. But in 1843 the question was not one which affected Catholics only; it affected all Irishmen, and the whole of Ireland. To carry a measure, therefore, which affected all Ireland, and to carry it by moral force against the wish of England, O'Connell should have had all Ireland at his back. But this he had not; and therefore he had not in 1843, as he had in 1829, sufficient moral force to carry his measure through. If all Irishmen had been as united in 1843 on the question of repeal as all Irish Catholics were united in 1829 on the question of emancipation, we cannot doubt that O'Connell would have obtained either a repeal of the Union, or some other measure of what is now called Home Rule. All admit that there are grievances in Ireland which require redress. When will they be redressed? If they affect Catholics

only, when all Catholics shall unite in demanding justice;
if they affect all Irishmen and the whole of Ireland, when
all Irishmen shall be united in demanding their rights.
There is no demand which Irishmen can make, and which
is consistent with loyalty to the Throne, which they will
not obtain when union amongst themselves shall bring
sufficient moral force to bear upon England. O'Connell,
besides being the liberator of the Catholics of the United
Kingdom, taught, in his way of fighting, a great lesson to
the whole world. But he has taught that lesson in vain,
if moral force can no longer be brought to influence the
action of the British Legislature; if it cannot do here
what was done in South Africa by the unerring aim of the
Boers.

We have thus seen a slight sketch of the various organizations of the Irish Catholics from the year 1727 until the
passing of the Emancipation Act. The history of Ireland
during the whole of that time is most interesting and
instructive. Various historians have written of that period
or of some special portions of it. But I am not aware that
any one has had for a main object, in treating of the events
of those days, to show the rise and progress of a great
political power, the difficulties from within and from without which it encountered, the conquests which it made, and
the defects in its working which have prevented its consolidation as an engine of enduring strength. The long and
persevering struggle which ended in the brilliant victory of
1829 ought to have been the prelude to the establishment
in Ireland of a power which would have made the British
Legislature yield to every just claim of the Irish people,
and which would have compelled the Executive to administer the laws "without favour or affection, malice or
ill-will."[1] Any man or any set of men who may be fired

[1] Words which occur in the oath which is administered to constables.

with the desire to obtain full justice to the Catholics of Ireland must be thoroughly convinced of the truth of this proposition—that the Irish Catholics are powerless when they are not united, and all-powerful when they are. When divided amongst themselves they are indeed worse than powerless; for they not only cannot obtain what they want from England, but they keep up an irritation amongst themselves which weakens their strength, and gives those who have to make laws for them an excuse for saying that they do not know what the Irish people want. It has been said in a former page of this history that the first statesman who will govern the sister island well, will be the one who shall legislate for her as Irish and Catholic. Such a statesman is not to be entirely self-made: nor are we to expect him to be providentially raised up by God without that co-operation on the part of God's creatures which Divine Providence expects to be used. The fable of Jupiter and the Carter must not be forgotten on the other side of St. George's Channel. The late Sir Robert Peel was one of England's greatest statesmen. He did many wise and good things. Amidst all his works the two measures which will be the most remembered in connection with his memory are Catholic Emancipation and the repeal of the Corn Laws. In the wisdom which he showed in forcing those two measures, he is not entitled to be called a self-made statesman. He had opposed Catholic Emancipation and the repeal of the Corn Laws up to the very moment when he changed his policy. What was it that made him change? It was the Catholic Association and the Anti-Corn-Law League. The bold front of the association made Peel a great statesman in 1829; the bold front of the league made him a great statesman in 1846. The same observation applies to the passing of the first and greatest Reform Bill in 1832. On that occasion

Peel did not yield: but it was again the bold front of the Political Unions which gave Earl Grey the strength to pass the measure. Within the last sixty years we have, then, three great examples of the practical wisdom which is forced into the minds of statesmen by a compact union amongst those who are demanding relief. It is true that a man like O'Connell does not appear twice in a thousand years. But it does not require a man like O'Connell to organize and lead an association of men who are willing to be led in a cause which they have at heart.

Cobden was a mere pigmy in comparison with O'Connell, and yet he effected great things; and men of less power than Cobden could sustain the spirit of an association formed to protect cherished rights. Supposing that it had been possible for any large section of the English people, to injure all the rest by a course of action which would have been against the spirit of the Reform Act, or the Act which repealed the corn laws, can we believe for a moment that a combination would not have been formed, and if necessary kept in permanent existence, to protect and preserve the right which had been so dearly won? Many men would have been found in England able and willing to begin and keep alive an association always ready for defence, and sometimes for attack. A permanent association of the Catholics of Ireland united in their work would have ensured a much fairer line of conduct on the part of England, and probably would have left Ireland at this day nothing to complain of. Let me take one example to illustrate my meaning. If England had legislated for Ireland on Irish and Catholic and not on English and Protestant principles, the Irish Catholics would at this time have a chartered university. Education in these days is a matter of the highest importance, and to establish the education of all on a sound

Catholic basis is an object for which a people might well bind themselves together. The legislation of the last forty years in respect of education in Ireland has been but a poor tinkering job. Demands are made in Ireland; in England the minister is threatened if he yields to them; he is between two fires, neither of which is strong enough to beat the other, so they both maintain their places, and with both he must make terms. The settlement is unsatisfactory; perhaps one party absolutely condemns it, as in the case of the "Godless colleges." Ever since the Act of Emancipation, all legislation for Ireland, of which the legislation on education is but an example, has been only half-measures and patchwork. If there be an exception it is the disestablishment of the Irish Church; but even that was a compromise in which the English and Protestant notions prevailed to an extent at least equal to those which are Irish and Catholic. In framing measures for Ireland an English minister anxious to do full justice would always have opposed to him two mighty powers—the jealousy in England of Ireland's prosperity, and the hatred of Englishmen against Ireland's religion. The history of Ireland during the present century shows that there is only one power which, during ordinary times, can overcome the enormous power of England's prejudice and English bigotry; and that power is the united and organized Irish people demanding justice. I say in ordinary times; because when England is threatened with war, only a slight murmur from Ireland is sufficient to bring Englishmen to a sense of what is right, and a rapid and unanimous determination to do it. But occasions of this kind do not so often occur. "England's adversity is Ireland's opportunity," is a well known and oft-repeated apophthegm. But, happily for England, unhappily for Ireland, England's adversity does not so often occur. Still it does sometimes occur, and it occurs often enough to exempt Irish Catholics from that class of persons spoken of in the trite quotation from Horace :

"Rusticus expectat dum defluat amnis ; "

and it happens often enough to make it imprudent to wait for the event. Between the intervals much mischief is done which renders redress more difficult. In opportunities England certainly has the best of it. For if England's adversity be Ireland's opportunity, certainly Ireland's *un*unanimity—if I may coin an expression—is England's opportunity ; and whereas adversity here is only of fitful occurrence, and therefore Ireland's opportunity only seldom appears, the differences amongst Irish Catholics are so chronic that English opportunities succeed each other in a very rapid course. To what extent English statesmen deliberately foment differences and quarrels amongst Irish Catholics, I must leave those to judge who are in the secret of government. But the soundest piece of advice which could be given to the Irish Catholics, if they were just beginning to exercise civil rights for the benefit of their religion and country, would be to tell them, first and above all things, to beware of allowing any one to create disunion amongst them. If the Irish wish to see the day when a statesman will arise who will govern them as they ought to be governed let them be united, and the man will soon appear. Englishmen are quite capable of being educated in the science of governing Ireland well. Nothing would sooner educate an Englishman up to the proper standard in this most necessary branch of political learning, than a positive demand from a united people. If Irish Catholics were united amongst themselves, both nations would be greatly benefited : the Irish would get what they want and what they ought to have ; the English would soon find a middle term to prove at least the practical use of the new order of ideas. Some would say, "Well, after all, it is only just;" and others, after a good deal of grumbling, would settle quietly to their own business, on the principle that "what can't be cured must be endured." If that most desirable of all political unions, union amongst Irish Catholics, could be brought about, and have a lasting existence, the happiness resulting from it would be so complete and so enchanting, that the idea of repealing any other union would never enter into men's minds. Irish Catholics in permanent union amongst themselves would soon obtain not merely equal laws, administered with impartiality, but laws suited to the genius and character of the Irish people. What more would they need? Pitt's famous statute, after eighty-five years of perhaps very merited abuse, would at last rest in peace.

If such a state of things could be brought about, what glorious days we should have: glorious for the Irish nation and glorious for the Irish Church. The nation would thrive and be strong under liberties gained as Emancipation was gained, and the Church would have that influence which is her due, an influence which may perhaps be the only thing wanting in the United Kingdom to preserve in the hearts of millions the fear of God and the honour of the Sovereign. If faith and loyalty are to be preserved in these islands, they will be preserved by the Catholic Church. No Irishman can complain of the remarks I have made about the want of union amongst his countrymen. The same remarks have been made by every Irishman who has written the history of Ireland or any portion of it. It is impossible to take up any book which treats of Irish history, and not, after a few pages, see the fatal effect of disunion. Open the volume where you please, you will be delighted at first by the noble schemes which ought to lead to glorious results. But, alas! you will come before long to the inevitable paragraph, which might remind a lawyer of the first recital in a deed of separation of husband and wife: "Whereas various unhappy differences have arisen," etc. The proof of what I have written is in the facts stated and the admissions made by Irishmen themselves. The truth, indeed, in this matter is patent to all; and to us on this side of the Channel, if distance does not lend enchantment, it certainly lends clearness to the view.

The remarks here made have been dictated by the sincerest possible friendship for Ireland and the Irish. They have been made in the firm belief that union amongst Irish Catholics, and, as far as possible, union amongst Irish and British Catholics, is the chief blessing to be desired for the Church in the United Kingdom. Nothing could be more unbecoming in the mouth of an English Catholic than an ill-natured reproach of the Irish for not being united amongst themselves; at the same time it would be impossible to write truly about the state of the Catholics in these islands without alluding to what is a patent and an important fact. It would be well if some Irish Catholic were to collect together the various instances in which, during the last hundred years, disunion amongst Irish Catholics has either led to failure, or at least materially injured the work to be done. If the facts could be brought to a focus, they might perhaps cause the truth to be seen more clearly than it is now, under a scattered and unheeded light. The Irish Catholics are a great political power, but by disunion amongst themselves this power is wasted and lost.

CHAPTER XI.

FIRST SCOTCH RELIEF ACT.

English and Scotch bigotry—The Church in Scotland—The Act of 1793.

BEFORE beginning the history of English Catholics during the present century, the reader should know the progress of events in Scotland. The riots in Edinburgh and Glasgow have been noticed in a former chapter. Considerable damage had been done to the property of Catholics, and Mr. Burke loudly demanded full compensation. Some compensation was made, but not half enough to cover the loss. The venerable Bishop Hay, so well known in all English-speaking communities by his excellent works, received nothing for the loss of his valuable library.[1]

Nothwithstanding the fierce bigotry and opposition of the Scotch Presbyterians, which rendered the effort useless, Charles James Fox, whose thorough Whig liberal principles ought to shame those who call themselves his disciples in our day, proclaimed in the House of Commons that it was time to relieve the Catholics from the persecution of those laws which Burke said were as severe, though not quite so bloody, as the laws of Draco.[2] Nothing, however, in the way of relief from the penal laws was done. Every-

---
[1] Walsh's "History of the Catholic Church in Scotland," p. 525.
[2] Ibid.

thing was done by the ministers and elders of the Presbyterian Church to keep up an excitement against the Catholics. The Scotch Catholics did not benefit by the more kindly feeling and the spirit of greater toleration which, amongst the English Protestants, succeeded the passing of the Relief Bill in 1778. On the contrary, the indulgence shown to the English Catholics only increased the virulence which existed in the hearts of the Scotch against the Church. So that when the Act of 1791 legalized the Catholic religion in England, it was still proscribed in Scotland, and every effort made to prevent it from growing, and, if possible, to stamp it out. In 1792, the only chapel in the city of Glasgow was a small room, into which a few Catholics stealthily entered on a Sunday morning. This room was indeed the only place where Mass was said in Glasgow until the year 1797, four years after the first Scotch Relief Act, about which I shall presently write. There can, I think, be no doubt that there is a greater and more deeply rooted hatred of the Church in Scotland, even to this day, than in England. North of the Tweed the hatred is directed more intensely and more immediately against the dogmas of faith. That this hatred exists in England is true; but it does not exist so universally, nor is it so pointedly directed against the great truths of religion as in Scotland. In England a pseudo-hierarchy, claiming to be descended from the old Catholic hierarchy, has kept up the old form of Church government. The English have acknowledged the authority of bishops and priests, and object only to Catholic bishops and Catholic priests. But the Scotch abolished all episcopal and sacerdotal authority, and therefore speak of bishops and priests with a virus unknown in England; and this virus is so bitter that no social laws of courtesy or good manners can keep it within the bounds of propriety. Besides this, the work of destruction was so completely done at the time of the Reformation, that the Christian feasts which were respected by the Anglicans were abolished by the Scotch. John Knox and his followers knew that to root out everything that was Catholic, they must destroy as far as possible everything that was Christian. And so great was their desire to put an end to everything Catholic that they determined to obliterate from the minds of Scotchmen the recollection even of the great feasts of the Church. The feasts of Christmas, Good Friday, Easter, and Whitsuntide were abolished. With the abolition of the feasts, the reality of the mysteries celebrated lost their hold on men's minds; until at this day the words Christmas Day, Good Friday, Easter, and Whitsuntide bring to the minds of Scotchmen, even of educated Scotchmen, no idea whatever in any way connected with religion.[1]

It has been noticed in a former chapter that in England there is a great deal that is political, as distinguished from dogmatical, in the hatred which is directed against the Church. Although the foundations and the more solid portion of the superstructure of British liberties were laid in Catholic times, the enemy of mankind has succeeded

---

[1] "Whitsunday" brings no other idea to the minds of Scotchmen than that of paying or receiving rent and interest, or of *flitting* from one tenement to another, Whitsunday, by Act of Parliament, always falling on a week day. A caricature which appeared in *Punch* a few years ago, when Christmas Day fell on a Sunday, is not in the smallest degree an exaggeration. An Englishman, detained by business, has the misfortune to spend Christmas Day in a town on the other side of the Tweed. No Englishman who can by possibility afford to appear at least merry on Christmas Day, ever thinks of looking anything else. Going out in the morning, in a good and merry humour with everybody, he meets a Scotch acquaintance, and, as every Englishman or Irishman would do on a like occasion, he cries out, "A merry Christmas to you." "That's nae an epithet, I'm thinking, to put before the sabbath," is the only answer he receives from the sad-looking, long-faced hypocrite.

in possessing the English mind with the absurd but most deplorable delusion that the Catholic religion is opposed to the liberties of the people. Hence, all that miserable cant about "popery and slavery" is so constantly uttered, to the unspeakable disgust of all British and Irish Catholics. But in Scotland hatred of doctrine absorbs every other sentiment. Scotch Presbyterians seem to have this hatred always ready for expression. And as they emphatically hate the Catholic Church, so they appear to hate the members of the Church, and especially, of course, the priests of the Church. A Catholic priest cannot walk the streets of a town in Scotland without seeing in the countenances, and sometimes hearing from the mouths, of at least one half of the Scotch people whom he may meet, signs and expressions which convey the idea that they are saying in their hearts what the Pharisees of old cried out against our Lord, "Crucify Him, crucify Him!" And the religion of these people well fits them to hate what is good and true. The Church would look for its worst enemies amongst those whose religious thoughts were full of sadness and gloom. It is said in Scotland that the ministers who are most followed, are those who show the most cleverness in persuading those who "sit under" them that they form a portion of the elect. But in meeting these saints coming from church on a Sunday, a person might fairly judge by their appearance—awful in every respect—that the minister had undoubtedly convinced them that they were all predestined to eternal loss.

From this the reader will easily imagine that the number of converts in Scotland is much smaller than that in England. It is a very rare thing for a person of purely Scotch blood, and a Presbyterian, to become a Catholic. In the city of Glasgow it is estimated that there are about one hundred and twenty thousand Catholics. Of these there may be about one thousand whose parents were both Scotch, and the greater part of them are Highlanders, or of Highland descent. The Church in the Lowlands of Scotland, though it includes several large communities in Edinburgh, Glasgow, and Dundee, and many lesser ones who live either in small towns, or scattered in the country in the neighbourhood of smaller towns, is almost purely Irish. At the time of which I am writing, the Lowlands had been almost entirely cleared of Catholics; and it is comparatively of late years that there has existed any Catholic chapel between Edinburgh and Berwick-on-Tweed. On the Western Border, especially in Dumfries, Catholics were better off. But at the beginning of this century there were probably fewer Catholics by far in the Border counties of Scotland than in any part of England of the same respective extent. It was not so in the Highlands. Amongst the Macdonalds on the western coast, and amongst the Chisholms and Frasers, and a few other clans, there have always been many Catholic families in which the faith has never been lost. The district of Moidart, for example, is almost entirely Catholic to this day.[1] Some of the Western Islands are also almost exclusively Catholic.

During the bad times religion was kept alive in Scotland, as it was in England, by missionary priests, amongst whom were several members of the Society of Jesus, to whose labours Scotland is indebted for the preservation of the faith in some districts. The most remarkable man at the time of which I am writing was Bishop Hay. The author of the "Memoirs" prefixed to the last

[1] The author was present some fifteen years ago at a school-feast held in a school established on Loch Sheil by the late lamented Mr. Hope Scott, of Dorlin and Abbotsford. There were about forty children present, and all except two answered to the name of Macdonald.

edition of his works says, "Since the religious revolution of the sixteenth century, to no man has the Catholic Church in Scotland been so much indebted as to Bishop Hay. He is pre-eminently her bishop of the last three hundred years." He was born in 1729, and at the age of sixteen he followed the army of Prince Charles Edward into England, as assistant to his professor, Mr. George Lander, who was appointed head surgeon to the army. On his return to Scotland he was taken prisoner and sent to London, but was liberated in 1747. He went back to Scotland, and in 1747 he was received into the Church by Sir Alexander Seaton, a Jesuit missioner. Shortly after he accepted the appointment of surgeon on board a trading vessel bound for the Mediterranean, and, having to pass through London before embarking, he there made the acquaintance of Bishop Challoner. In 1751 he entered the Scotch College in Rome. After eight years' study he was ordained priest, and returned to Scotland, where he laboured as a missionary, and in 1769 he was consecrated bishop. He died in the year 1811.

The number of Catholics in Scotland at the beginning of this century is supposed to have been about thirty thousand. Of this number the great majority were Highlanders. And in most of those towns where a few Catholics began to collect together, as at Glasgow, Greenock, and Paisley, they were chiefly, if not entirely, from the Highlands. And the number remained small until God sent the Irish people to swell to large proportions the members of His Church, and to sing the song of the Lord in a strange land.

The Scotch establishments abroad shared the same fate as had befallen the English. "The miserable state of the Scottish mission," says Walsh,[1] "and its great loss

[1] "History of the Catholic Church in Scotland," p. 530.

by the French Revolution, was brought before some of the members of the British Government by Bishop Hay and some liberal Protestant friends. The Government considered that both justice and humanity demanded that something should be done for the Scotch Catholic clergy. The chief difficulty in the way was the danger of giving offence to the fanatical or intolerant portion of the community, lest "No Popery" riots should ensue. And such was the dread by the Government of that day of this faction, that it was deemed necessary that all should be kept a profound secret in regard to the relief given. The Government granted to the two bishops, who were Vicars Apostolic, the sum of one hundred pounds a year each, also to the Catholic priests in Scotland a sum sufficient to make up their salaries, including what could be got from other sources, to twenty pounds a year each. The two Catholic seminaries of Aquhorties and Lismore were to get fifty pounds a year each, with a contribution of six hundred pounds a year each for its erection. This grant was no doubt useful at the time, but it was not continued even to the end of the war with France. The full amount of the grant, as far as we can learn, was never paid. It was at first given very reluctantly, and with fear and trembling, and after three years it was entirely withdrawn." It will be observed that the clergy to whom the Government gave this temporary relief were not foreign refugees, as those were to whom the nation behaved so generously in England. The refugees who came to Scotland were Scotch priests. From this it would appear that the resources of the Scotch Catholics were much less than those of the English Catholics, as the latter were able to support the English clergy who returned to their own country at the time of the French Revolution. There were certainly fewer families in Scotland than in England of the wealthier class, and therefore fewer who could give funds and hospitality to the exiles. Another thing to be remarked in the above extract from Walsh's history, is how the Government of the day was almost completely dominated, in dealing with the Scotch Catholics, by public opinion in Scotland. This public opinion was not only adverse to Catholics, but it was informed by the bitterest hate of our religion, and the most bigoted spirit of intolerance.

Such being the state of things in Scotland, especially as regards the feelings of the Presbyterians towards their Catholic fellow-subjects, it is no matter of wonder that the first Relief Act was delayed for fifteen years after the first Act for the relief of the English. Of this first Scotch Relief Act I will give the account in the words of Mr. Butler.[1] " On Monday, the 22nd of April, 1793, the Lord Advocate of Scotland stated, in the House of Commons, that 'his Majesty's Catholic subjects in Scotland were then incapacitated by law either from holding or transmitting landed property, and were liable to other very severe restrictions, which could not then be justified by any necessity or expediency.' He therefore moved 'that leave should be given to bring in a bill to relieve persons professing the Roman Catholic religion from certain penalties and disabilities imposed on them by Acts of Parliament in Scotland, and particularly by an Act of the 8th of King William.' On the following day the lord advocate proceeded to observe that 'the Roman Catholics of Scotland laboured under many hardships and disabilities on account of their adherence to their religion. By one law an oath, called a formula, or solemn declaration, was imposed upon them, which they could not take without renouncing the religion which they professed, and if they refused to take it, their nearest Protestant relation might deprive them of

[1] "Historical Memoirs," vol. iv. p. 104, edition of 1822.

their estates.' His lordship stated that 'it was repugnant to justice and humanity that a subject should be deprived of his estate for no other reason than that he professed the religion most agreeable to his judgment and his conscience, or that he should be placed in the wretched situation of holding his estates at the mercy of any Protestant relation who might be profligate enough to strip him of it by enforcing this penal law. The liberality which had induced the House last year, and on a former occasion, to grant relief to the Roman Catholics of England, would, he was persuaded, induce them to extend relief also to the Roman Catholics of Scotland, whose loyalty and conduct gave them an equal claim to the indulgence of the Legislature. He admitted that the particular law to which he referred was too odious to be often carried into execution, but if it was not fit that it should be executed at all, it ought not to be suffered to remain, merely as a temptation to the profligate to strip honest and meritorious people of their property.' He said he was extremely sorry to inform the committee 'that there was, at that moment, a suit actually depending in the courts of law in Scotland founded on this particular statute. A Roman Catholic gentleman, as respectable and amiable in character as any man in this or any other kingdom, was possessed of an estate of £1000 a year, which had been in his family for at least a century and a half. This gentleman, loved and respected by all who knew him, was now on the point of being stripped of his property by a relation, who could have no other shadow of claim to it than that which he might derive from this penal law, which he was endeavouring to enforce. In the courts as much delay as possible was thrown in the way, but it was to be feared that he must succeed at last, and reduce to beggary a gentleman in every respect a most meritorious subject. If it was too late to save him from such a misfortune, the Legislature, he trusted, would interpose, and take care that he should be the last victim to a cruel law, and that it should never operate in future to the destruction of any other person; for surely it was no longer to be endured that a man should be placed in the horrid situation of either renouncing the religion of his heart, or, by adhering to it conscientiously, forfeit all his worldly substance.' His lordship concluded by moving 'that the chairman should be directed to move the House for leave to bring in a bill requiring an oath of abjuration and declaration from his Majesty's Roman Catholic subjects in that part of Great Britain called Scotland.' Colonel Macleod having declared his ready concurrence in the measure proposed, the question was unanimously carried, and the bill having passed through all its stages without opposition, it received in due course the confirming sanctions of other branches of the Legislature."[1] Thus we see that only ninety-one years ago the penal laws were, at least in one instance, in active operation.

Mr. Butler, in his "Historical Memoirs," sets out the whole of the long preamble to this first Scotch Relief Act. It is not necessary to insert it here; but the conclusions which Mr. Butler draws from it are worth notice. He says, "Both the general tenor and the language of this Act are very remarkable. They appear to imply, or rather to express in clear and unambiguous terms, that the Parliament who passed the Act understood, first, that Popery consists in the Pope's right to temporal power in this country;[2] secondly, that a Roman Catholic, taking the oath of supremacy, denies by it the Pope's temporal

[1] For this account Mr. Butler refers to the "Annual Register" for the year 1793.
[2] Butler adds in a note, "If this be true, there is now no Papist."

power, but does not deny by it his spiritual power;[1] thirdly, that this spiritual power was, in a political view, merely a speculative and dogmatical opinion; fourthly, that the oath of 1778 was, and had been found, a proper and sufficient test of the loyalty of the persons by whom it is taken; and fifthly, that an uniformity of oaths is desirable." To this Butler adds, quoting from Lucan, "Quid quærimus ultra?" and then concludes the chapter by saying that "Catholics solicit from Parliament nothing more than that they should legislate, in their regard, upon these principles, in a manner suitable to their high wisdom and liberality, with a due regard to the honour and conscientious feelings of those whom they profess to relieve."[2]

What the Catholics of the United Kingdom seek for is that we should not be governed as Catholics according to the notions of English Protestants and English freethinkers. In all matters relating to religion, and where we ought to be free, we say to English Protestants and English freethinkers what the little doll's dressmaker is constantly saying about certain people in one of Dickens' novels, "I don't like your ways and your manners."

When freethinkers in religion proclaim that all the Queen's subjects should be allowed to worship God in the manner which most approves itself to the conscience of each one, and at the same time perseveringly endeavour to banish the teaching of any religion from the schools, and so prevent us from giving that instruction which we conscientiously believe we ought to give to our children, we do not like such conduct. When Whigs ally themselves with freethinkers to preserve themselves in power; when they sacrifice principles to party; when they themselves,

---

[1] Butler adds in a note to this, "But it has, we apprehend, been shown in a former part of the work that the oath of supremacy is not susceptible of this construction."

[2] "Historical Memoirs," vol. iv. p. 110.

or at least the more respectable portion of them, profess to fear God and honour the Sovereign, but by an unholy alliance help their supporters to prevent us from doing the same, we do not like such behaviour. When a prime minister, thwarted by the bishops of the Catholic Church in his scheme for educating the Irish according to his English Protestant notions, chafes under his disappointment, and writes pamphlets to raise a mischievous "No-Popery" cry against us, we do not like "his ways and his manners." When the Tories pander to Orangemen, and endeavour to keep Catholics in the background; when, professing the same loyalty to God and the Queen which we profess, they refuse an alliance with us, which would help them to preserve Christianity and loyalty amongst the people, we do not like and we cannot understand such behaviour. When all parties and all men are governed in their dealings with us by the cry of a thoughtless and ignorant mob, urged on by the jealousy and malice of those who would lead it, we do not like such "ways and manners." Who would? "Quid quærimus ultra?" says Mr. Butler. We seek now for "a fair field and no favour." We seek for that appreciation by those who govern us which is due to men who, through evil report and good report, for better and for worse, have always loved and clung to their country; who among the loyal are the most loyal; and who, should their mother country ever be in need, will prove themselves the children who love and honour her the most.

CHAPTER XII.

THE RESIGNATION OF PITT IN 1801—THE VETO.

The resignation of Pitt—Lord Stanhope on Pitt's resignation—The Veto—Gregory XVI. and Lord Melbourne.

THE question of the complete emancipation of Catholics, by opening to them the two Houses of Parliament, began to be discussed at the very commencement of this century. After twenty-nine years of agitation, the right was finally conceded in the reign of George IV. In the year 1800, the Catholics of Ireland were the only Catholics in the United Kingdom who could even vote for members of Parliament. The Catholics of England and Scotland did not obtain the franchise until the year 1829.

On the second of July, in the year 1800, the Act for the Legislative Union between England and Ireland received the royal assent, and it took effect from the 1st of January, 1801. On the 22nd of January, the first united Parliament met. Amongst the many things, fair and foul, which were done to ensure the passing of the Act of Union, one was that Mr. Pitt allowed the Irish Catholics to be aware of his determination to propose a measure for admitting them into Parliament. There is no doubt that Pitt had not only made up his mind to do this act of justice, but he also considered an Act of Relief as a necessary accompaniment of an Act of Union. He made

this expressed determination of his an inducement to
obtain the consent of the Irish Catholics to the union. To
such an extent did Pitt's determination operate, that most,
and perhaps the far greater majority of the Irish, thought
that they were more likely to obtain emancipation from
the united than from the separate Parliament. At the
same time, it certainly does not appear that Pitt ever gave,
or authorized any one to give in his name, a distinct
explicit pledge that he would bring in a bill to admit the
Irish Catholics into Parliament, though something very
like a pledge was implied. Mr. Pitt's intention being, as
we have seen, "the last question," says Dr. Aikin, "discussed in the Cabinet previously to the King's illness, was
the extension of all political privileges to the Roman
Catholics of Ireland, which Mr. Pitt had given them every
reason to expect."[1] The intention of the minister, and the
discussion in the Cabinet, were of course made known to
the King. The knowledge so preyed upon the mind of
George that it caused a return of what was commonly
called in those days "the King's illness," but which was,
in fact, insanity. His mind had been previously affected
in the year 1788. That George III. himself attributed his
"illness" in 1801 to Mr. Pitt's proposed emancipation of
the Catholics appears from what he himself said on the
subject: "On Friday, the 6th of March, the King . . . was
clear and calm in mind. . . . With respect to Mr. Pitt, his
Majesty used the following words—'Tell him I am now
quite well. . . . But what has he to answer for, who is the
cause of my having been ill at all?' Pitt was deeply
affected; and, before Mr. Addington, authorized Dr. Willis
to tell his Majesty that during his reign he would never
agitate the Catholic question—that is, whether in office or
out of office. . . . Dr. Willis, in a letter to Pitt, says, 'I

[1] "Annals of the Reign of George III.," vol. ii. p. 107.

stated to him' (the King) 'what you wished, and what I had a good opportunity of doing; and after saying the kindest things of you, he exclaimed, " Now my mind will be at rest!" Upon the Queen's coming in he told her your message, and he made the same observation upon it.'"[1]

Pitt resigned his office of prime minister, and, to quote the words of Dr. Aikin, "the sole reason assigned by him for resigning the post he had so long held with the applause of a great part of the nation, was his inability to carry the proposed measure in favour of the Catholics; and in a paper circulated in his name throughout Ireland, which he did not disavow, he assured the Catholics that he would do his utmost to establish their cause in the public favour (though he could not concur in a hopeless attempt to force it now), and prepare the way for their finally attaining their object."[2]

Great efforts were made to prevent Pitt from carrying out his determination to resign. "After a month of unexampled confusion," says Lord Campbell, "during which it was difficult to say in whom the executive Government was vested, the attempt to retain Mr. Pitt at the head of affairs on his renouncing all his measures for the relief of the Catholics failed, and his administration came to a close."[3] Several of Mr. Pitt's colleagues in the Cabinet followed him on his retirement from office; and he was succeeded in his post of prime minister by Mr. Addington, the speaker of the House of Commons.[4]

That George III.'s scruple about the admission of

---

[1] Lord Stanhope's "Life of Pitt," p. 302, et seq.
[2] "Annals of George III.," p. 107.
[3] "Life of Lord Eldon," p. 107.
[4] This Mr. Addington was a bitter enemy of Catholics. Some years afterwards, as Lord Sidmouth, and home secretary, he compelled Mr. Weld, of Lulworth, to send forth from hospitable asylum a community of Trappist monks, who had taken refuge on the Lulworth estate from the persecution inflicted on the Church by the French revolutionists.

Catholics to Parliament being inconsistent with the coronation oath was the great obstacle to an Emancipation Act, is well known. It would be difficult for a minister, whether Whig or Tory, to find himself in a more difficult position than one in which he has to choose between denying an act of justice to several millions of his Majesty's subjects on the one hand, and on the other hand, the certainty of driving his Majesty (and such a Majesty as George III.) out of his senses. There is no doubt that Pitt's intended resignation on the Catholic question drove the good old King mad. And Catholics must always look upon him as the good old King. With the exception, of course, of James II., he was the first King of England who did not persecute the Church since the time of Henry VIII., who made England to sin. He looked kindly upon Catholics, and decidedly set his face against persecution. He did much more; he gave an unhesitating and a cordial assent to the Relief Acts of 1778 and 1791. But he could not go a step further; he could not admit Catholics into Parliament. It was a conscientious scruple; but it was a mere scruple, and is now generally admitted to have been such. Lord Stanhope says, " I am far from denying . . . that there were several weighty arguments to allege against the Roman Catholic claims. But most certainly the supposed breach of the coronation oath is not to be numbered among these. It has been long since, and almost by common consent, abandoned as untenable."[1] So great and so universal was the respect entertained for George III., that Catholics, who among the loyal are the most loyal, would never have urged on the question at the risk of bringing on the same misfortune which had been caused in 1801. The question was often discussed during the regency; but it was not

[1] "Life of Pitt," vol. iii. p. 263.

until the year 1820 that, to use Mr. Butler's words, "proceedings for our final and complete relief were begun."[1] The administration which followed that of Mr. Pitt was therefore essentially anti-Catholic. This was made pretty evident when Parliament met in January, 1802. Lord Stanhope says, "On the 23rd, the King went down and delivered the opening speech. He exhorted the two Houses 'to maintain the true principles of the Constitution in Church and State,' an allusion, as some persons deemed it, to the Roman Catholic claims." And he adds in a note, "'They have put Church and State into the speech; I think I guess why:' so wrote Canning from London. 'It could only be to revive what led to Mr. Pitt's going out of office.' So said Mr. Rose at Bath."[2]

A question has arisen amongst historians, biographers, and writers in reviews, whether Pitt's real, or at any rate dominant, motive for resigning office in 1801 was that the King would not allow him to bring forward the question of emancipation. As the question is one which would afford interesting matter for speculation to any one, and is especially interesting to Catholics, the reader may perhaps not dislike a few remarks on the subject.

At the time that Mr. Pitt resigned in 1801, the question of making peace with Napoleon was being discussed. As time went on, it became evident that peace must soon be made.[3] Pitt saw that peace was inevitable, and as he had always been in favour of war, and of war carried on vigorously against France, the act of making peace would have been to him one of great humiliation. It has, therefore, been said that the great minister resigned in

---

[1] "Memoirs of English Catholics," 1820.
[2] "Life of Pitt," *ut supra*.
[3] The preliminaries of peace were signed in London on the 1st of October, 1801, and the treaty of peace was signed at Amiens on the 27th of March, 1802.

reality because he did not wish to be the one to make peace; but that, not liking to own this, he gave as the reason his inability to pass in favour of the Catholics an Act of Relief. Pitt's own account of his resignation, as given by Lord Stanhope, is as follows:—" On the 16th of February, in answer to Sheridan, Pitt said, 'I have been accused of having refused to give the House an explanation upon the subject of my resignation. Sir, I did not decline giving the House any explanation on that subject; but I must be permitted to observe that it appears to me a new and not a very constitutional doctrine, that a man must not follow his sense of duty—that a man must not, in compliance with the dictates of his conscience, retire from office without being bound to give to this House and to the public an account of all the circumstances that weigh in his mind and influence his conduct. Where this system of duty is established I know not. I have never heard that it was a public crime to retire from office without explaining the reason. I, therefore, am not aware how it can be a public crime in me to relinquish, without assigning a cause, a station which it would be the ambition of my life and the passion of my heart to continue to fill if I could do so with advantage to the country and consistently with what I conceive to be my duty. As to the merits of the question which led to my resignation, though I do not feel myself bound, I am willing to submit them to the House. I should rather leave it to posterity to judge of my conduct; still I have no objection to state the fact. With respect to the resignation of myself and of some of my friends, I have no wish to disguise from the House that we did feel it to be an incumbent duty upon us to propose a measure on the part of the Government which, under the circumstances of the Union so happily effected between the two countries, we thought of great public importance, and necessary to complete the benefits likely to result from that measure. We felt this opinion so strongly, that when we met with circumstances which rendered it impossible for us to propose it as a measure of Government, we equally felt it inconsistent with our duty and our honour any longer to remain a part of that Government. What may be the opinion of others I know not, but I beg to have it understood to be a measure which, if I had remained in Government, I must have proposed. What my conduct will be in a different situation must be regulated by a mature and impartial review of all the circumstances of the case. I shall be governed (as it has always been the wish of my life to be) only by such considerations as I think best tend to ensure the tranquillity, the strength, and the happiness of the Empire.' " [1]

Such being Pitt's account of the reason for his resignation, I will give a few opinions offered by different writers. Mr. Therry, who, as the friend of Canning, and the editor of his speeches, must often have heard this matter spoken of, accepts Pitt's statement without reserve. He says, " Pitt resigned in consequence of his inability to carry a measure of relief, which he had given the Irish every reason to expect as the result of the Union." [2] Alison is of a different opinion. He says, " The personal objections of the King to the removal of the Catholic disabilities, to which Mr. Pitt considered himself pledged as a consequence of the Irish Union, afford at least the ostensible reason for the resignation of that minister and his personal adherents, which took place on the 1st of February ; the real cause, more probably, was the reluc-

---

[1] "Life of Pitt," vol. iii. p. 285.
[2] "Canning's Speeches," edited by Therry, vol. v. p. 359. Mr. Therry was afterwards, and for many years, well known in Australia as Judge Therry.

tance of Mr. Pitt to be personally concerned in concluding peace with France, which he saw could not be much longer delayed."[1] Mr. M'Cullagh Torrens, one of the most impartial of writers, does not seem able to accept of Pitt's statement.[2] He says, "Pitt, after eighteen years' experience of the incoherency and intolerance of George III., picked a quarrel with his Majesty about religious disabilities, and threw up his office when he could not prevail. After three years' exile, he discovered that his *sine qua non* might with honour be waived; and he came back without being able to give any logical account of why he had quitted."[3] Lord Stanhope maintains that the reason assigned by Pitt was the true one. "It has often been said," he writes, "both in England and abroad, and even now perhaps the rumour has not wholly died away, that the cause assigned by Mr. Pitt was only his ostensible, and not his real motive. It has been asserted that he withdrew from office on account of the difficulties which he experienced or expected in the way of making peace. Lord John Russell and another eminent critic have some years since sufficiently disposed of this hostile allegation. The original documents bearing on the question, some of which have lately come to light, must, I am sure, convince every careful and dispassionate reader that any such idea is entirely unfounded."[4]

The refusal of the King to allow Pitt to carry a measure to which he was implicitly, if not explicitly, pledged, was a sufficient ground for resignation. It was something more than a sufficient ground for resignation.

[1] "History of Europe," Epitome, p. 184.
[2] Mr. M'Cullagh Torrens is almost the only Protestant writer of repute who, in writing about Catholics and Catholic affairs, makes use of respectful and correct phraseology.
[3] "Life of Lord Melbourne," vol. i. p. 341.
[4] "Life of Pitt," vol. iii. p. 309.

To resign, under the circumstances in which Pitt did resign, was the only course which a high-spirited minister could adopt. There was no necessity, therefore, for seeking any other reason. And as Pitt declares what his reason was, it would not be just to assign any other reason unless that other reason were evidently the motive. That Pitt was glad to escape from the responsibility of making peace with Napoleon was no doubt true, and it may have been a consolation to him not to be minister when the peace was made; but there is no reason for supposing that if the King had been willing to do justice to Ireland, Pitt would not have cheerfully undertaken the responsibility of making peace, or any responsibility which a continuance in office might have thrown upon him.

I will now give the reader some of Lord Stanhope's reflections on the King's determination to resist the Catholic claims. "Few things in our history," says his lordship, "are perhaps more to be lamented than the inflexible determination of the King, in February, 1801, against the Roman Catholic claims. Even the adversaries on principle of those claims would probably in the present day partake in that regret. They would argue that the concession should not have been made at all; but they would allow that, if made, it would have been attended with much greater benefit, or with fewer evils by far, in 1801 than it was in 1829. How fierce and long was the intervening conflict! How much of rancour and ill-will— and not on one side only, but on both—did that conflict leave behind! It is true, indeed, that even in 1801 there would have been a resolute resistance to the measure— a resistance headed by the primate in England, and by the primate in Ireland. But I think it certain that, had the king been favourable, or even remained neutral, the measure would have passed, not easily indeed, but still by a large majority. The feelings of the English people had not been stirred to any considerable extent against it. There had been none of that violent conduct and violent language on the part of Roman Catholics which at a later period provoked so much resentment on the other side. In 1801, it would have been a compromise between parties; in 1829, it was a struggle and a victory of one party above the other. And, further still, the measure that was carried by the Duke of Wellington was far less comprehensive than the one proposed by Mr. Pitt. It did not comprise any settlement of the Roman Catholic clergy which in 1801 might have been most advantageous, and which thirty years later became not only disadvantageous, but impossible."[1] Such are Lord Stanhope's reflections upon the failure of Pitt to carry a Relief Bill.

Very different are the reflections of most Catholics on the same thing. Few things in our history are perhaps more to be rejoiced at than the inflexible determination of the King in February, 1801, against the Roman Catholic claims. It is quite certain that if Pitt could have carried a Relief Bill he would have done so; and it is equally certain that he would have charged the Relief Bill with clauses, giving what in those days would have been called "securities" on the part of Catholics. These "securities" would have been a veto, or something in the nature of a veto, on the election of bishops, and a State provision for the Irish clergy. Securities!—new chains to be fastened on as soon as the old penal chains had been removed. That we have been delivered from a new slavery, we owe to the inflexible determination of the King. "How fierce and long," says Lord Stanhope, "was the intervening conflict." But the very fierceness and length of the conflict made the Catholics more feared, with that whole-

[1] "Life of Pitt," vol. iii. p. 281.

some fear which keeps the tyrant from the intended victim. Lord Stanhope seems to look upon the violent language used, as he says at a later period, as an unmitigated evil. We may presume he alludes chiefly to the language used by O'Connell. As we get nearer the time of emancipation, we shall see it admitted that if O'Connell had not used the language he did, he never would have won emancipation. "In 1801," says Lord Stanhope, "it would have been a compromise between parties." Yes, it would have been a compromise; and thank God it was not. A compromise between Catholics and the English Government means Catholics giving up something they have a right to, in order to get something else they have a right to, but which is being unlawfully kept back from them. "In 1829," continues Lord Stanhope, "it was a struggle and a victory of one party above the other." But the victory of the Irish Catholics made them politically respected, and feared with a wholesome fear. In 1829, the Catholics of the United Kingdom felt that it was as useful a thing to have amongst them a man who had brought England on her knees, as all the King's subjects felt it a useful and comfortable thing to have amongst us the man who had made Napoleon turn his back upon the British lines at Waterloo. Though I do not wish to give a very decided opinion, I am inclined to think that if O'Connell had a political defect, it was the same which in military affairs Maherbal charged upon Hannibal, that he knew how to conquer, but not how to use his victory. "And further still," continues Lord Stanhope, "the measure that was carried by the Duke of Wellington was far less comprehensive than the one proposed by Mr. Pitt." When the reader understands that this desirable comprehensiveness would have comprehended the security clauses, the veto, the State payment of the clergy and other new claims, he will be inclined to say: Thank God that the bill which was introduced in 1829 was far less comprehensive than the one William Pitt would have drawn. When we consider our present position in the British Isles, and still more when we consider that the hitherto abandoned fruits of victory are still within our reach if we choose to take them, not only are we inclined to say, but we do say, with the deepest feelings of heartfelt gratitude: Thank God for the "inflexible determination of the King in 1801, against the Roman Catholic claims."

It was not until a few years after the beginning of this century that the word "veto" was heard in connection with any designed interference of the British Crown with the government of the Church in this country. The idea of obtaining the consent of the bishops of the United Kingdom and of the Holy Father to such interference had occurred to William Pitt some years before the name of veto was heard. As we have seen, some concessions on the part of Catholics were expected by the minister, and they formed a part of the plan framed by him for our complete emancipation. As the question of making concessions in Church government as the price of emancipation, was for many subsequent years debated amongst both Catholics and Protestants, it may be well, before proceeding with the history of the question, to explain, as clearly as I may be able, what the veto meant.

When, by custom of ancient standing tolerated at Rome, or by the tacit consent of the Holy See, or by the usurpation of the civil power, or by what is called a *concordat*, the sovereign power in any country exercises any portion of that authority which of strict right belongs to the Holy Father, that power may either be a positive or a negative power. A positive power would be (to take the example of the choice of a bishop to fill a vacant see), when the civil government should nominate a person to fill the office, and either present him to the Pope for institution, or direct the chapter to elect him for such presentation. A negative power, in the instance I have taken, would be where the civil power should exercise the right of objecting to any person canonically elected for presentation to the Pope. The difference between these two powers is theoretically great. The positive power is a direct exercise of authority in a spiritual matter, by a person to whom it does not naturally belong. The negative power enables a person who has naturally no power in a spiritual matter, to prevent one who has that power from exercising it. But the difference between the two powers is in practice not so great as it is in theory. For instance, the civil power in a State might exercise the negative power in the appointment of a bishop, so as to prevent the institution of any one to a vacant see, except the person whom the civil power might itself choose. If, for example, by a *concordat* the right of objecting to those elected by the chapter should be limited to a certain number of times, still the exercise of the power might sometimes prevent the election of any one of those whom the chapter might think fit to fill the office of bishop. The proper exercise of a negative power would depend on many circumstances. It might be in the hands of one of sound judgment or of unsound judgment, of a man of fair or unfair disposition. One man might consult only the interest, as he would understand it, of the Church and of the see to be filled; another man might look only to what he would consider the interest of the State, ignoring completely the interests of the Church and of the See. One minister might object to a priest being made a bishop, on the ground that he was what he would call a proselytizer, and this simply because he had been a successful controversialist; another less bigoted might despise such a reason. There are men who would decide such a question from unworthy personal motives, and there are others who would rise superior to such imperfection. The veto nominally in the hands of the Crown, might be actually in the hands either of a Protestant or a Catholic minister. In this country it would, of course, be most likely in the hands of a Protestant; and if so, that fact alone would make the Holy See decline such a power, or even refuse to tolerate its exercise, unless under very great compulsion. And if in the hands of a Catholic, the interests of the Church might fare no better in the exercise of the right of exclusion. It has happened that some years ago a Catholic, closely connected with Government, was asked whether, in a matter affecting the interests of the Church, but not actually touching faith, he would act in the interest of the Church or of his own political party; and he unhesitatingly replied that he would give the interests of his party the first place.[1] The Holy See would not be well content that a veto upon the election of a bishop should be in the hands of such a minister.

In relation to this subject, and as an example of what might happen if the English Government were allowed to exercise a veto in the election of bishops, I may cite a remarkable passage from the "Greville Memoirs." Mr. Greville says, "I told him" (Lord Melbourne) "that I had been long of opinion that the only practicable and sound course was to open a negotiation with Rome, and to endeavour to deal with the Catholics in Ireland and the ministers of the Catholic religion upon the same plan

---

[1] The reader will observe that it was his *party*, not his *country*, to which he would give his preference.

which had been, *mutatis mutandis*, adopted universally in Germany and almost all over the Continent, and that there was nothing the Church of Rome desired so much as to cultivate a good understanding with us. He then told me a thing which surprised me, and which seemed to be at variance with this supposition—that an application had been made to the Pope very lately (through Seymour), expressive of the particular wish of the British Government, that he would not appoint MacHale to the vacant Catholic bishopric—*anybody but him;* notwithstanding which the Pope had appointed MacHale, but on this occasion the Pope made a shrewd observation. His Holiness said that 'he had remarked for a long time past that no piece of preferment of any value ever fell vacant in Ireland that he did not get an application from the British Government asking for the appointment.' Lord Melbourne supposed he was determined to show that he had the power of refusing and of opposing the wishes of Government, and in reply to my question, he admitted that the Pope had generally conferred the appointment according to the wishes of Government."[1] If the English Government had possessed the right of the veto, whether it had been in the hands of a Protestant or a Catholic, it would, in the particular instance mentioned by Lord Melbourne, have been undoubtedly exercised to exclude Dr. MacHale, and Ireland would have been deprived of a great bishop.

In the above extract we see that Greville thought that the fact of His Holiness having declined to accede to the request of the British Government to exclude Dr. MacHale from the episcopate, was at variance with the preconceived idea that Rome desired to cultivate a good understanding with us. It does not appear to me to militate against

[1] Vol. iii. pp. 269, 270, June 30, 1835, conversation with Lord Melbourne on the Irish Tithe Bill.

such an idea. Lord Melbourne told Greville, as we have seen, that "the Pope had generally conferred the appointment according to the wishes of Government." This, surely, is quite sufficient to show the inclination of Pope Gregory XVI. to meet the wishes of the English Government. It is ample proof of his desire not to exercise his authority in a way to offend the Crown of England unnecessarily. It would be ridiculous to say that, to show his good-will, His Holiness must in every case yield, in the appointment of a bishop, to the desire of the State. From what Lord Melbourne said, it would appear that the desire to interfere on the part of England was continual and becoming a great deal too frequent, and that Pope Gregory was resolved to show that there must be a break in the compliance with the requests of the State. It may, indeed, have crossed the mind of the vigilant pastor that, if every interference were allowed and every request acceded to, in a series of years a kind of right to interfere would have at last been claimed. His Holiness may have thought that it was time to stand on his right, lest, without even a *concordat*, an unauthorized power might have crept into the relations between England and Rome. He may have seen the shadow of the veto and taken alarm. The action of His Holiness in the case of Dr. MacHale does not show any recoiling from a desire to be on friendly terms with England. It shows that he wished to prevent a continual favour from becoming a recognized custom ; and to do so, he chose the case of one to whom the British Government objected, but who was a learned and pious priest, and who would be most acceptable as a bishop to the Irish people. In acting as he did, Pope Gregory also taught a good lesson to the English Government. The State should have no right, in any case, to interfere, except where it can show good proof that the loyalty of the person objected to is at least questionable. They could not show this in the case of Dr. MacHale. A man is not to be suspected of disloyalty to the crown of England because he can paint in strong colours the wrongs of his country and call out against the oppressor. Attwood, at the head of the political unions in 1831, and Cobden, the leader of the Anti-Corn-Law League, were not chargeable with disloyalty in their respective positions. The wrongs of Ireland were far greater than any wrongs suffered by the English. Church and landlord oppression, occasionally leading to a discharge of musketry upon the people from British soldiers, were grievances harder to be borne, than the want of suffrage, by the Birmingham gunmakers, or bread a little dearer than it has been of late years. Pope Gregory would have been ready to comply with the wishes of the English Government, if it could have shown that Dr. MacHale was not a loyal man; but perhaps he was rather glad to show that he would not refuse to confirm the election for the reason that Dr. MacHale was troublesome to the English Government, because he was a patriot. The loyalty of Dr. MacHale to the Crown of England was in every respect superior to the loyalty of those, the number of whom increases every day, who are only loyal to the Crown so long as the Crown satisfies all their desires. If English Statesmen, instead of objecting to the election of Dr. MacHale, had given the attention which it deserved to the voice from St. Jarlath's, it is most probable, indeed it is certain, that the relations between England and Ireland would not have been, to use an expression much in vogue now, so strained as they have been of late years and still are. Lord Melbourne was probably a little annoyed that His Holiness would not veto the election of Dr. MacHale; but he was not the man to resent it. He very likely secretly admired the independence and firmness of the Pontiff.

Some of my readers may probably be surprised to know, from what Lord Melbourne said to Greville, that the English Government does interfere so often in the election of Catholic bishops of the United Kingdom, particularly those of Ireland. But besides the authority of Lord Melbourne, I have heard on very good authority that such interference does occur much oftener than many would be inclined to suppose. The state of things revealed by Lord Melbourne's words is not altogether unsatisfactory, for that very state may prevent any recurrence to the question of a veto. If English statesmen would govern their relations with the Holy See on the same principles and good feeling which governed Lord Melbourne, no one could reasonably complain of the fact of those relations, or of the manner in which they were conducted. It is surely a good thing that the Holy See and even a Protestant Government should be on speaking terms. A hard and fast line between the two which would prevent any communication, might lead to a severity of conduct on both sides which would produce an unwholesome enmity rather than useful conciliation. If the English Government would take in a proper spirit and not be offended at some refusal to comply with its request, the Holy See would not object to a suggestion, and even to a remonstrance, when respectfully made, and would undoubtedly always be inclined to listen to reasons, and, where it could, comply with requests. In this way an English statesman who should have a share in what a Frenchman called in William Pitt "that prodigious good sense," would carry on affairs with Rome in a much more satisfactory manner than is done by those who look to written forms and agreements for their undeviating rule. England has it in her power to be a model for other nations to copy in their relations with the Holy Father. English statesmen can, if they choose, prove practically to the world that such odious things as forced concessions, vetoes and *concordats* are fit only to be matters of history.

Every power claimed and exercised by the State in spiritual matters is, of course, objectionable. The positive power is in every case a usurpation, or, what amounts to a usurpation—a concession which in no circumstances would be obtained unless extorted by superior force. The negative power—or, in other words, the veto, is less objectionable, but nevertheless so objectionable that the State would never be allowed to exercise it if the Church felt herself free to refuse it. In the history of the veto question in this country there was no attempt to claim in theory any positive power. All that was spoken of was a negative power, or the veto. And supposing that, unfortunately, any negative power in the nomination of bishops had been granted to the English Government, it would in all probability have been a limited negative power. A limited negative power is when the State has the power of setting aside only a certain number of names at each episcopal election. In an unlimited negative power, the State can set aside as many names as it pleases; and thus, when exercised to its full extent, it amounts in practice to a positive power. There can, however, be little doubt that the men in power in England when the question of the veto was being discussed, intended to obtain such a right to veto as would enable them practically to fill the Irish sees with men of their own choice. When we come to the history of the question, the reader will perceive from words publicly uttered, that some Protestants thought that, by obtaining the veto they would almost entirely subject the Catholic Church in the United Kingdom to the power of the State. It will be sufficient now to cite one proof of what has been said. Dr. Milner says, "The personage whose opinion he considered to be of the greatest weight in this business explained that the effect of the veto was to make it exactly correspond with the *Congé d'élire*, by which the Protestant bishops are appointed. 'I will suppose,' he said, 'myself to be his Majesty's Minister to whom you present a list of three candidates, whom your prelates judge worthy of the vacant chair. Very likely I may say to you: Neither Mr. A. nor Mr. B. nor Mr. C. is approved of, but if you choose Mr. F. he will be accepted.'"[1] From this we see what use would have been made of the veto if it had been obtained by the Government.

Having given the reader some idea of what the veto is, and of the power it would have given the English Government in the appointment of bishops in England, I propose in the next chapter to commence the history of the question as it was agitated in England and Ireland until it was swept away in the grand march of O'Connell's Catholic Association.

[1] "Supplementary Memoirs," p. 133, note. Milner does not say who the personage was whom he mentions in the above extract. It was probably in the year 1808 that the words above cited were said to him. If so, the No-Popery Ministry of the Duke of Portland was then in power; and Milner is not likely to have spoken to any member of that Ministry on the subject. The personage he alludes to may perhaps have been Lord Grenville.

CHAPTER XIII.

THE VETO QUESTION.

Origin of the Veto Question in the United Kingdom—Burke on the Veto—Resolutions of the Irish bishops in 1799—First public mention of the veto—Milner's interview with Ponsonby—Debate in the Commons—Milner and Ponsonby—Indignation in Ireland—Milner's " Letter to a Parish Priest."

THE earliest allusion to what was afterwards called "the Veto Question," so far as I have been able to discover, occurs in Edmund Burke's famous " Letter to a Peer of Ireland on the Penal Laws against Irish Catholics." The letter is dated February 21, 1792, and towards the end of it he writes as follows:—" Before I had written thus far, I heard of a scheme of giving to the Castle the patronage of the presiding members of the Catholic clergy. At first I could scarcely credit it: for I believe it is the first time that the presentation to other people's alms has been desired in any country. If the State provides a suitable maintenance and temporality for the governing members of the Irish Roman Catholic Church, and for the clergy under them, I should think the project, however improper in other respects, to be by no means unjust. But to deprive a poor people, who maintain a second set of clergy, out of the miserable remains of what is left after taxing and tithing—to deprive them of the disposition of their own charities among their own communion, would, in my opinion, be an intolerable hardship. Never were the members of one religious sect fit to appoint the pastors to another. Those who have no regard for their welfare, reputation, or internal quiet, will not appoint such as are proper. . . . It is a great deal to suppose that even the present Castle would nominate bishops for the Roman Church of Ireland, with a religious regard for its welfare. Perhaps they cannot, perhaps they dare not, do it. But suppose them to be as well inclined, as I know that I am, to do the Catholics all kind of justice, I declare I would not, if it were in my power, take that patronage on myself,— I know I ought not to do it."[1]

The next mention which I have found of the veto is in a letter from Dr. Hussey to Edmund Burke.[2] The letter was written from Dublin, and is dated January 29, 1795. Dr. Hussey says, "Some plan is likely to be thought of by Parliament for the appointment of Catholic bishops. The *election* to rest with the clergy, and the election of one out of three so elected to be in government, or something similar."[3] To this Burke replies on the 24th of February as follows:—"This is a great crisis for good or evil. Above all, do not listen to any other mode of appointing your bishops than the present, whatever it is; no other elections than those you have; no Castle choices."[4] Thus we see how jealous the great philosopher and orator was of any interference with the rights of those

---

[1] For further excellent remarks on this subject see the "Letter" in Burke's works. The "Peer of Ireland" was Lord Kenmare.

[2] Dr. Hussey was at one time attached to the Chapel of the Spanish Embassy in London; during which he was employed by the English Government in a delicate negotiation at Madrid. He became afterwards the first President of Maynooth College, the establishment of which, Charles Butler says, was principally due to him. He was subsequently appointed to the bishopric of Waterford.

[3] "Correspondence of the Right Hon. E. Burke," edited by Lord Fitzwilliam, vol. iv. p. 268.

[4] Ibid., p. 285.

whose cause he advocated: how clearly he saw the true interests of the Catholic Church in Ireland, and how anxious he was that they should not be injured by any secular power. As the next date in the history of the veto is after the death of Burke, this may be a good place to pay a very short tribute to his memory, and to say that of all the great men who advocated Catholic claims, not one was more sincere and faithful than Burke. And one thing entitles him to hold the first place among those Protestants to whom we owe respect and gratitude: in all he did for us, he seems to have had in view, not mere political expediency, not only the restoration of civil rights, but the well-being and perfect liberty of the Church in the United Kingdom. In giving Burke the first place, some may be inclined to think that I detract from the merit of our illustrious advocates Grattan and Canning. But it must be remembered that, as we shall see in the course of this history, Grattan and Canning were Vetoists, Burke was not.[1]

Between the years 1795 and 1799, the question of the veto was no doubt often discussed by Pitt and the other ministers who were meditating the Act of Union. Pitt, as we have seen, intended an Act of Emancipation to accompany the Act of Union. And he further intended that some concessions on the part of Catholics should be a condition of the Act of Emancipation. It was supposed that these concessions would render harmless the emancipated Catholic Church. But it is difficult to suppose that a statesman of such "prodigious good sense" could have really thought that the Church and State of England would have anything to fear when Ireland should be freed

[1] Charles James Fox must of course have a foremost place amongst our advocates; but he must rank after Burke, and as he died in the year 1806 he could not give us the continued support which was given by Grattan and Canning.

from her penal chains. He most probably thought that the concessions would render the Bill of Emancipation less unpalatable to the English people.

Whatever might have been Pitt's chief motive for wishing to shackle the Church in Ireland, in the year 1799 while he was maturing his plans for the Union, he commissioned Lord Castlereagh, who was Chief Secretary to the Lord Lieutenant, to sound the Irish bishops on the subject of the veto, and of a State provision for the clergy.[1] Lord Castlereagh having received his instructions, it happened that ten of the Irish bishops who were trustees of Maynooth College were assembled in Dublin "to attend to its concerns."[2] Amongst the ten were the four Metropolitans. There were at that time twenty-nine bishops in Ireland; so that, as Dr. Milner observes, the number assembled in Dublin was "little more than a third part of their whole number,"[3] and they were not met to attend to the general interests of the Irish Church, but only to the interests of Maynooth College. Lord Castlereagh took advantage of this meeting of the ten Episcopal trustees of Maynooth to proceed in the execution of his instructions, "and to consult them on the double plan of a State provision for the Catholic clergy, and of a government interference in the appointment of their successors."[4]

The reader must here note well, that the proposals for a State veto and a State provision for the Catholic clergy did not come from the Irish bishops to the Government; but came to the Irish bishops from the English Government—from Mr. Pitt, through Lord Castlereagh. This

[1] Lord Castlereagh's speech in the House of Commons on May 25, 1810, cited from Keating's Report, in Butler's "Memoirs," vol. iv. p. 112.
[2] Milner's "Supplementary Memoirs," p. 115.
[3] Ibid.
[4] Ibid.

fact should be remembered, because, as Milner says, "it has been asserted by a great many ill-informed and self-interested writers and speakers, that the Irish prelates who, to the number of ten, met together in Dublin in 1799, were the original authors of the veto. . . . No assertion, however, can be more false."

The ten bishops considered and discussed the proposals made to them by Lord Castlereagh. The reader will no doubt be interested in knowing the result of their deliberations, an account of which I take from Plowden's "History of Ireland since the Union."[1]

"*Resolutions of the Roman Catholic Prelates in* 1799.

"At a meeting of the Roman Catholic prelates, held in Dublin, the 17th, 18th, and 19th of January, 1799, to deliberate on a proposal from Government, of an independent provision for the Roman Catholic clergy of Ireland under certain regulations, not incompatible with their doctrine, discipline, or just principles:

"It was admitted, that a provision through Government for the Roman Catholic clergy of this kingdom, competent and secured, ought to be thankfully accepted.

"That, in the appointment of the prelates of the Roman Catholic religion to vacant sees within the kingdom, such interference of Government as may enable it to be satisfied of the loyalty of the person appointed is just, and ought to be agreed to.

"That, to give this principle its full operation, without infringing the discipline of the Roman Catholic Church, or diminishing the religious influence, which prelates of that Church ought justly to possess over their respective flocks, the following regulations seem necessary:—

"1. In the vacancy of a see, the clergy of the diocese to recommend, as usual, a candidate to the prelates of the ecclesiastical province, who elect him, or any other they may think more worthy, by a majority of suffrages; in the case of equality of suffrages, the Metropolitan or senior prelate to have a casting vote.

[1] Vol. iii. Appendix, n. ii. p. 9.

"2. In the election of a Metropolitan, if the provincial prelates do not agree within two months after the vacancy, the senior prelate shall forthwith invite the surviving Metropolitans to the election, in which each will then have a vote; in the equality of suffrages, the presiding Metropolitan to have a casting vote.

"3. In these elections, the majority of suffrages must be *ultra medietatem*, as the canons require, or must consist of the suffrage of more than half the electors.

"4. The candidates so elected to be presented by the president of the election to Government, which, within one month after such presentation, will transmit the name of the said candidate, if no objection be made against him, for the appointment to the Holy See, or return the said name to the president of the election, for such transmission as may be agreed on.

"5. If Government have any proper objection against such candidates, the president of the election will be informed thereof within one month after presentation; who in that case will convene the electors to the election of another candidate.

"Agreeably to the discipline of the Roman Catholic Church, these regulations can have no effect without the sanction of the Holy See, which sanction the Roman Catholic prelates of this kingdom shall, as soon as may be, use their endeavours to procure.

"The prelates are satisfied that the nomination of parish priests, with a certificate of their having taken the oath of allegiance, be certified to Government. (Signed) Richard O'Reilly, Edward Dillon, P. J. Plunkett, Daniel Delany, James Caulfield, Thomas Bray, P. Moylan, Edmund French, John Cruise."[1]

"*Subsequent Resolution of the Roman Catholic electors.*

"The prelates assembled to deliberate upon a proposal from Government of a provision for the clergy, have agreed, that M.R. Doctor O'Reilly, M.R. Doctor Troy, and R.R. Doctor Plunkett, and such other of the prelates who may be in town, be commissioned to *transact all business with Government* relative to said proposal, under the substance of the regulations agreed on and subscribed by them. Dublin, January 28, 1799."

[1] I conclude that Dr. Troy also signed the resolutions.

This subsequent resolution was signed by seven bishops, making with the three named in it the ten above-mentioned.

Several things have to be noticed about these resolutions, both as to their substance and their circumstances. In the first place, the proposals of Lord Castlereagh were not made to the bishops of the Irish Church assembled to deliberate upon matters which were vitally important, but merely to a small portion of their lordships accidentally meeting in Dublin to discuss the affairs of Maynooth College. Nor could these ten bishops be said in any way to represent the rest of their order in any matter not coming within the scope of their trust. And yet Mr. Butler, in his "Memoirs," so words his account of the Castlereagh proposals as to leave an impression on the mind of the reader that the negotiation was with all the bishops. He heads the section in which he writes of this affair with this title: "Resolutions of the Irish Prelates in favour of the Veto." And whenever he mentions the resolutions, he speaks of them as "the resolutions of the Irish Prelates." To do Mr. Butler full justice, I must mention that after having repeatedly spoken of the assembled bishops as "Irish Catholic Prelates," he does mention, quite at the end of his account, that they were ten in number. And he cites a passage from the speech of Lord Castlereagh in 1810, already referred to, in which he does speak of the *ten* bishops; but his lordship's words are so chosen as to convey the idea that if all the bishops did not sign, all of them deliberated upon the resolutions. Castlereagh's words as cited by Butler from Keating's report are as follows :—" The expediency of making, without delay, some provision for their clergy, under proper regulations, was so generally recognized, even by those who were averse to concessions of a political nature, that a communication was officially opened with the heads of their clergy upon the subject. The result of their deliberations was laid before Government, in certain resolutions, signed by ten of their bishops, including the four Metropolitans, in January, 1799."[1]

The words "the heads of their clergy" certainly means the bishops, and in a matter of this vast importance would surely imply all the bishops either personally or by authorized representation. And the succeeding words, "the result of their deliberations," would confirm the same impression; for who would suppose that the result of the deliberations of ten members of a council of twenty-nine, the nineteen not even knowing that the deliberations were going on, would be formally announced in Parliament as the result of the deliberations of all the Irish bishops? In mentioning the ten bishops, Lord Castlereagh does not say that only ten deliberated, but that only ten signed. No doubt the question would arise as to the opinions of the remaining nineteen. But taking all that Lord Castlereagh said on this occasion, I am inclined to think that the impression left on the mind of his hearers would be that all the bishops had been consulted, that ten of their number had signed, perhaps authorized by the rest and therefore representing them, or perhaps that the ten were the only ones who would sign, the others declining to do so, but willing to let the thing pass without protesting against it. They certainly did not protest, for the very sufficient reason which we shall have again to allude to, namely, because they had no knowledge whatever that the resolutions had been passed, nor even that the subject of them had been broached. However much Mr. Butler may have approved of the resolutions, he should not, in a matter of such consequence, have left this portion of

[1] "Historical Memoirs," vol. iv. p. 117. Edition of 1822.

his "Memoirs" to be *spotted* by his great antagonist, Dr. Milner.[1]

The next thing I have to call the reader's attention to in the above resolutions is the three concessions contained in them: the interference of the government in the election of bishops; the acceptance of a State maintenance for the clergy; and the certificate to be sent to Government of the nomination of parish priests, and of their having taken the oath of allegiance. That the first of these was a concession is of course plain enough. With regard to the second, namely, the State maintenance of the clergy, it was an important concession, because it gave up that freedom from control which must necessarily hamper every one who depends upon another for his subsistence. The pensioner of a Tory family dares not vote for a Whig; and a priest paid by the State dares not always be too zealous for the interests of the Church. As to the third, that the appointment of parish priests and their having taken the oath of allegiance should be certified to the Government, it was a degrading concession and a gross insult to the Irish Catholics to require such a thing. What is loyalty if the Irish clergy have not been loyal during the last hundred years? Burke, as we have seen in a former chapter, told the electors of Bristol that the Catholic priests of London should have been called up to receive the thanks of both Houses of Parliament for having held back the Irish during the Gordon riots. And on several occasions during the last hundred years the Irish clergy have deserved

---

[1] If Mr. Butler had written his "Memoirs of the English Catholics" as carefully as he wrote his Notes to Coke-upon-Littleton; if he had elucidated the facts of history as clearly as he elucidated difficult and abstruse points of law, he would have left us a valuable work. But when he wrote the latter he wrote as an impartial lawyer: when he wrote the former, he wrote as a prejudiced partisan. And so it almost always is: the student in history cannot read with the same confidence as can the student at law.

the same recognition of their services. It has frequently happened that a partial insurrection has not ended in a general rebellion solely because the Irish clergy stood boldly out to oppose revolt. What has more than once prevented a universal rising? Who are they who could have caused a rising and have not done it? The bishops and priests of Ireland could at any time during this century have roused the whole people, as O'Connell used to say, from Giant's Causeway to Cape Clear, from Connemara to the Hill of Howth, against English rule. And they have not done it. And why have they not done it? Because they have been loyal, with a loyalty guaranteed by their religion. And yet these are the men whose loyalty is held up by English statesmen as something which cannot be trusted, unless a clause in some miserable concordat shall prescribe an oath of allegiance.

It may have happened in the course of the last hundred years that the priests of a people ground down by the bigotry and jealousy of a more powerful nation, have, in the spirit of religion and patriotism, cried out, and cried out aloud against the oppressor. It may have happened that, smarting under the lash of the tyrant, they have said words which but for the provocation they never would have uttered. Let these cries and these words be repeated by an unscrupulous Press, in order to make the English people believe that the clergy of Ireland are not loyal men: what in the name of all reason and common sense is the worth of such evidence, when against it we have the fact that the bishops and priests could at any time have raised a universal rebellion in Ireland, and they have not done it?

Another matter to be noticed in the resolutions, and which indeed we have already alluded to, is that, to use the words of Milner, "the ten bishops . . . were not the representatives of the prelates of Ireland, for they did not so much as inform their absent brethren of the business in question. Hence the answers which they gave to the secretary's questions were never considered by them, nor can they in justice be considered by others, as expressing anything more than their *their own private opinion in the existing circumstances*, on the points proposed to them."[1]

The next observation on the resolutions cannot be better expressed than by again quoting from the " Supplementary Memoirs." "Then," says Milner, "as to the purport of these very answers; they will be found, on a strict examination, to fall very short of that contained in the veto, as it was generally understood; for the Maynooth trustees approved of the interference of Government in episcopal elections, barely as far as was necessary to *ascertain the loyalty of candidates.* They, moreover, stipulated for their 'own just influence,' and also for the *consent of the Pope* in this important business."[2]

But perhaps the most extraordinary circumstance in connection with these resolutions was that the "Maynooth trustees" not only did not inform their absent brethren of the business in question before their communication with Lord Castlereagh; but they did not inform them of the communications after they had taken place. The nineteen absent bishops knew nothing of the resolutions until the year 1808, nine years after they had been passed; and Milner says that the resolutions remained equally "unknown to Catholics and Protestants in both islands."[3] And Francis Plowden says that "the resolutions of the clerical trustees of Maynooth College never came fully to light till 1810."[4]

[1] "Supplementary Memoirs," p. 115.
[2] Ibid.
[3] Ibid.
[4] "History of Ireland since the Union," vol. iii. p. 663 note.

Whether any further steps were taken in the matter of the resolutions, and whether the committee of bishops appointed to "transact all business with the Government," in any way exercised the power given to them, no published history, so far as I am aware, has revealed. As the resignation of Mr. Pitt in February, 1801, put a stop to the project of emancipation, all question of any concessions on the part of Catholics also dropped.

The next mention of any interference on the part of the Government with Church matters in the United Kingdom occurred in Parliament during the session of 1805. In the month of May in that year "a petition from the Roman Catholics of Ireland to be relieved from the civil disabilities under which they laboured, was introduced into the House of Lords by Lord Grenville, and into the House of Commons by Mr. Fox."[1] Speaking of the debate in the Commons, Butler says, "*The first public mention of the veto* appears to have been made by Sir John Cox Hippisley."[2] And Butler gives a long extract from the speech, in which there is no mention of the appointment of bishops, but suggestions that bulls and papal rescripts should be subject to State inspection, and that priests and schoolmasters should produce certificates of character. Francis Plowden's report of the debate does certainly contain a hint of the veto. He says, "Sir John Cox Hippisley, by way of meeting the objections of those who opposed the motion upon the ground of its incompatibility with the coronation oath, mentioned that the Constitution of Corsica, as ratified by his Majesty, stipulated that the Roman Catholic religion in all its evangelical purity (such

---

[1] Aikin's "Annals of the Reign of George III.," vol. ii. p. 165. Butler, in his "Historical Memoirs," says that the motion for referring the petition of the Irish Catholics to a committee of the whole House, was made by Mr. Grattan. This is a mistake: it was made by Fox and supported by Grattan.

[2] "Historical Memoirs," vol. iv. p. 134.

were the words of the Act) should be the only national religion of Corsica, and all others tolerated; and that Parliament should concert the discharge of the functions of the bishops with the see of Rome. His Majesty, also in the year 1794, appointed Mr. Macdonald, a Roman Catholic priest, to a Catholic Fencible Regiment raised in Great Britain."[1] Butler concludes his notice of what Sir J. C. Hippisley said, in the following words:—" By this speech the arrangement of the veto was first brought before the public; but it mentioned it only in very general terms; little more respecting it was intimated than that it should be formed on the model of the legislative provisions of France against Papal encroachments; and that it was to supersede altogether the sanguinary provisions, enacted, ostensibly at least, for that purpose, by Queen Elizabeth and her Parliaments."[2]

In neither the House of Lords nor the House of Commons was the negotiation with the Irish bishops mentioned; and it remained unknown to all but a very few. But though the resolutions were not spoken of, " the subject of them," says Dr. Milner, " was frequently discussed by leading men of both communions, at least on this side of

[1] "History of Ireland since the Union," vol. ii. pp. 148, 149. When the Highland chiefs cleared their estates of the small farmers, in order to create sheep-walks for the Lowlanders, many of the Highlanders were employed in the works of the Glasgow manufacturers. The Glasgow trade suffered so much from the breaking out of the war with France in the year 1793, that the Highlanders could no longer find employment. The Rev. Alexander Macdonald (afterwards the first Bishop of Upper Canada) conceived the idea of getting the men out of work embodied in a Highland corps. This plan was effected, and Mr. Macdonald was appointed and gazetted chaplain to the regiment, which did service in Guernsey and afterwards in Ireland. It was disbanded at the peace of Amiens. For the information contained in this note I am indebted to the Rev. William Forbes Leith, S.J.

[2] "Historical Memoirs," vol. iv. p. 139. Sir J. C. Hippisley afterwards published the substance of what he said, and of what he intended to say, in a good-sized pamphlet with notes and appendices. This pamphlet is now very scarce; but is to be found in some of the older Catholic libraries.

the water."[1] Sir John Hippisley in particular busied himself in the subject, and according to Milner he was endeavouring to dispose Catholics "to accept with cheerfulness certain legislative restraints on the appointment of bishops, and their intercourse with the Apostolic See, the management of which, by means of an office to be created for that purpose, he expected would be put into his hands."[2]

To bring about a settlement of the Catholic question was Sir John's hobby. He began well, and was acknowledged to be our friend both by the Irish bishops and by Milner. But he ended by being a mischievous meddler; and at last he "meddled and muddled" to such an absurd degree, that he drew upon himself the ridicule of the House of Commons, excited by one of the wittiest speeches Canning ever made. There was no further public mention of the veto and other concessions until the year 1808. In that year, and up to and including the year 1810, the history of the veto question presents one of the most interesting and extraordinary portions of the annals of the Catholic Church in the United Kingdom during the last hundred years. It must be confessed that during this period there was a certain amount of *muddling* which was not confined to one side. But a good Providence which has so kindly and so wonderfully watched over our renascent Church, brought us unscathed through the mistakes and the misdeeds of good and bad.

Before going back to the year 1800 to mention other matters, it may be well to continue the history of the veto, at least up to the year 1810. In the year 1807 the Irish bishops requested Milner to act as their political agent in London. The reader should know that Milner

[1] "Supplementary Memoirs," p. 117.
[2] Ibid.

was now the Vicar Apostolic of the Midland District, having been appointed by the Holy See Bishop of Castabala, and consecrated at Winchester on the 22nd of May, 1803. In order to ensure his continual residence in London, several of the Irish bishops interested themselves to obtain an exchange between Dr. Milner and Dr. Poynter, the coadjutor vicar apostolic to Dr. Douglas, who was then the Vicar Apostolic of the London District. This proposed arrangement was not carried out; but, to effect the object of it another way, Pope Pius VII. granted to Milner a dispensation from the obligation of residence in his own district, and gave him permission to reside in London, if he should deem it advisable.[1] On the 20th of May, 1808, Dr. Milner arrived in London as the agent of the Irish bishops. His reason for coming at that time was that a debate on the "Catholic disabilities" was about to come off in the House of Commons. On the morning after his arrival in London, Milner was "conducted by Lord Fingall to Mr. Ponsonby," who was going to take a leading part in the debate. But Lord Fingal did not inform Milner of the subject that was to be treated of between himself and Ponsonby. We may, however, naturally suppose that Milner knew that the interview was to be on the subject of the debate on the "Catholic claims," though he did not know the special point on which he was to be questioned. It is necessary to notice this, because the special point was the veto, and the public were afterwards led to believe that the opening of the question began with Milner. In the course of the conversation, Ponsonby asked Milner, "as agent to the Irish prelates, *what power they were disposed to attribute to his Majesty in the choice of future Catholic bishops?*" To this question Milner answered as follows:—" I know very

[1] Husenbeth's "Life of Milner," pp. 132, 133.

well that they cannot, conformably with their religion, attribute to his Majesty *a positive power* in this business, but I believe, on good grounds, that they are disposed to attribute *a negative power* to him. However, as I have no instructions from them on the subject, I cannot positively answer for them." " This admonition," says Milner, "the writer" (that is, Milner) "repeated several times." Ponsonby did not say a word intimating an intention of making a proposal of the kind in Parliament, and was so little satisfied with Milner's "answer respecting the disposition of the prelates, that he requested him to write out of hand to them on the business, which he did by sending letters to five of them that very evening."[1]

Having given this account of his interview with Mr. Ponsonby, Milner then writes as follows:—"Reflecting, however, as he returned from the conference, that the necessity of the Pope's authority in any new regulation of discipline had either not been mentioned, or not sufficiently expressed, he wrote a hasty note to Mr. Ponsonby to supply the defect, into which, however, he introduced several unconnected subjects, on which he had conversed with the member, and among others the process by which, *in case the Pope and the prelates agreed to this plan*, the Catholic bishops in Ireland would be appointed in future. That this ill-digested paper was a mere hypothesis, and not a fixed plan for Mr. Ponsonby to act upon, is plain from the concluding words of it, which are these: ' Dr. Milner has not, of course, had an opportunity of consulting with the prelates of Ireland on the important subject of the Catholic presentations, but he has every reason to believe that they will cheerfully subscribe to the plan traced out in the first page of this note.' "[2]

[1] "Supplementary Memoirs," pp. 124, 125.
[2] Ibid., p. 125. Milner adds a note at this place, saying, "see the Hon. Robert Clifford's ' Origin and Progress of the Veto,' p. 3."

The debate in the House of Commons came off on the 25th of May. Milner was present in the gallery. Several petitions having been presented by Grattan, Sheridan, Sir John Newport, Mr. Butler, and Mr. Fitzgerald, Grattan rose and moved a Committee of the whole House to consider the petition of the Irish Catholics for a repeal of the penal laws. In this speech he was the first to introduce the question of the veto. He said, " I have a proposition to make, a proposition which the Catholics have authorized me to make ; it is this. That in the future nomination of bishops, his Majesty may interfere and exercise his royal privilege, and that no Catholic bishop be appointed without the entire approbation of his Majesty. In France the King used to name ; in Canada the King names ; it is by no means incompatible with the Catholic religion that our King should name ; and I do not see any difficulty on this head. Thus the objectors cannot refuse to go into the committee with consistency. They say they have no repugnance to the civil capacities of the Catholics, but they object to the nomination of their bishops by a foreign power. Here, then, they may get their wishes on both subjects ; if the danger will exist under the further admission of the Catholics, it exists now ; if Bonaparte has that ascendency over the Pope, if the Pope has that ascendency over the bishops ; and they—that is, the clergy—over the people, it follows that the Catholics in the army and navy, and the Catholic freeholders, are affected by a foreign power : so that a very great danger now exists, and a further measure is necessary. Here is the measure."[1]

[1] With all due respect to so great a man as Grattan, I must say that his manner of proving the ascendency of Bonaparte over the Catholic soldiers and sailors in the British service, may remind us of the old absurdity of proving that a battle was lost for the want of one nail. I don't know whether it is necessary to apologize to the present generation for what I believe to be a

Ponsonby spoke after Grattan. When the reader shall have seen what this gentleman said, he will be able to form some faint idea of the astonishment and grief which filled the heart of Milner when he heard the words. It is necessary to bear well in mind what was said, and what was not said, in the conversation which Milner had with Ponsonby. Ponsonby did not tell Milner that he was going to make a proposal in Parliament on the subject of the veto; on the contrary, he left Milner to suppose that he had no such intention. Milner did not *authorize* Ponsonby to say anything, nor did he even suggest to him that it would be well to say anything on the subject; on the contrary, he told Ponsonby, in his "hasty note," that nothing could be done without the consent of the Pope. The reader may now imagine what Milner's feelings were when he heard what Ponsonby said: "As to the danger to be apprehended from the Pope's connection with the Irish Catholics arising out of the dominion of Bonaparte over that personage, he appealed to the common sense of the House whether anything were to be apprehended from that quarter. What motive could the Pope have to promote the wishes of Bonaparte? He certainly could not be prompted by affection or interest to do so. But in order to remove all apprehension on that head, *he was authorized to say*, that the Catholic clergy were willing, in the event of the measure before the House being acceded to, that the appointment of every Catholic bishop in

---

"Joe Miller," but the proof was this: for want of a nail the shoe was lost; for want of the shoe the horse was lost; for want of the horse the man was lost; for want of the man the battle was lost. This proof is quite as good as the other, from Napoleon to the blue-jacket. At any rate, the influence of Pope Pius VII. produced no bad effect a year and a half before in Trafalgar's Bay; unless, indeed, it was His Holiness who raised the storm which marred the "spoils of Trafalgar."

Ireland should in future finally rest in the King; that the Catholic bishops had no objection to make the King virtually the *head of their Church;* and that a bishop appointed by the Pope, if disapproved by his Majesty, should not *be allowed to take upon himself his spiritual functions.* Mr. Yorke expressed a wish to know upon what authority Mr. Ponsonby grounded his statement relative to the disposition of the Irish clergy as to the future appointment of their bishops; that circumstance, if well founded, must serve to remove a principal objection to the Catholic claims. Mr. Ponsonby answered, that he made the statement on the authority of Dr. Milner, who was a Catholic bishop in this country, and who was authorized by the Catholic bishops of Ireland to make the proposition, in case the measure of Catholic emancipation should be acceded to. The proposition was this, that the person to be nominated to a vacant bishopric should be submitted to the King's approbation; and that if the approbation were refused, another person should be proposed, so that the appointment should finally rest with the King."[1]

"These assertions," says Milner, "as they filled every one else who heard them with astonishment, so they pierced the writer's heart (who equally heard them, and on whose authority they were stated to be made) with grief and confusion." When Ponsonby "had concluded his speech, he sent for Lord Fingal and Dr. Milner to meet him in the lobby of the House, where he asked them both the question—'if he had not gone too far?'"[2] In the year 1810, Ponsonby said in the House, according to

[1] *Vide* Plowden's "History of Ireland since the Union," vol. iii. pp. 655, 656; and Milner's "Supplementary Memoirs," p. 126. The above account of what passed in Parliament is taken partly from what Milner himself heard, and partly from the report of the debate as quoted by Francis Plowden.

[2] "Supplementary Memoirs," p. 126.

Keating's report of the debate on the Catholic question, that on the occasion of his asking the above question, Lord Fingal said, "No; you are quite exact." Milner's conduct we must give in his own words. "Certain it is," he says in the "Supplementary Memoirs," "that the writer hung his head down, and made no answer at all, being resolved early the next morning to print a disavowal of the heterodox sentiments which had been ascribed to him on so solemn an occasion." Accordingly, on the following morning, Milner, who never procrastinated an hour when he had anything of importance in hand, had printed a Protest, which he had probably written overnight, and posted copies of it to the Irish and English bishops, and to several other persons. He took one himself to Ponsonby. This gentleman said to Milner, and, as we should express it in these days, in the coolest possible way, "I am not surprised at your alarm; I do not pretend that you authorized me to say all that I did say; but I was at liberty to argue as best suited my cause. For the rest, this paper (the Protest) is a fair paper, and you have my consent to circulate it."

On the 27th of May, Lord Grenville presented the Catholic petition to the House of Lords, and moved that it be referred to a committee. In his speech he introduced a proposal of the veto. Butler, who said and wrote all he could to make the public believe that Milner was in favour of the veto, says in his "Historical Memoirs" that "Lord Grenville made a proposal of the veto in the House of Lords, at the suggestion of Dr. Milner." Milner, in his "Supplementary Memoirs," says that if such a charge were advanced in the hearing of Lord Grenville, his lordship "would flatly deny it." Milner had, in person, presented a copy of his Protest to Lord Grenville, and "all that then passed consisted in his lordship objecting to the restriction on Government proposed in that paper, namely that its negative power should be confined to avowed civil grounds." [1]

The report of the debates in Parliament, and that of Ponsonby's speech, caused universal indignation in Ireland. Clergy and laity, all joined in condemning the extraordinary and unwarrantable assertion which had been uttered. The bishops, says Milner, "both in conversation and correspondence, universally disavowed Mr. Ponsonby's language." [2] But before publishing any authoritative condemnation of what had been said in Parliament, the bishops thought it more prudent to wait until they could all conveniently meet together to discuss the question. Mr. Butler takes advantage of this delay to say that the Irish bishops continued to adhere to the resolutions of 1799.[3] Butler also says that "the Irish Prelates distinctly expressed to many their approbation of what had been said on the veto by their parliamentary advocates."

Milner, who was their agent, says, as we have seen, that they universally disavowed it. How are these two statements to be reconciled? The explanation is no doubt this, that the Irish prelates approved and expressed their approval of a good deal that had been said in Parliament by Ponsonby and others, which was not only not objectionable, but was much to be praised and to be grateful for as

---

[1] "Supplementary Memoirs," p. 124. The reader of Plowden's "History of Ireland since the Union," in perusing the note at page 662, vol. iii., must bear in mind that that note was written ten years before the publication of the "Supplementary Memoirs," and that therefore Plowden most probably did not know that Milner had called upon Lord Grenville between the 25th and the 27th of May.

[2] "Supplementary Memoirs," p. 128.

[3] At page 151, vol. iv., of his "Historical Memoirs," edition of 1822, Butler heads a chapter in the following words:—"Continued adherence of the Irish prelates to their resolutions in 1799, until their meeting in September, 1808."

powerful advocacy of the Catholic claims. But that the bishops approved of such language as that which conveyed to the House of Commons, on the authority of Dr. Milner, that their lordships were willing "to make the King virtually the head of their Church," no sane man can believe. And yet Butler asserts, without any qualification, that "the Irish prelates distinctly expressed to many their approbation of what had been said on the veto by their parliamentary advocates." This surely is not history; it is not an historical memoir, but a memoir of the wish which was father to the thought. The paragraph which in the "Memoirs" immediately precedes the words just quoted, seems to show the truth of the remark I have made upon them. It is as follows:—"The effect produced in favour of the Catholic cause by what was said in both Houses of Parliament, of the willingness of the Catholic prelates of Ireland to accede to the veto, was very great; even their most determined adversaries seemed to consider that it had gained them their cause. This was the general language within the walls of Parliament; the first impression which any Catholic heard from his Protestant acquaintance, on the following day, was a congratulation on the turn of the debate, and the event which occasioned it."

As Butler does not in any way protest against the language held by Ponsonby, it would certainly appear from the above extract that he received with unalloyed pleasure the congratulations of his Protestant friends.

The reader will now be surprised to hear that Milner himself advocated the veto. But judgment upon this act must be suspended until the whole of the story has been told. Amongst the letters which Milner received from Ireland in consequence of the unwarrantable speeches of Lord Grenville and Ponsonby, was one from an Irish bishop, written to him, as Milner says, "too sharply and indignantly on the subject." Milner was not a man who, in expressing his opinion, ever minced matters himself; nor was he always over-nice in the choice of words. He generally used strong words to express strong opinions. What *he* thought was too sharp and indignant, must have been sharp and indignant indeed.[1] Milner was evidently annoyed at receiving the rebuke. He had said nothing in London which he was not amply justified in saying as the agent of the Irish bishops; and, to say the least, he had not gone further in any expression favourable to a veto than some of the bishops themselves had gone in the resolutions which they had passed in Dublin.

The mind of Bishop Milner on the subject of the veto was probably this: any interference of the Government in Church matters is bad, especially at this time when the minister would desire to have the appointment of bishops in his own hands; but a negative voice, a right of veto limited as to the number of times it may be exercised, and the reason of the objection to any particular person confined to the question of his loyalty, would be, along with complete emancipation, a better state of things than a continuance of the penal laws. Stung by the letter he had received, he wrote a letter in answer to it. He printed this letter, calling it "A Letter to a Parish Priest." The letter was not printed for publication, but only for private circulation. Only fifty copies were struck off. It was dated August 1, 1808. The fifty copies "were distributed," Milner tells us, "exclusively among the higher order of the

---

[1] Husenbeth, who, we may suppose, was supplied with all extant letters to Milner by those who have the custody of them, does not mention the name of the Irish bishop who wrote so "sharply and indignantly," nor does he give a single extract from the letter itself. If that letter should be in existence, it would be an interesting document in the matter about which I am now writing.

clergy, with the exception of a single copy given to Lord Fingal."[1] Taking this letter by itself, without any of the surrounding circumstances to explain it, it is undoubtedly an advocacy of the veto. "One of the copies of the letter, unfortunately," says Milner, "fell into the hands of the writer's adversaries, who published it, to his indescribable mortification."[2] When Charles Butler read it, he was, of course, in a high state of delight; to him it was, to use a vulgar expression, *nuts to crack*. But the letter "was not a serious advocation of any kind of veto." This Milner positively tells us in his "Supplementary Memoirs." And when he asserts this, he adds that it was "merely *a mooting essay*, to use a lawyer's term, for the perusal of his friend, a Catholic prelate of Ireland, who had written too sharply and indignantly to him on the subject."[3] Milner also says that Charles Butler was "frequently assured" of the real nature of the letter. But notwithstanding this, Butler continued to speak of it as a serious advocacy of the veto, and so long after as the year 1819, when he published the first edition of his Memoirs, and in all subsequent editions, he heads a section with the words, "Dr. Milner's advocacy of the veto, in a pamphlet entitled, 'A Letter to a Parish Priest;'" and he begins the section by saying, "In Dr. Milner the veto found both an able and zealous advocate;" and he praises the argument and the eloquence of the letter. This was not very fair on the part of Butler. He was bound to accept the positive assurance of Milner as to the sense in which Milner's own words were written. Butler was a lawyer, and a lawyer should be the last man to fix an advocate with a personal assent to the views which he puts before a judge in a

[1] "Supplementary Memoirs," p. 130.
[2] Ibid.
[3] Ibid. The italics are Milner's.

question for that judge's decision. It must happen often every day that a barrister, simply doing his duty to his client, puts before a judge an opinion which he does not himself believe to be the correct one. He does this in the interest of his client, and if he did not do it he would be arrogantly assuming to himself the office not of advocate, but of judge. An advocate defending a man charged with murder may believe—indeed, he may know from the man's own mouth—that he is guilty, and yet he may adduce such strong arguments to prove the innocence of the culprit as to cause the jury to bring in a verdict of "Not Guilty." Would it be fair to say that the barrister really believed the man was not guilty? It would not only be unfair, but it would be absurd and ridiculous. And the same thing may occur in an argument on a point of law. Council may put before a judge a view of a case which he does not believe to be good law, and he may even obtain a decision in his favour. Is he to be taxed with being a bad lawyer, and with seriously holding an opinion which is bad law, when the decision of the court below shall have been reversed in an Appeal Court? Certainly not. Milner maintains that his advocacy of the veto was an advocacy of this kind, and is he to be taxed with seriously holding an opinion which he only put forth for the sake of argument?

Husenbeth, in his "Life of Milner," hardly does justice to Milner's real opinion. He says that Milner, "in his eagerness to defend himself, certainly went a great way in favour of a certain negative power being attributed to the Government in the appointment of Catholic bishops."[1] But Milner, by asserting that the letter was a mere *mooting essay*, prevents any one from asserting with correctness that he went any way at all towards a serious advocacy of any

[1] "Life of Milner," p. 154.

kind of veto, or that the letter was in reality anything more than the argument of an advocate to show that if emancipation could be obtained on no other condition, the kind of veto which he proposed might not be too great a price to pay for it.

END OF VOL. I.

www.ingramcontent.com/pod-product-compliance
Lightning Source LLC
Chambersburg PA
CBHW030321240426
43673CB00040B/1232